PRAISE FOR
THE SECRET HISTORY OF BIGFOOT

"Hilarious. An unforgettable blend of comic hijinks, barn-burning journalism, and beautiful writing. *The Secret History of Bigfoot* places a peculiarly American phenomenon on the continuum of crackpot ideas and believe-whatever-you-want fantasies embedded in our past and present, tracking its life and legend while parsing various subtexts of belief, from Salishan mythology to modern day 'cryptozoology,' from clear-headed skeptics to conspiratorial kooks. His affection for Bigfooters is matched only by his honest and revelatory assessment of their beliefs. Simply one of the funniest and most entertaining books I've read in a very long time."

Kirk Wallace Johnson, bestselling author of *The Feather Thief* and *The Fisherman and the Dragon*

"There's nothing more fun than diving down a rabbit hole, and *The Secret History of Bigfoot* drops the reader into one that is deep, wide, and mysterious. Packed with fascinating characters and compelling history, O'Connor made me care about something I'd never given a moment's thought before. A heckuva lot of fun."

Daniel Barbarisi, author of *Chasing the Thrill*

"Tales of monsters dwelling in the forest dark endure around the world, but there is something conspicuously, poignantly, and out-landishly American about Bigfoot. John O'Connor takes us on a jubilant journey coast to coast and across the centuries to understand why a mythic figure that seems always to be disappearing just as it comes into view has such an enduring presence. The truth may or may not be out there; *The Secret History of Bigfoot* is a reminder of how much fun the search for it can be."

Peter Manseau, author of *The Apparitionists*

"I might be a Bigfoot skeptic, but this book reinforces my belief in the power of great nonfiction writing. John O'Connor is a masterful and very funny guide through a subculture that is much larger and far more interesting than I ever imagined."

Sam Apple, author of *Ravenous*

"In *The Secret History of Bigfoot*, John O'Connor explores a piece of American culture that has often had a buff of exuberant goofiness on its outside, but what O'Connor's wonderful debut shows us is that beyond that sheen is something far more fascinating and profound than Bigfoot. Intoxicatingly adventurous and deftly insightful, this book is magical."

John D'Agata, author of *About a Mountain*

"Ostensibly, this is a book about the legend of Bigfoot and the cabal of seekers who studiously attend to its myth, but it is actually a book about wildness, desire, faith, hope, loss, and the various things we sense in our bones but cannot account for. John O'Connor is a deeply smart, funny, and tenderhearted writer, and *The Secret History of Bigfoot* is a remarkable debut, full of wit, insight, and a devout reverence for the mysteries at the heart of our existence. I loved this book. It made me feel as though both everything and nothing are possible."

Amanda Petrusich, author of *Do Not Sell at Any Price*

"John O'Connor doesn't just search fearlessly for Bigfoot wherever he may be but hunts intrepidly for the enduring heart of our common culture. Along the way he picks up the scent of the American psyche and never lets it go. The result is a charming, thoughtful, frankly brilliant investigation into what we believe, and why we need to believe it."

John Glassie, author of *A Man of Misconceptions*

"I had little interest in Bigfoot or Sasquatch before picking up John O'Connor's book, but from page one, his reportorial rigor, wide-ranging intellect, and Bill Bryson-esque humor had me hooked. In haunting the ground where the creatures have purportedly been sighted—from Washington to Arkansas, California to Kentucky — and spending time in the woods with those who search, he uncovers not a beast but a portrait of our time with profound insights about solitude, landscape, belief, science, and the American character."

John Jay, editor of the *Library of America's Charles Portis: Collected Works*

"John O'Connor takes us on a thrilling double journey—through mountain trails and desert passes in search of Bigfoot, but also through the mysterious reasons why some people devote years of their lives to tracking down the monster (or trying to). Although skeptical that the power of belief should prevail over hard scientific truths, O'Connor nonetheless embraces this community of searchers, whose Bigfoot quests have given their lives meaning. Come for the thrill of the chase, stay for evocative descriptions of some of the last remaining American wilderness, and leave with insights on what history, religion, and psychology can teach us about the true meaning of the Bigfoot phenomenon. After reading this book, the next time you hear a strange noise in the woods, or glimpse a mysterious shadow flitting through the trees, you, too, will want to step into the world of possibility."

Derek Baxter, author of *In Pursuit of Jefferson*

THE
SECRET
HISTORY OF
BIGFOOT

Field Notes *on a* North American Monster

JOHN O'CONNOR

Published by Sourcebooks
P.O. Box 4410, Naperville, Illinois 60567–4410
(630) 961-3900
sourcebooks.com

Cataloging-in-Publication Data is on file with the Library of Congress.

Printed and bound in the United States of America.
LSC 10 9 8 7 6 5 4 3 2

For Cassie

TABLE OF CONTENTS

"The search is not for a wild man but for how wildness has left men, then to bring that wildness back."

—DANIEL C. TAYLOR

"In a deeply tribal sense, we love our monsters."

—E. O. WILSON

"But let me tell you what I see."

—SWAMP DOGG

PROLOGUE

"The genius of Melville is that he saw that this
is a country that needs a monster."

—CARLOS FUENTES

I once spent the better part of a year writing a film script about a group of eco-warriors who blow up a fracking well owned by a nefarious Big Oil outfit in a Pacific Northwest forest. The explosion rocks a Bigfoot hub, killing scores and unleashing the "Wrath of the Squatch," who descend on the eco-warriors and oil company guards in a spree of freakish, primeval violence. Resistance is futile:

EXT. GENERATORS / FRACKING SITE—NIGHT

Cue the BLOODBATH: The GUARDS reach the generators to find them ripped apart and on fire. They switch on night vision goggles (nods). Large indistinct forms stalk them.

A SQUATCH thuds beside one of the GUARDS, who pops off a few shots, but the SQUATCH tears into him—his body explodes, coming apart at the seams.

Another GUARD views the carnage through his nods before

finding his partner's upper body and torso connected by a
string of entrails.

BLOOD bubbles from the fallen GUARD'S mouth and his
legs twitch.

Page after page of this. My screenwriting partner, the novelist
Farooq Ahmed, called it "memorable." But we'd had a bad connection and maybe what he'd really said was "regrettable"? Either way,
neither of us had thought to do much research, so the script was written in a fog of ignorance. Extractable natural gas in a PNW forest?
Not a thing. All we knew was what everyone knows: Bigfoot lived
there, and you didn't screw around with Bigfoot. Bloodthirsty hom-
icidal Bigfoots, I'd eventually learn, were also far outside the norm.
It'd probably been a mistake to abandon our Sasquatch screwball
comedy—the original elevator pitch was *The Hangover* meets *Harry
and the Hendersons*. We'd even written a part for M. Emmet Walsh
(this reference will elicit smiles from .01 percent of readers) for a
cinema verité splatter fest with a ham-handed allegory about nature's
revenge. But that was where Bigfoot led us. Shockingly, Hollywood
(unlike predatory Bigfoots) didn't bite.

While working on the script, I started seeing Bigfoot everywhere. On CBD oil and air fresheners. On car polish and coronavirus masks. On scented candles and Nalgene bottles and maple syrup
and vile, undrinkable IPAs. Why hadn't I noticed this before? And
what did it all mean? I gradually and glumly realized that Farooq
and I had gotten hold of the wrong thread. Or that I, at least, had
boiled my fascination with Bigfoot into lowbrow genre schlock
when what I really wanted was to understand where Bigfoot came
from. Questions abounded: If we'd bothered to do any research,

what would it have revealed about the folklore and anthropological backstory of Bigfoot? Was it an actual zoological possibility or a human-wide cultural delusion, a manifestation of a universal desire to believe in the unbelievable? What was Bigfoot's appeal, not only to know-nothings like Farooq and me but to whoever we imagined was our more Bigfoot-savvy audience? Why, despite no definitive proof of the creature's existence—no body, bones, conclusive DNA analysis of skin or hairs, just a bunch of blurry videos and obscenely large footprints seemingly left by Harry himself—was interest in Bigfoot soaring?

A mere asterisk in the script but arguably its unwritten hero was an eccentric Bigfooter named Kennerson (Walsh). He roamed isolated woods, moved only under cover of darkness, and was endearingly absent from social media (as it turned out, we weren't far off here). Only now, late in the game, do I see that Kennerson was more complex than he appeared. Brilliant, charming, and a little bit crazy, he spoke for those who felt seductively bored by everyday life and scorned and neglected by the world at large. As sure as he was about Bigfoot's existence, he knew the rest of us had it coming—for our ecological sins, our gull-wing Teslas and legacy admissions and summer homes on the Cape. He was passionate about this but far more passionate about the startling scientific discovery he sensed was closer at hand. Until, that is, he got eaten by a Bigfoot.

Who were the real Kennersons out there—the Bigfooters—and where did they spend their weekends? What evidence had they found? Could I tag along? While I had my doubts about Bigfoot, the point wouldn't be to prove or disprove whether it existed but to try and set aside my own convictions, unpeel the oniony layers of belief, and understand something about Bigfooters and the culture that shaped them. This time, I'd do my research. Knowing as little as I did, I thought America itself might even poke its head out from behind Bigfoot's shadow.

1

SHADOW COUNTRY

"Now I have come to where the phantoms live,
I have no fear of phantoms, but of the real."

—DEREK WALCOTT

Sometime in the night, the noise started. Quietly at first. Then less quietly. Then it grew urgent. Then livid. Until it was positively beside itself. A free-form, sphincter-shuddering howl, attended by a near-subliminal reverb, coming just beyond my tent. I'd been lying there, trying to sleep, feeling overly proud, feeling exultant really, at having huffed up from the road that morning carrying way too much—up sidewinding cloisters of Douglas fir, across scrubby fields of red hawthorn where crickets pinged off my trekking poles, into meadows of pale valerian and purple heather and tangy wild blueberries hardly bigger than Nerds, over shattered rockfall, past weird hummocky deposits of turf that turned out to be marmot dens, along a narrow culvert whose edges tipped into the void, and onto this imposing yet minor summit of the Northern Cascades, where, sweating and cursing like a farmhand, I'd plopped a flimsy tent below an abandoned fire lookout and climbed inside—when the howling commenced.

Suddenly I was eight years old again. As the night air shuddered, I shuddered too. I'd been deluded in coming here, had once more distilled my neurotic, citified, armchair jones for wilderness into a Sierra Club fantasy. Yet here I was, fifteen, maybe twenty miles from another soul. Twenty-five from asphalt. One hundred from the nearest Wendy's. It was a place where two hikers, including an ex-Marine, had gone missing in recent years. Like the narrator of the Rosemary Tonks poem—"I'm being broken / At this very moment"—I sensed prefrontal slippage, mass losing solidity.

Before bedding down, I'd strung a bear bag among sagging, cliff-side spruce. But an inedible trail bar, the kind that gums up your intestines for seventy-two hours, lingered in a coat pocket. Ditto a sodden, ziplocked tangerine. To the proper audience, I was a rack of lamb. Only once, in the Smokies, had I encountered a wild bear. This high up, at this time of year, on this solitary spur, a bear would be odd. So I told myself.

What then? Marmots? These adorable beefcake guinea pigs occupied the shoulders of my perch in a colony several dozen strong. When I'd first heard their shrill, graveyard screams, it had shaken me to my core. But this wasn't that, was it? Maybe the northern harrier I'd seen wheeling about? Stone-cold killer, that one, trailing death across hill and dale but possessing a battle cry that was ludicrously pipsqueak.

Which led me, by way of a certain line of thinking, to Bigfoot, or Sasquatch if you prefer. The "strange and ghostlike" forest being that local Sauk-Suiattle and Skagit Indian legends describe. The humanoid giant that European fur trappers and railroad men, loggers, and miners claimed to have encountered during their westward ravages. The "abominable snowman" that two boys, Mark Meece, sixteen, and Marshall Cabe, fourteen, ran into just east of here, at Cub Lake, in 1969. The "monkey or gorilla" that tourists saw crossing Highway 504 over in Cowlitz County. The source of eerie yowls, "like people yelling," that elk hunters heard recently on Spencer Butte. The seven-to-nine-foot-tall beast with a "cone-shaped head" and "matted and dirty, but not stringy" hair that a man spotted "lumbering along" a hillside near Darrington. The ogre, trickster, cave monster, mountain devil, wild man, and cannibal child slaver that nearly every Indigenous American culture has a name for: Bakwas, Dzunuḵwa, Kala'litabiqw, Kchi Awas, Nik'inla'eena, Omah, Ste-ye-hah'mah. The tabloid curiosity. Skulker of the old growth. Model of Arcadian simplicity. Transient and scary-ass figment of my dreams. Imaginary herald of our oldest and most hard-dying myths, or long odds candidate for a real yet undiscovered hominid species.

Whatever it was, marmot or missing link, it circled, footfalls crunching frosted stonecrop, claws scattering talus. In my barricade of fleece and down, I lay perfectly still, eyelids bolted shut, my only weapon, a plastic spork, clutched tightly to my chest. There came a surgical howl, followed by another, my own this time—a feral, child-like, trombone wail—and the crash of rock on rock.

We all have our coping mechanisms. Mine was to burrow deeper and hum a few bars of Little Feat's "Willin'" while weeping inwardly. Later, when the noise subsided, I pulled myself together. Wriggling free of my bag, I slipped on my headlamp, unzipped the tent, and stuck my face into the darkness. It was the bottom of the ocean: pure black above and below, the weensie glint from my headlamp illuminating fuck all. I clapped, as you're meant to do with bears. Nothing. Stepping outside, I found a loose tent peg being dashed against the rocks by the wind, its guyline snapping in a frenzied dance. Thus had a seam opened between tent and rain fly, creating that unfathomable howl. Which should've been obvious from the comfort of my bag.

David Rains Wallace, in his book *The Klamath Knot: Explorations of Myth and Evolution*, describes a bout of visions and night terrors that troubled him in California's Siskiyou Mountains, a region of frequent Bigfoot sightings. "Lying in the dark, I couldn't close my eyes because intensely vivid faces would appear, mouthing incomprehensible words. The faces seemed so real that I had trouble reassuring myself that they came from my mind, and I afterward saw them at other camps, as though I'd been sensitized to something." He entertains rational explanations—a microbe, exhaustion—as well as other possibilities. "It made me wonder where the mind ends and the forest begins." A similar kind of residual illness, I felt, had struck me just beneath the surface. Could it all have been a trick of the imagination?

After so much excitement, I decided to make coffee. This was early September. The wind was a wet wrench. But the eastern sky trended blue gray as the sun began its interminable crawl over the mountains.

What a balm the daylight provided. To the south, I could make out the ten-thousand-foot Glacier Peak, its summit wreathed in clouds. Directly opposite was another ten-thousand-footer, Mount Baker, a black dorsal fin breaking a blue line of surf. Due east, beneath the crest of Sinister Peak, the fast-retreating Chickamin Glacier (eighty-six hundred feet), and to the west, the chossy flanks of White Chuck Mountain (seven thousand feet). I was aboard the palpably inferior Green Mountain, sixty-five hundred feet of andesite cinder and humble pie. Usually snow-packed till midsummer, it swarmed now with bluebells and silvery sedge. Fox sparrows, golden-crowned kinglets, and my favorite of all, the ubiquitous juncos, on holiday from Mexico, bounded past on mysterious errands. Smoke from wildfires farther south, around Mount Rainier, gathered in the valley below. Behind me, standing like a fez cap on the summit, was a shuttered fire lookout, its east flank crumbling into a boulder-strewn gully, mist coiling from its steepled roof.

This extraordinary tableau was the reason I'd come here. Or half the reason. The other half being the stated subject of this book. Long story short, I wanted to write about Bigfoot: its myth and meaning, where it comes from, why it bewitches, confounds, and occasionally terrifies us. Most crucially, I wanted to meet Bigfooters. Months back, midway through the pandemic, I'd gotten caught up in the spirit of our strange times. I couldn't stop myself. If you'd asked me then, I'd have said that Bigfoot was a beautiful yet harrowing intimation of the future, a terminal cocktail of hope mixed with discontent and a twist of climate apocalypse. Or some such. On Green Mountain, I could read a lot of the personal and public dread of 2020 into that thinking. While it seemed clear that fear and self-delusion were intertwined with Bigfoot, I was also made painfully aware of our uneasy rapport with nature. But I still knew virtually nothing about the Big Guy. I had a lot to learn.

In truth, one rarely thinks about why they're looking into something until long after they've begun. Bigfoot was probably always there, in the back of my mind. Perhaps I thought it would fade. Instead it gained momentum. After abandoning my blockbuster film treatment, "Wrath of the Squatch," I began imbibing the Bigfoot literature, the podcasts and chat room banter, Instagram posts and Facebook rants. I watched the unwatchable films, spoke to believers and non, diehards and weekenders, clearheaded skeptics and fervid charlatans, plumbing the thin margins between credible and contrivance, between reasoned inquiry and unhinged pursuit of a creature whose exact location no one could specify but whose existence was taken as a matter of faith. "Other people's obsessions don't turn me on," Saul Bellow once said. Other people's obsessions are precisely what turn me on. They become my own obsessions, propelling me down uncertain paths, making life more interesting. With Bigfoot, there are innumerable paths. You can find him everywhere. While I planned to hit all points of the compass on my Bigfoot walkabout—north, south, east, west—it's in the Pacific Northwest, as everyone knows, where Bigfoot's story begins.

I hadn't left my bed in years, it seemed. When it became possible, in the fall of 2021, I flew from Boston to the Washington Cascades, laden with instant noodles and COVID-19 self-tests. Not exactly to look for Bigfoot but to see the landscape, arguably the biggest Bigfoot country in the Lower 48, a sixty-thousand-square-mile glaciated column that backed all the way up into Canada. I had it on good authority that the Mount Baker-Snoqualmie National Forest, and expressly this very Darrington Ranger District, was a favored Bigfoot haunt of late.

Plus, it'd be big fun. Sleeping under the stars, lying with a book under leafy crowns. To be moving again, "taking part in the existence of things," as Keats put it, with nary an eyebrow raised at my quarantine hair and waistline, not knowing what the days would bring, knowing only they wouldn't bring the drudgery of sameness, felt as vital as a beating heart. "Comes over one an absolute necessity to move."—D. H. Lawrence. "If you're edged 'cause I'm weazin' all your grindage, just chill."—Pauly Shore. Translation: I had to go. Every sensible argument for not going be damned.

I'd been in such a yank to get here. And here I finally was. *The* spot to begin my "fieldwork," as I was calling it, a dark and unfathomable forest where eight-hundred-pound monsters roamed undetected and where the imagination could lurch, unmediated, from one vision to the next. It was the most beautiful place I'd ever been, but I couldn't stay another minute. Its sheer beauty served only to intensify a desire to leave. Rattled by my sleepless night, I struck camp, humped on my pack, and headed down to my car.

An hour later, I met a ptarmigan hen and cock on the trail, and lower down, a pika—a short-eared and pissed-off cousin of the rabbit—scampered from its ferny den to eyeball me. I could hear everything that was going on. A nuthatch whistling. A crow flapping. Grass stirring. Slowly, the trees closed in, growing bigger and taller: Douglas fir and Engelmann spruce, western hemlock and bristlecone pine, their branches tied together in feathery loops. Stopping for a drink, a rifle shot cracked uncomfortably close by. It was two weeks before the high hunt. Picking up my pace, I crossed a hilltop and caught sight of a tarp and camp stove stashed away in some bushes. Other people, armed people, hadn't been so distant after all.

Finding my car at the trailhead, I shook a beer from the Styrofoam cooler in back, stifling the urge to pour it directly onto my face. The car was a rental. I drove it too quickly down a rutted Forest Service road, every spin of the wheels producing a hammer strike to the buttocks, and made camp on the Suiattle River, a mile from Buck Creek. The site had a firepit with a circle of stones and a log bench on which someone had scrawled "Sasquatch 2021" in hunter orange.

The river was massive. It ran the color of dishwater around sandy islands choked with young alder and cottonwoods. From the center-most island, a few treacherous rock leaps away, I turned and stared back at the vertiginous world I'd left behind. A place I'd been so eager to leave suddenly exerted a gravitational pull. Bigfoot, I knew, like bears, would more likely appear near the river, a reliable food source. Still, I couldn't help but feel deflated. And ashamed at having fled the upper air for the lower elevations, realizing too late that I'd succumbed to the lamest of clichés: Irrational fear is revealed to be exactly that. While the mountains had felt so alive, the chaos of the river, beating past like a train, drowned out even the birds. Pollock-y swirls of dog tracks littered the banks, and a few bear prints. But no sign of Bigfoot. Unless Bigfoot wore a size-9 Teva.

————

Bigfoots, you may be surprised to learn, aren't all that rare. In fact, by most accounts, they're quite common, or no less widely dispersed than, say, bald eagles or Starbucks. Each year, hundreds of Bigfoots are sighted across the United States and Canada, from Alberta to Alabama, Saskatchewan to South Carolina, and thousands more "encountered" via footprints, calls, and "wood knocks," a form of communication that entails pounding on trees. Visitors to Ohio's scanty twenty-six-square-mile Salt Fork State Park, which is flanked by some of the Midwest's busiest highways, have recorded dozens of sightings. The Bigfoot Field Researchers Organization (BFRO), a group of investigators dedicated to obtaining "conclusive docu-mentation of the species' existence," keeps a database of more than seventy-five thousand eyewitness reports in North America. That's just since the mid-1990s, when Matt Moneymaker, a bankruptcy lawyer from Los Angeles, founded the group. While only a sliver of sightings[1]—between five and six thousand—are deemed credible enough to make the BFRO's meticulously curated, user-generated website, and ten thousand more are judged hoaxes, the remaining sixty thousand are merely "unsubstantiated," or what Moneymaker calls "a driving-down-a-turnpike-in-the-middle-of-the-night sighting," meaning their details couldn't be confirmed.

The volume of reports rises and falls over time, mostly depending on what happens to be on TV. Between 2011 and 2013, when Animal Planet's *Finding Bigfoot* was at the height of its popularity, sightings skyrocketed. But Moneymaker, a *Finding Bigfoot* cast member, said fluctuations seem to have as much to do with the day of the week as with the power of suggestion. "Of all the marvelous consistencies we've seen, Wednesdays, for some reason, are big sighting days. Historically that's when we get the most. We were told once that doctors golf on Wednesdays, so there are lots of people in offices with more time on their hands to report sightings. Who knows? Fridays are when we tend to get the least amount. I have no idea why. People got better shit to do on Fridays, I guess."

What's striking about the reports is their narrative cohesion. Eyewitnesses from every niche of the continent describe pretty much the same creature: shaggy, bipedal, nocturnal, shy, standing seven to ten feet tall, weighing about seven hundred to eight hundred pounds, and smelling to high heaven. An aspiring pescatarian, Bigfoot is known to cave to the occasional rodent, deer, sheep, goat, cow, or horse. (Among certain Bigfooters, the digestive outcomes of this are a matter of earnest speculation.) Though capable of random acts of violence, the "consensus description" of Bigfoot behavior, as

---

1 The BFRO ranks sightings on a "credibility" scale—Class A through C—given their circumstances and the potential for misidentification.

the late British primatologist John R. Napier once put it, is "leisurely
and unafraid," its attitude "inquisitive rather than aggressive," even
toward hunters taking potshots. Exuding a stoner-ish gait, Bigfoot
walks "slightly stooped, with a swinging motion of the arms" and has
a comically pigeon-toed footfall, like Ratso Rizzo. Still, one's instinct
upon seeing a Bigfoot, as virtually every BFRO eyewitness report
attests, is to flee in terror.

———

In the spring of 2005, the writer Peter Matthiessen traveled to this
same stretch of the Suiattle on a similar mission. He nursed a long
fascination with Bigfoot, stemming from an incident in the Dolpo
region of Nepal in 1973. He'd gone there with wildlife biologist
George Schaller, who was studying rare Himalayan blue sheep called
bharal. Out walking one day near the Suli Gad River, Matthiessen
saw a "dark shape" dashing behind a boulder: "I glimpse the creature
only for an instant," he wrote in his famous account of the expedition,
The Snow Leopard. "It is much too big for a red panda, too covert for
a musk deer, too dark for wolf or leopard, and much quicker than a
bear." What could it have been? The obvious culprits—a snow leopard or Asian black bear—didn't resemble this puzzling figure. "All
day I wonder about that quick dark shape that hid behind the rock,"
he went on, "so wary of a slight movement on the far side of a rush-
ing torrent; for I was alone, and could not have been heard, and was
all but invisible in the forest shades." Although he eventually decided
it was a musk deer, "it is hard to put away the thought of yeti."

The *yeh-teh*, or "man-thing of the snows," Matthiessen wrote,
was familiar to Sherpa villagers. "Described most often as hairy,

reddish-brown creature with a ridged crown that gives it a pointed-head appearance," it never attacked men—nevertheless the Nepalese government forbade killing one—but seeing a yeti brought bad luck. Matthiessen's guide, Tukten Sherpa, told him that yeti had once been common in the Khumbu region around Mount Everest but had been poisoned and killed off by locals to prevent them from raiding their crops. According to Tukten's grandfather, who witnessed the carnage, "There were dead yetis everywhere."

Matthiessen was surprised to find that Schaller, one of the world's leading field biologists, believed in the yeti, though he had doubts about its North American cousin the Sasquatch. Schaller had been persuaded by photographs of humanlike footprints taken in 1951 by a group of British mountaineers, including the writer Eric Shipton, on the western slope of Everest during the race to conquer the mountain. The discovery made the pages of *Newsweek*, igniting another, ultimately futile, race to find the yeti. The Irish big-game hunter Peter Byrne cobbled together a search team. As did Japan, France, and Switzerland. The Soviet Union, under the auspices of its "Snowman Commission," sent expeditions into Tajikistan's Pamir Mountains.

The Snow Leopard, while nominally about its titular animal, which Matthiessen never succeeded in catching sight of (or did and mistook it for a yeti), is also his Squatchiest book. At least I've always thought of it that way. Again and again, he mulls over the possibility of the yeti's existence, wondering if he has seen something more extraordinary than a snow leopard. Matthiessen was nudged along by Schaller, the eminent scientist, who had little doubt "that an animal unknown to science occurs here."

"From a biologist's point of view...most of the Himalayan region is still *terra incognita*," Matthiessen wrote. "As [Schaller] says, almost nothing is known of the natural history of the snow leopard, and we are walking a long way indeed to find out some basic information about the relatively accessible Himalayan bharal." Unlike Schaller, Matthiessen didn't see why, if the yeti were possible, the Sasquatch wasn't. "A strong argument against the existence of both sasquatch and yeti (and the whole world-wide phenomenon called 'Bigfoot') is that man's expeditions in pursuit of these elusive creatures have all failed. However, this may only prove that Bigfoot habitat is virtually impenetrable, and that after long centuries of hiding, these rare creatures are exceptionally wary."

Three years later, Matthiessen glimpsed another strange bipedal figure, this time in Oregon. After dashing across the road in front of his car, it scaled a pile of felled trees with freakish agility, then vanished. When Matthiessen tried to follow, he didn't get far. The logs were too perilous. No human could've climbed them.

His Bigfoot trifecta culminated on the east bank of the Suiattle. Here I have to amend what I said earlier. Another reason I'd come to Washington State was a prurient interest in this expedition of Matthiessen's, a writer I admire. I wanted to see precisely where his Bigfoot quest had taken him. With him were two friends, John Mionczynski, a wildlife biologist for the U.S. Forest Service, and Jeff Meldrum, an anthropologist at Idaho State University who specializes in foot morphology and locomotion in hominids. Meldrum was about to publish a book, *Sasquatch: Legend Meets Science*, for which Matthiessen had written a blurb: "Fascinating…bound to encourage a more open mind in other biologists as well as naturalists and general readers in regard to sasquatch."

They camped a half mile from the wilderness boundary, timing their arrival to coincide with a spring salmon run. Recent floods had gouged out chunks of riverbank, leaving sandbars of impacted sediment that were good for tracking. "We figured we'd be able to find evidence of Bigfoot gleaning salmon along the river," Meldrum told me when I reached him at his ISU office.

The upper Suiattle has a well-worn Bigfoot history. *Suiattle* may be a Salish term for Sasquatch, which itself is an Anglicization of the Halkomelem Salish word *Sesquac*, or Sésq̓əc, meaning, roughly, "wild men."[2] In the 1910s, American naturalist Nels Bruseth collected oral stories among the area's Stillaguamish, Sauk, Skagit, and Suiattle tribes about a Bigfoot-like animal called "Steetathls" that "had to be appeased or guarded against...There were certain trails that were unsafe; strange tracks had been seen on them. There were noises in the night...and disappearances of Indian children, all charged to the Steetathls." Salish legends feature various "border monsters" that dwelled in mountain passes. The Puget Sound Indians, as recounted by anthropologists Hermann Haeberlin and Erna Gunther, believed in "wild tribes" of the interior called *ste'tat* "who traveled by night and attacked lone wayfarers" and "spoke a language unintelligible... The Sound Indians said that the *ste'tat* used to be savages but they had become civilized now." Nonnative sightings date back to the 1700s, when French Canadian voyageurs reported encounters with wild men. In 1792, Spanish naturalist José Mariano Mociño, traveling through the Pacific Northwest, recorded a tale from the Nootka people of a dreaded "Matlox," an "inhabitant of the mountainous

---

2 "Sasquatch" was coined by John W. Burns, a white schoolteacher on British Columbia's Chehalis Indian Reserve, who introduced the term to a national audience in a 1929 article for the Canadian magazine *Maclean's*. "Bigfoot" didn't enter the lexicon until 1958, when sixteen-inch footprints were found on a logging road in northern California.

districts, of whom all have an unbelievable fear. They imagine his body as very monstrous, all covered with stiff black bristles; a head similar to a human one but with much greater, sharper and stronger fangs than those of the bear; extremely long arms; and toes and fingers armed with long curved claws. His shouts alone (they say) force those who hear them to the ground, and any unfortunate body he slaps is broken into a thousand pieces."

In 2004, tracks had been found on the Suiattle's sandbars that, according to Meldrum, were either an elaborate hoax or "a stunning example" of impressions left by Bigfoot. The men set up wildlife blinds and motion-sensor cameras. They went on hikes in search of tracks. But the weather was against them. The temperature soared to 112 degrees, sending snowmelt gushing down from Glacier Peak, washing out the Suiattle's sandbars. After ten days, no tracks had been found. Nothing unusual turned up on the trail cameras. Disappointed, they went to bed, planning to leave the next day. In the morning, Matthiessen noticed that a large rock near his tent had been stood on its edge, like a tombstone. Other rocks were stacked in cairns. Their camp equipment had been rifled through. Footprints larger than a man's were found nearby, with "enough suggestion of anatomy that you had to at least entertain the possibility" of Bigfoot, Mionczynski said. Something had come through their camp that night. Bigfoot? Hikers pulling a fast one? They didn't see how it could've been faked. There were no human footprints. It was a long hike from the road. Although it was hardly the evidence he was after, Matthiessen was spooked. He returned home to New York and to a Bigfoot novel that would occupy him on and off for the rest of his life.

———

After Green Mountain, the plan had been to visit Peter Byrne down the coast in Oregon. Byrne, who had just turned ninety-five, was a prominent Bigfooter in the 1950s, '60s, and '70s. Before that, he was a big game hunter in Nepal. Before that, he was a tea planter in Bengal. Before that, he was part of an elite Royal Air Force sea rescue squadron in the South Pacific. He seemed to have stumbled straight out of Kipling, in other words, neat Glenfiddich in hand. Now he's retired and living in *Goonies* country.

I'd been taken with Byrne's book *The Hunt for Bigfoot* and its assessment, based on his understanding of the habitat and dietary needs of large mammals, that Bigfoot couldn't cut it east of the Rockies. Viable territory stretched upward from northern California through the coastal ranges of Washington and Oregon, over to the Cascades, and farther north into British Columbia and Alaska. That was it, with patchy exceptions for western Idaho. Claims of Bigfoot popping up in, say, French Lick and the Tampa exurbs were, Byrne said, "misinformed" and "gullible," with "no basis in reality." He estimated that 85 percent of eyewitness reports he'd investigated over the decades were bogus, many of them hoaxes. Which is perhaps why, by his own admission, Byrne was a widely loathed figure in the field. (His fondness for Stetsons and paisley cravats probably hasn't helped.) As one young Bigfooter told me, "Peter Byrne is the enemy."

So of course I wanted to meet him. On the phone, he was a gentleman. Sharp, garrulous, with an accent from somewhere north of the River Shannon. "I went to Texas to investigate sightings there," he'd said, "there" sounding like "tar." "I went to New York State. I went to Illinois. I went to Ohio. And there was absolutely no substance to any of them. Bigfoot habitat is west of the Rockies and nowhere else." This cut so sharply against the contemporary Bigfooter grain that part of me wondered if Byrne was settling old scores without naming names. We'd planned to meet at his local pub. At the last minute, he begged off. He was feeling under the weather. The Delta variant wasn't quite finished with us, and as much pleasure as it would've given some Bigfooters, I had no wish to kill Peter Byrne.[3]

I decided to drop in on Robert Michael Pyle. Pyle's 1996 book, *Where Bigfoot Walks: Crossing the Dark Divide*, is far and away the most literate of the Bigfoot literature. By the lenient standards of the genre—which, like its subject matter, has remained unchanged for centuries—it's a work of excoriation, with a scientist's rigorous devotion to reason. The possibility of Bigfoot, though, is always there. "To dismiss the unknown out of hand is even more foolish than to accept it unquestioned, more foolhardy than to fear it," Pyle wrote with his typical arms-length parity. It was the first book I'd read during my research, which was probably a mistake, as it seemed to have said it all. Fortunately, Pyle centered things around an obscure roadless area in western Washington—the "Dark Divide"—and neglected to quote Pauly Shore at all. In a 2017 reissue, he reckoned with decades of immersion in the subculture, with the "gold fever" that can strike Bigfooters, leaving tattered lives in its wake. "It is easy to disappear into the shadow of this particular chimera and never come out." I wanted to ask him about that, to see what he thought of Bigfooting today, how things had changed.

When I arrived, Pyle was standing in his yard staring at butterflies. This makes sense when I tell you that he does this for a living.

---

3 I mention him as a way of acknowledging the sometimes fractious nature of Bigfooting and my own trepidation about involving myself in it. Cliff Barackman, a *Finding Bigfoot* cast member and a widely *loved* figure in the field, told me he'd received several death threats. "Bigfooting is a vitriolic cesspool of bloodthirsty vipers," he said. "Acrimony," the anthropologist David J. Daegling has written, "is the signature of the field."

A lepidopterist, his first books were on moths and butterflies, including his excellent *Chasing Monarchs: Migrating with the Butterflies of Passage*, about the nine-thousand-mile monarch migration from British Columbia to Mexico. He's also a poet and novelist of serious renown.

Pyle's house, an old Swedish homestead, sat in the hills above Washington's last remaining covered bridge. It was surrounded by rhododendron, laurel, black walnut, and a lone sugar maple. One massive oak had been the tallest in the state until it was topped after an ice storm. The butterfly, by the way, was a fritillary, a black and carroty spangled beauty that, like its larger cousin the monarch, is a prodigious pollinator. The evidence of this crowded out Pyle's yard: currants, blueberries, Asian pears. The overall impression was of a home being reclaimed by its resident flora.

Pyle was expecting me. Which isn't to say that I was invited, not strictly speaking. But I had brought beer. Drinkable beer, not some IPA crap. We sat on his porch as the day's heat wore off. Pyle had a bushy white beard, matching shoulder-length locks, and toenails painted brilliant cornflower blue, courtesy of a niece. A neighbor dropped by with a cooler of razor clams. This was what passed for an afternoon in Washington: porch beer. Fresh-caught clams. Butterflies in a currant-scented breeze. I loathed Boston just then.

Talk turned, as it does, from Bigfoot to Trump. Bigfooting didn't start with Trump. In its modern iteration, Bigfoot has been with us for nearly three-quarters of a century. But the beast's dual nature—legitimate dark horse prospect or pathetic, demented caricature?—had inevitably drawn the Orange Lord into the conversation.

"Any massive enthusiasm, when your life is not wholly satisfactory, can carry you away," Pyle said. "And I think that's exactly what's happened, in such tragic and massive forms, with Trump."

I asked whether he meant that Bigfooting and Trumpism were related phenomena—expressions of disproportionally white, male, middle-aged American angst?

"Yes. There's a lot in common. As with the January 6th people, Bigfooters are all white guys. And they love their gear and their big trucks and their big guns and all of their infrared things. It's not exactly the same crowd as January 6th, but it's some of the same people. Think of a Venn diagram. Probably there's overlap with racists and white supremacists and other kinds of mental maladies too. Which the germ is just making worse. And I suspect a lot of them won't be vaccinated." Like Trump, Pyle said, Bigfoot "kind of hits people like a storm. Many are mild mannered until they get into this gyre of craziness."

Early on, when I began dabbling in Bigfoot, I came to know a few people whose lives had fallen into disrepair. One in particular, I mentioned to Pyle, had been accused of hoaxing and lying about sightings. We'd spoken a few times. He seemed like a nice guy but eggshell brittle, carrying an almost violent armature of persecution, along with a near-hysterical devotion to the irrational. From others I'd learned that he had grown estranged from his daughter and son-in-law over the hoaxing business, had moved cross country to separate himself, and that he and wife had begun communicating nightly with ghosts.

"The Shakespearian, tragedian figure," Pyle said, someone "driven by their demons" deeper and deeper into escapist fantasy, was a familiar Bigfooter meme. At first, Bigfoot could be an exhilarating ride. There was an *Alice in Wonderland* quality of stepping through a door to an anomalous exterior, at once mythic and real, a world larger than you'd ever imagined. But as often as not, there were more and more doors to be opened. The spark of curiosity led to endless searching, which fed a temptation to goose up "evidence," which spun some Bigfooters into the outer reaches of the mind and imagination. So desperate you were for the White Rabbit to appear again, so tormented you became with waiting, that it torpedoed your life.

"Say a person actually has an experience," Pyle said. "Life suddenly becomes interesting. They're not just another Forest Service grunt. They're special. People are writing articles about them. They start a Bigfoot group. And then nothing else happens. They don't find more tracks. No more sightings. Now what? So they get into hoaxing. They get into orbs and flying saucers. This happens over and over."

In an early chapter of *Where Bigfoot Walks*, Pyle wrote of the eerie nocturnal dance of ghost moths, one of "nature's most spectacular displays of sexual energy and adornment," not unlike that of birds of paradise. Male ghost moths, after spending most of their lives in the larval stage, emerge from their pupa and, for an hour or so, swarm together in a collaborative courtship shimmy, swaying back and forth above the ground, trying to attract females. At twilight, these undulating orbs—many dozens at a time—resemble "glowing spirits hovering." At first glance, Pyle admits, "they do seem to be phantoms." Which is what some folks take them for. "These fleeting lives leave powerful visions behind, beguiling a small number of lepidopterists while giving shivers to dusk-watchers and night-campers who haven't a clue what to make of these strange sights," he wrote. "I have little doubt that many UFOs, fairies, and specters could be handily explained in lepidopterological terms." The "flying saucer" orbs of one woo-like visionary, he tells us, are simply mosquitoes filmed out of focus and backlit by a camp lantern.

"Denial, and the will to be gulled, is very strong," Pyle said. "I'm afraid the number of reasonable people in Bigfooting is vanishingly small. There's a lot who range from mentally unstable to having no filter. It's a sad pathology of our times."

Pyle got up and went inside. He came back with an LP that he'd cut with Krist Novoselic, the Nirvana bass player, who lived nearby. *Butterfly Launches from Spar Pole*—a spar pole is a tree stripped bare for logging, a symbol of a plundered forest—contained eleven of Pyle's poems recited over Novoselic's arrangements of guitar, dobro, mandolin, and accordion. It made a certain sense that Pyle would collaborate with Novoselic, whose recent work, as part of the band Giants in the Trees, is synchronous with Bigfoot.

While Pyle had contempt for the Trumpers and magical thinkers, he was equally contemptuous of those who dismissed Bigfoot out of hand.

"How can you say, 'This cannot be'?" His voice, I noticed, suddenly became more forceful. His palms were upturned in the manner of someone addressing a jury. "I'm a scientist. I know what a null hypothesis is. I know how to establish deniability. I filter everything through parsimony, and Bigfoot passes the test. Not only is it parsimonious to think of the animal evolutionarily, but biogeographically it's not a problem. And the food dynamics—a big hairy ape surviving on what's available—hold up. There's also Native American traditional knowledge of great depth. Very few areas of doubt cannot be confronted with parsimony. Not to mention that parsimony does not easily admit a hoax of such grand design and coordination. Talk about a conspiracy theory!"

Twenty-five years is a long time. When Pyle started *Where Bigfoot Walks*, he assumed the creature lay beyond the realm of biological tenability. When he finished, he was on the fence, though more inclined toward accepting Bigfoot than not. He'd never seen one, but the physical evidence, he felt, was overwhelming. By 2017, when he added a new chapter, he found Bigfoot "very difficult to dismiss," he told me. "I was eighty to eighty-five percent convinced it was real." He was careful not to put too fine a point on it. "I've never been an advocate for believing in Bigfoot. That's not my job or objective. All I'm advocating for is having an open mind."

Then in May 2021, while driving home from a butterfly field trip, Pyle had his first sighting. He was coming over White Pass from Yakima on U.S. 12. Dusk was falling. A herd of elk was crossing the highway in front of him. After nearly hitting one, he slowed to a crawl.

"I'm driving along and all of a sudden, up a steep bank, I see an animal moving. I'm expecting an elk, so I turn and look up at it— this is a matter of seconds—I see this thing and I say, 'Holy, holy shit!' I only see two legs, and they're big thick legs, and I see a big arm hanging down. Barely saw the head. And then it disappeared between two trees, and I saw its ass and it did not have a big white butt, which elk have. If I had hallucinated an elk and turned it into an ape, it should've had the big white ass. But I saw this brown butt, with a vertical mass above it, taller than any elk, disappear between two trees. And that's the last thing I saw."

I asked him if he believed what he'd seen that night had been a Bigfoot.

"I *think* it's what I saw, but I don't *believe*. Belief is faith. I have no faith in it. I just have belief in probability. And I don't have a better hypothesis. The simplest explanation is often the one that applies. But the light was fading. I saw it for only five or six seconds, which is a serious liability. There's suggestion and projection to consider. I'm subject to it like everybody else. This could've been projection operating in overtime."

I confess when Pyle first told about me his sighting back in July, I was unsettled. *Where Bigfoot Walks* had played a decisive role in my decision to write this book. By exposing the legend to wider scrutiny, Pyle gave me permission of sorts to poke my head in the rabbit hole. I worried that he too had vanished "into the shadow of this particular chimera," succumbing, almost inevitably, to the trope of heroic fatigue. Sitting on his porch, however, I began to vibe on his experience. Granted, three beers in, Pyle found me in a suggestible state. But the power of his telling, the simple but subversive thrill of what he'd maybe/maybe not seen, dispelled whatever hesitancy I had. It marked the birth of an eagerness to continue with my Bigfoot search that, until then, I hadn't quite possessed. At the same time, I became conscious of the fact that I was, in a hard-to-define way, probably guilty of the kind of intellectual foreclosure Pyle abhorred, with a mind that wasn't totally open but only slightly ajar.

"I *think* it's what I saw, but I don't *believe* it." I wondered, basking in Washington's soft afternoon glow, whether it was even possible to separate the two.

Pyle hadn't been back to the spot of his sighting. I suggested I follow up, head over there in a few days to see what I could find. Before seeing me off, he drew me a map with GPS coordinates. "Extraordinary claims require extraordinary evidence," he said, quoting Carl Sagan. "Unless you've been confronted with extraordinary proof, you won't be convinced."

———

The next day, feeling pumped after my visit with Pyle, I arrived at Mount Saint Helens. The volcano is in Skamania County, the first to pass an ordinance—in 1969, amended in 1984—prohibiting the killing of Bigfoot. It was a publicity stunt with the dual purpose of preventing overeager Bigfoot hunters, who were flocking to the area after a rash of sightings, from accidently shooting each other.

One of the most infamous of all Bigfoot stories sprung out of Skamania in July 1924. Five men working a gold claim on Mount Saint Helens's southeast shoulder, two miles below the summit, claimed to have been attacked by a pack of "gorilla men" or "mountain devils." One miner, Fred Beck, later published an account called *I Fought the Apemen of Mt. St. Helens.* You can find it online. It's worth a read. Beck says they began hearing strange noises at night and discovered footprints measuring nineteen inches long. One day, things took an odd turn:

> Hank asked me to accompany him to the spring, about a hundred yards from our cabin... We walked to the spring, and then, Hank yelled and raised his rifle, and at that instant, I saw it. It was a hairy creature, and he was about a hundred yards away, on the other side of a little canyon, standing by a pine tree. It dodged behind the tree, and poked its head out from the side of the tree... The creature I judged to have been about seven feet tall with blackish-brown hair. It disappeared from our view for a short time, but then we saw it, running fast and upright, about two hundred yards down the canyon. I shot three times before it disappeared from view... Nightfall found us in our pine-log cabin.

Around midnight, the men were awakened by objects crashing against the cabin walls. The creatures, they discovered, were raining rocks on them from the canyon lip. Beck and Hank returned fire with their rifles while the others, "stunned and incredulous," cowered in a corner. At one point, the apemen climbed onto the cabin itself.

> We shot round after round through the roof. We had to brace the hewed-logged door with a long pole taken from the bunk bed. The creatures were pushing against it and the whole door vibrated from the impact. We responded by firing many more rounds... They pushed against the walls of the cabin as if trying to push the cabin over...
>
> Just as soon as we were sure it was light enough to see, we came cautiously out of the cabin... It was not long before I saw one of the apelike creatures, standing about eighty yards away... I shot three times, and it toppled over the cliff, down into the gorge, some four hundred feet below.

They eventually made it to the Swift Lake ranger station. As reported in the July 16, 1924, edition of the *Oregonian*, rangers J. H. Huffman and William Welch accompanied Beck to the cabin site and the cliff where he'd shot the ape-man. "A ranger scrambled down the supposedly inaccessible canyon and found—nothing." They decided the miners had made the whole thing up. Fifty years later, William R. Halliday, in his booklet "Ape Cave and the Mount Saint Helens Apes," rendered an even less flattering verdict: The miners' assailants, he claimed, were kids from a local YMCA camp who'd trekked to the canyon and tossed rocks into it, not realizing there were people at the bottom. The miners, seeing dark figures silhouetted by moonlight, mistook them for giant apes.

Something Beck didn't mention at the time of the incident, or at least didn't appear in contemporary accounts about it, was that he and his companions were "always conscious that we were dealing with supernatural beings" that were "not entirely of the world," he wrote in *I Fought the Apemen of Mt. St. Helens*, published in 1967, four decades after the events it describes. How else to explain that, after shooting one, they found no trace of the body? A self-diagnosed clairvoyant, Beck said he'd experienced "visions" as a boy in the Adventist Church and later spent years in "healing work." The ape-men—he referred to them as "Abominable Snowmen," a term then in wide use—passed back and forth between spiritual and material planes, appearing suddenly in this world, "followed by the super-natural exits back into their own realm." They were, he said, "from a lower plane. When the condition and vibration is at a certain frequency, they can easily, for a time, appear in a very solid body. They are not animal spirits, but also lack the intelligence of a human consciousness." Other apparitions appeared to the men, chatting amiably, and helping them locate their mine. An "aura of good or spiritual power surrounded" us, Beck wrote. Trouble started when one of the miners lost his temper and besmirched the reputation of a spirit.[4]

I Fought the Apemen of Mt. St. Helens is the earliest delineation I can find of what Bigfooters today call, in Seussian fashion, "woo." This is the idea that Bigfoot is but a star in the paranormal firmament, encompassing interdimensional travel, UFOs, shape-shifting, telepathy, spirit projection, cattle mutilations, infrasound, levitating

---

4 Beck's account is the only one from the Ape Canyon miners that survives.

orbs, Nephilim—i.e., the ur-Bigfoots, offspring of fallen angels who, in Genesis, "went into the daughters of humans, who bore children"—and a sense of indeterminant connection between them all. The term emerged around 2005, though its mystical antecedents can be traced to antiquity. Depending on the user, woo can be meant pejoratively—the cutting ripostes "aper" or "flesh-and-blooder" refer to the rubes who believe merely that Bigfoot is an undiscovered species of primate—or simply as a metonym for ever-murkier and convergent recesses of belief. As befits a childlike vision of the world, woo makes anything and everything possible, blurring the lines between the fantasy genre and more tenuous occult visions. Bigfoot's enduring elusiveness might be chalked up to interstellar wormholes, extraterrestrial moonbeams, Predator-like cloaking, the mercurial hand of a higher order, or a combination thereof. Some woo'ers claim to "mindspeak" with Bigfoot—communicate telepathically—others to have been zapped aboard spacecraft copiloted by the Big Guy and little green men. Most Bigfooters are conversationally fluent in woo, though few cop to an expression of faith. Suffice it to say, for a substantial number—Pyle referred to them as "the lunatic fringe"—the creature is far more than it appears, with powers and origins beyond our comprehension.

————

At the time of the Ape Canyon incident, the land around Mount Saint Helens was mostly virgin forest. Spruces later felled by loggers had trunks seventy-five to eighty feet around. Five-hundred-year-old Douglas firs, bare of branches for the first 150 feet, reached heights of forty stories. John Muir thought Mount Saint Helens—"Loowit" or "Lady of Fire" to Puyallup tribe and "Si Yett" or "the woman" to the Yakama—and its closest cousin, Rainier, were "the noblist [sic] mountains I ever saw, surpassing even Shasta in the beauty of their lines." The ancient forest surrounding them, "more wood than human beings could ever use, a limitless supply," one observer noted, were supposed to last forever.

Within sixty years, almost all of it was gone. Land rapers like the Weyerhaeuser and Georgia-Pacific lumber companies saw to that. Most harvestable old growth between the Cascades and Puget Sound was clear-cut, shipped to sawmills and plywood mills across the west and turned into ship masts, piles, joists, flooring, rafters, siding, and windowsills. Until it became a national monument, Mount Saint Helens, which lies inside the Gifford Pinchot National Forest, was managed largely at the pleasure of the timber industry. "Getting the cut out," a popular Forest Service phrase of the 1960s and 1970s, typified the agency's "multiple use" management philosophy, which laid bare public lands to private logging, grazing, mining, gas, and oil concerns. In some cases, the forest's very custodians—Forest Service employees—worked exclusively on behalf of the lumber companies and were promoted based on how many trees they helped extract. By 1982, when Mount Saint Helens gained monument status, prohibiting logging inside its boundaries, it was too late. Much of its old growth, and indeed, most of Washington's great primordial forests, like that of the eastern United States, Midwest, and South before them, had been leveled.

Auden got it right when he wrote, "A culture is no better than its woods." By removing mature, fire-resistant trees and replacing them with highly flammable plantations, clear-cuts create ideal conditions for wildfires. The week I traveled to Washington, fires raged across the west, eventually burning more than 2.5 million acres. The Schneider Springs fire, which had consumed one hundred thousand acres southeast of Rainier, was threatening more destruction. Evacuation orders had been issued for a triangular swath of land from the Naches River to U.S. 410 and over to Pinecliff.

Approaching Mount Saint Helens, I passed graveyards of gnarled stumps. Charred remains of leftover slash. Orange logging signs tacked or package taped to sprucelings and noble firs. Trees that from afar appeared so thickly arranged as to be immovable were, I saw when I pulled close, merely screens—"beauty strips," the Forest Service calls them—left by timber crews to obscure clear-cuts. It wasn't quite Burtynsky's *Manufactured Landscapes*, but a feeling of calamity, of having stumbled upon the scene of an accident, came over me.

A caveat: at Merrill Lake, a 280-acre alpine tarn framed by patches of second and third growth, I camped beneath spectacular Douglas firs. The area's topography had been completely transformed by logging, but it was stunning. A rich, diaphanous ochre from the southwest gave the water an eerie glow, as if a fire were raging above it. The lake was flies only. "Anglers, you are in bull trout country!" a sign read. I assembled my rod, pulled on my waders, and clomped down to the water, where a hex hatch was underway. Trout slurped at flies, their bulbous heads breaching the surface. With the place to myself, I landed one trophy trout after another... This is a pathetic joke. I'd brought neither my rod nor waders. All I could do was sit there, impotently, and stew.

It may be worth lingering a moment on the 1980 eruption. I knew nothing about it. For starters, Mount Saint Helens, I learned, is a stratovolcano, meaning it's made up of layers of ash, mud, magma, and rock. Geologically speaking, it's prepubescent, about forty thousand years old. Sicily's Mount Etna, by contrast, is around 350,000 years old. Over the last four thousand years of its life, Saint Helens has been the most active volcano in the country. According to the U.S. Geological Survey, of all Cascades volcanos, Saint Helens is the most likely to erupt again in our lifetimes. Since 1980, "seismic swarms" of small earthquakes, thought to be a sign of magmatic "recharging," have recurred frequently beneath it, as recently in 2019.

During the May 18, 1980, eruption, Mount Saint Helens's entire northern flank collapsed. Magma exploded from the crater, not straight up but to the side, sending avalanches called "pyroclastic flows" down the slopes. "Being in a pyroclastic flow is sort of like being in the most powerful hurricane on earth but with most of the atmosphere replaced by red-hot, pulverized rock. Such a flow can travel at speeds of hundreds of miles per hour up and over ridges, down valleys, and around obstacles. People die by suffocating on the stone dust that fills their lungs, by burns from the enveloping ash cloud, or by being torn apart by the force of the blast," Steve Olson wrote in *Eruption: The Untold Story of Mount St. Helens.*

There was no outrunning it. David Johnston, a thirty-year-old volcanologist, was at his observation post, Coldwater II, five and a half miles from Mount Saint Helens, when it erupted. Grabbing his two-way radio, he called his colleagues at a monitoring station sixty-five miles away—"Vancouver! Vancouver! This is it!"—before his radio went dead. Johnston's body was never found. On a nearby ridge, sixty-four-year-old ham radio operator Gerry Martin watched as the blast overwhelmed Johnston. Martin's last words, calmly announced to the local ham network, were, "It's going to hit me too." Fifty-five other people died. It was the single most powerful natural disaster in

U.S. history, releasing more energy than the 1945 atomic explosions at Los Alamos. Some 150,000 acres of forest were destroyed. Winds eventually deposited 520 million tons of ash eastward.

Also killed in the blast, legend has it, were Bigfoots. It's said that Bigfoot corpses were found in the Cowlitz River after the eruption; that the bodies were housed in a makeshift morgue until the Forest Service, in collusion with Weyerhaeuser and perhaps the U.S. Army, could airlift them out; that in Spokane, a Chinook helicopter was seen flying overheard towing a cargo net filled with dead Bigfoots. Max Brooks's epistolary barn burner, *Devolution: A Firsthand Account of the Rainier Sasquatch Massacre*, bears a strong family resemblance to this narrative. Brooks swaps out Saint Helens for Rainier—owing, perhaps, to the very real possibility of a pending Rainier eruption, in which three hundred thousand people and an unknown number of Bigfoots would have minutes to escape—and instead of pyroclastic flows sends a Bigfoot horde barreling toward an enclave of techy do-gooders, who're torn limb from limb. "Some of them realize, too late, that nature is anything but harmonious."

In *Who's Watching You? An Exploration of the Bigfoot Phenomenon in the Pacific Northwest*, Linda Coil Suchy repeats a story from a man named Fred Bradshaw, whose father worked for Weyerhaeuser during the eruption. The elder Bradshaw was sent to help out at Spirit Lake afterward. There, according to Suchy, National Guardsmen had piled carcasses of animals to be cremated. "Deer in one, elk in another, and so on." Bradshaw, his son told Suchy, was in charge of a pile.

> When the tarps were removed, he was amazed to see that the bodies were those of sasquatch. Some badly burned, and some not. They were placed in a large net and lifted into

the back of a truck, which was then tarped over. [Bradshaw] asked a guardsman what would happen to the bodies, and the guardsman replied, "They'll study them or whatever. I don't want to know. It's like other stuff, you don't ask." Later that day, his father and the rest were debriefed, told not to talk about what they had witnessed there that day, and sent home.

Such stories get recycled in blog posts, eliciting commentary. On one, a reader named Veronica wrote:

"I Was 11 yrs. old 1980 & watched Volcano on Mt. Saint Helens News. Got To See Male & Female Sasquatch being helped by Ambulances."

The response, by Bigfooter standards, was mild:

"No, no you didn't."—The Squatch

"Seriously, stop. You are ridiculous... This is why people will never take mysteries like this seriously."—Annie

"Sure you did. And Elvis was the ambulance driver right?"—Heath

"The Red Cross helped the sasquatch families get food and lodging for the week."—Bob

"This tall tale is...Muckady muckaroo."—Tom

It goes on like that. Until a man named Samuel came to Veronica's defense:

> "Now don't be so quick to discredit someone. It was the military and a few government agencies. That were helping them. [One Bigfoot] was taken out and had its injuries taken care of. There were like five total. Out of many more that did not make it. And [this] came from three sources. That live in different States. All had the same story... So explain that!?!???... The stories are out there. You just have to look and then listen to them."

Therein lies a succinct argument for keeping your kids off the internet.

At any rate, I wanted a glimpse of Ape Canyon, so I hiked up the volcano, skirting remnants of an eruption-era mudslide, onto a rocky steppe of scattered beardtongue and fireweed. A Steller's jay, with its European footballer's mohawk, darted past. There was a whisper of rain. And a rather bleak vista of fog. I could see nothing of Saint Helens. A pair of sodden mountain goats, grazing and bracing themselves against the wind, looked up, stared back at me, then resumed grazing. I pushed on toward Windy Pass, which lived up to its name, before circling back to Ape Canyon. A local Bigfooter had warned me against climbing down into the canyon itself. "It's a three-hundred-foot drop. You could very easily die," he'd said. I'd planned to camp on the canyon edge, at Pumice Butte, a stone's throw (as it were) from Fred Beck's cabin site. The cabin itself is long gone, but Bigfooters have guesstimated its location. Rain permeated everything. Soaked through to my underpants, I beat it down to my car, gobbled half a trail bar, spit it out, and went to find something warm to drink.

At the risk of stating the obvious, Washington is an absurdly well-caffeinated state. Its coffee IQ is through the roof. What surprised me was how widely dispersed it was. Everywhere, even in one-stoplight villages, there are wooden huts, Shackletonian in size and bearing yet decadently outfitted in state-of-the-art coffee-making tackle. In a rundown sawmill town on the Cowlitz River, my order of a drip coffee was tersely swatted away by a young barista. "Nothing brewed," she said. "I can make you an espresso, Americano, macchiato, cortado…" I had a latte. My first noninstant coffee in days. It was terrific.

———

It bears repeating: Peter Matthiessen, winner of not one but *two* National Book Awards—the only writer to win for both fiction and non—cofounder of the *Paris Review*, high priest of New York's literary demimonde, superintellectual, sane, solemn Peter Matthiessen, was a Bigfoot hunter.

"Peter was always reticent about that," Jeff Meldrum said. "He was cognizant of the potential negative fallout that might come from, you know, hanging out with us kooks." Still, Matthiessen was game enough to give a talk on ISU's Pocatello campus called "A Naturalist's Perspective on the Wild Man," which drew on Native American legends and the anatomical evidence for Bigfoot. He included images of footprint casts that Meldrum had collected over the years, many with musculature signatures and minuscule skin ridge details on the toes and plantar surfaces that Meldrum contends could only have been made by an apelike creature. "Sometimes even subtle evidence is compelling," he said, noting the preponderance of such prints around the country. "Show me how they're faked. It would have to be a massive hoax, incorporating knowledge of anatomy, not just of human feet but of nonhuman primates and early hominids, which only a few dozen people in the world have a working knowledge of. This kind of thing is lost on some people, but not Peter."

After a second trip to Nepal, Matthiessen returned to New York with photographs of footprints and a twist of reddish hair that Sherpas claimed was from an abominable snowman. The footprint turned out to be a bear's, the hair from a horse. Undaunted, Matthiessen announced, "As with the sasquatch of the vast rain forests of the Pacific Northwest, the case *against* the existence of the yeti—entirely speculative, and necessarily based on the assumptions of foolishness or mendacity in many observers of good reputation—is even less 'scientific' than the evidence that it exists."

Matthiessen's interest in Bigfoot led to an immersion in Native American myths and traditions and in turn to broader involvement in Indigenous struggles, as he noted in his 1983 book, *In the Spirit of Crazy Horse*, about Leonard Peltier and the American Indian Movement:

> My travels with Indians began some years ago with the discovery that most traditional communities in North America know of a messenger who appears in evil times as a warning from the Creator that man's disrespect for his sacred instructions has upset the harmony and balance of existence; some say that the messenger comes in sign of a great destroying fire that will purify the world of the disruption and pollution of earth, air, water, and all living things. He has strong spirit powers and sometimes takes the form of a huge hairy man; in recent years this primordial being has appeared near

Indian communities from the northern Plains to far northern
Alberta and throughout the Pacific Northwest.

In 2011, Matthiessen spoke at the Center for Fiction on Forty-
Seventh Street in Manhattan. I recall it being an uncommonly shitty
night. Horizontal rain. Umbrella-shredding gales. Which might
account for why the event was thinly attended. Despite arriving late,
I got a seat near the front. I'd not read much of him by then. *The
Snow Leopard*, half of *Far Tortuga*, but all of *Shadow Country*, twice.
I'm going to make enemies, but *The Snow Leopard* is an epic yawner.
Albeit a brilliant one, tenderhearted and moving, but excepting the
yeti cameo, entirely devoid of drama. Whereas *Shadow Country*,
about a murderous Florida planter named Edgar J. Watson, is harrowing, every page soaked with blood. For a while, I was subsumed
by it, in a way I liked to imagine that Matthiessen himself was by the
real-life Watson. In a flash of inept literary forensics work, I went to
the Everglades, boated out to the mangrove islands where Watson
had lived and died, the sundry grounds where his bullet-riddled body
had been interred, dug up, and reburied. I tracked down folks who
Matthiessen had talked to. He spent three decades collecting stories about Watson and the people who'd killed him. It was typical
of Matthiessen to commit himself so relentlessly to an investigation
that the reader feels exhausted in his own bones. I understood this
obsession, this long-haul narrative endurance, as an elemental part of
his modus. I also understood that I had none of it in me. I was there
a week, tops, and fed up with it by then. But I've loved Matthiessen's
work ever since.

Matthiessen sat with his interlocutor on a dais, in roughshod
khakis and an oxford, hands in his lap. He smiled a lot. Mostly what

I remember is his voice: casual, friendly, acerbic, sad, with humor sidling up to high melancholy. He more than met Adam Zagajewski's definition of a true artist: "maximally sober, at once melancholy and joyful...a whole being, happy and sad at the same time." During the Q and A, someone asked why, despite having grown up in Manhattan, he hardly ever wrote about New Yorkers and was instead preoccupied with Florida gladesmen, Sherpas, Lakota Sioux, etc. "I like to write about people with real problems, not people with neuroses," Matthiessen replied. Zing!

Someone else asked what Matthiessen was working on. I have no memory of what he said. He wouldn't have copped to Bigfoot. Bad press. But it's a safe bet that was indeed what occupied him: the novel he'd begun in the '70s and continued to struggle with, tinkering with it only when he tired of another book, *In Paradise*, which became his last published work. Matthiessen never finished his Bigfoot novel. Part of the problem, I suspect, was he'd mellowed on the topic. "I think he had reached the point in his life and in his study of the creatures where he felt confident that he knew what they were about," Jeff Wheelwright, Matthiessen's nephew, told me, "i.e., they hovered somewhere between myth and reality." Whereas with the yeti, "he believed that the biological possibilities were more secure there." When Matthiessen died in 2014, a fifty-thousand-word manuscript of his Bigfoot novel, too rough to publish, was found on his desk. Also left behind were notes of what he called his "Bigfoot Travels."

Lance Richardson, Matthiessen's biographer, told me the novel was little more than fragments. A copy is among Matthiessen's papers at the Harry Ransom Center at the University of Texas at Austin, where Richardson spent his days. "Pretty hard to even follow for the most part. He kind of wrote iteratively, refining and refining," he said.

Technically speaking, it was Matthiessen's *second* attempt at a Bigfoot novel. The first had broken down, taken on entirely new form, and sailed off somewhere else. "You've read it already. Let's just say the Watson trilogy evolved a lot from how it was originally conceived."

This wasn't surprising. The themes of *Shadow Country*—corporate greed, environmental destruction, wanton slaughter of wildlife—were ones Matthiessen revisited throughout his career. His first nonfiction work, *Wildlife in America,* was a call to arms in the cause of endangered species. Wild animals, he wrote, "embody a human longing no less civilized for being primitive, no less real for being felt rather than thought." Yet beneath that longing lay a shabby truth: when the book appeared in 1959, more than two hundred of our native species had already gone extinct, with more on the way. "Pinned in or chivvied out of its last redoubts by the convulsions of blind progress," American wildlife, Matthiessen worried, was fast approaching "the end of the wilderness road." Typical was the ivory-billed woodpecker, which had vanished from the "dark cypress silences of the southern swamplands," succumbing to habitat destruction and predation. It was last seen in 1944. Evidence of the birds' persistence, including scattered sightings and blurry videos, were "problematical, at best," Matthiessen wrote. But he remained open to possibilities, lest he miss something amazing. "I'm all for mystery," he once said. "I think it's going to be a very dull world when there's no more mystery at all."

In 2005, the ivory-billed woodpecker was rediscovered in an east Arkansas swamp. Ornithologists and birders flocked to the area, but none could capture convincing images or sound recordings. Given the bird's resemblance to the common pileated woodpecker, its comeback became confused and obscure. Sightings dried up. As in a fairy tale, the ivory-billed quietly slipped away, consigned once more to the imagination. But as Matthiessen knew, endings are rarely as clear as we think. In fantasy fiction, the dragon often isn't really dead, only biding its time until the sequel.

———

One of the last things I did in Washington was to follow up on Bob Pyle's Bigfoot sighting. I wanted to get a feel for the kind of place Bigfoot might hang out and to picture things as Pyle had seen them in May. It had the added bonus of eventually plopping me onto S.R. 123, due east of Rainier. On the 123, I'd find a trailhead for the Shriner Peak fire lookout. If I hustled, I could squeeze in a summit hike with a 360-degree vista of Rainier, Saint Helens, and Mount Adams. The 123 would then spit me onto U.S. 410 and back to Seattle.

The day dawned in garish Technicolor. Barn swallows chattered across a radioactive sky as the highway became a thin, spiraling chicane. The Columbia River, still as a martini, curled along beside me. So much more is possible on the road. One can fulfill their youthful promise, disentangle from the corporate mortal coil, turn decades of stagnation and decline on their head and start fresh. *I'll take cooking classes! Learn to play the banjo and habla español!*

Outside the village of Skamokawa, I got stuck behind a public transport van that showed no signs of approaching the posted speed of 35 miles per hour. It moved like it was dragging an anchor. When I finally got around it, I saw that written on its side was "Bigfoot is tired of social distancing. Get vaccinated." Vaccine hesitancy was in the news a lot then. COVID quackery abounded, no doubt aided by Trump's claim that 99 percent of coronavirus cases were "totally harmless." Some seven hundred thousand Americans had already died. There was a belief that vaccines were dangerous, even though numerous scientific studies had concluded the opposite. What was dangerous was *not* being vaccinated. But tens of millions of Americans were unmoved. Around then, the *New York Times* reported that the use of "water witches"—people who claimed they could locate underground water sources with dowsing rods, a practice that hydrogeologists described as "totally without scientific merit"—was on the rise in drought-stricken California.

I'd been thinking of what Pyle had said about parsimony and null hypotheses. Mostly because I didn't know the meaning of either and had to look them up. Scientific parsimony, sometimes called Occam's razor, holds that the best explanation for a phenomenon is usually the simplest one—whichever requires the fewest addenda or suppositions. It's a restraint placed on theoretical cul-de-sacs, such as Bigfoot eluding detection by teleporting aboard an Imperial Star Cruiser. A null hypothesis is a way of avoiding biases and false beliefs. When researchers come up with a hypothesis they think explains a phenomenon, they also propose its opposite—a null hypothesis—which they then try to disprove. If they can't disprove the null hypothesis, the hypothesis fails. According to the philosopher Karl Popper, this marks a crucial dividing line between science and pseudoscience: while science deliberately seeks evidence that falsifies a hypothesis, pseudoscience seeks only confirmation. Science is testable. Pseudoscience is not. While a pseudoscientific theory may be true, its validity is always in doubt because it can't be tested. Scientists acknowledge that the best hypothesis or theory is always tentative, as it may eventually be proven wrong. Pseudoscientists, on the other hand, regard their hypotheses as true simply because they haven't been falsified.

This figures into Bigfooting because many of its assumptions, like conspiracy theories and religious beliefs, are unfalsifiable. There's no evidence, for instance, that could disprove a null hypothesis that Bigfoot doesn't exist. The result, as the political scientist Michael Barkun says of conspiracism, is "a closed system of ideas" in which "every attempt at falsification is dismissed as a ruse." Turning an argumentative liability on its head is the oldest rhetorical trick in the book. Psychologists refer to it as the "burden of proof fallacy," a claim that attempts to avoid the burden of proof by shifting it onto someone else. Bertrand Russell, when challenged to explain why he was an atheist and not an agnostic, since he couldn't prove that God didn't exist, famously replied, "If I were to suggest that between the Earth and Mars there is a china teapot revolving about the sun in an elliptical orbit, nobody would be able to disprove [it]."

Further complicating matters is the fact that pseudoscience can seem to gain credence by mimicking the appearance of actual science. Bigfooters, who tend to be science literate[5], often begin scientifically, making bold claims—*this* is the way the world truly is, although it would be unlikely—and giving token expression to parsimony and null hypotheses (true parsimony would account for every possibility first before Bigfoot). They often then swerve away from scientific method, pointing to all kinds of evidence that supports their theories but rarely searching for evidence that could disprove them. Anecdotal claims from eyewitnesses, as many Bigfooters themselves admit, fail every test of scientific rigor. They're a matter of faith, not of evidence.

Which isn't to say we should dismiss Bigfooters' claims out of hand as cleverly packaged snake oil. Such knee-jerk judgment, as Pyle

---

5 I often heard the term "citizen scientist" from Bigfooters to describe their work. For the sake of splitting hairs, "citizen social scientist" would be more accurate, since their laboratory is in the field.

pointed out, is itself contrary to the pursuit of scientific knowledge. Rigorous thinking requires being open and exploratory. It also means accepting uncertainty. One of the insights of Werner Heisenberg, the German physicist and a founder of quantum mechanics, is the uncertainty principle, which holds that no physical events, not even atomic events, can be described with absolute certainty. Quantum theory provides only for probabilities. There are limits to what we can know about the electron, for instance, which reveals only so much information. "We always have to acknowledge that we might be mistaken," the philosopher Simon Critchley wrote. "All we can do is push deeper and deeper into better approximations of an ever-evasive reality. The goal of complete understanding recedes as we approach it." This is as true for Bigfoot as it is for quantum mechanics.

Pyle's coordinates led to a turnoff between Indian Creek and Tieton River Road. I parked and mooched around for a while. The time was midday. I didn't find much, except a pile of shattered elk bones and a leathery hide lying in the sun-beaten grass. The animal appeared to have been hit by a car. Someone had come along and sawed off its antlers. I followed a trail up into the trees and met a young couple headed in the opposite direction. They said the trail ended at a ledge with sweeping north-south views that locals called "the Top of the World." There, I found bottle caps and cigarette butts scattered among tufts of grass poking through volcanic rock. For some reason, the place was swarming with wasps. And it wasn't high up enough to escape the growl of ATVs tearing ass around the Clear Lake shallows below. Waving away wasps, I finally glimpsed Saint Helens, sixty miles west. Broken neatly in half by pines directly in front of me, the summit appeared to float in two jigsaw pieces on a brown haze of smoke.

The weather that summer had been extreme. A northwest heat-wave killed more than five hundred people, many in and around Portland, Oregon, where temperatures reached a record 116 degrees and the air quality index was worse than Chernobyl's. Heat, high winds, a historic drought, and a century of clear-cutting had contributed to one of the worst wildfire seasons in Washington's history. Where I stood was a few miles outside the Schneider Springs burn zone. The smoke soon had me coughing and rubbing my eyes.

When I reached the turnoff for S.R. 123, I found it closed due to fires. This threw my GPS into a tizzy. Unsure how to reach Seattle, I stopped to ask for advice at the Yakima ranger station. That too was closed. I drove until I found a convenience store. The guy behind the counter said the 410 was open but dicey. He suggested the less scenic interstate. Sensing my disappointment, he stabbed a finger onto the map spread before him. "This," he snapped, tracing a circle around Bigfoot's home range of south-central Washington. "This here's all gone."

2
ENTERING SQUATCHACHUSETTS

"The ultimate monster is always the self."

—DEAN YOUNG

When word came that a tornado had touched down near Albany and was barreling straight for us, I figured we had time. One always had time. Albany was what, an hour's drive away? How fast could a tornado possibly travel? No one knew. Except Google. And Google said...quite fast, actually. Upward of 60 miles per hour! Though it was also true that tornados trended in the far more outraceable 10–20 miles per hour range, advancing not in a straight line, typically, but meandering drunkenly about, swerving every which way, occasionally hovering in place, sucking the air out of things, before losing contact with the ground. As I said, plenty of time.

Meanwhile, thunder boomed. Lightning detonated. The wind whipped the trees into a blur. While those of us who'd arrived too late for the night's hunt were thumbing our phones, other folks were out there, no doubt drenched, combing the woods for Bigfoot. One by one, empty tents came loose of their moorings, stakes pried from the loamy earth, and rolled like tumbleweeds across our campsite. Mine held firm. For now. But the rain cared not for its lofty designation of "waterproof." The stupid thing had been so enthusiastically reviewed on gear websites, its virtues extolled so uncategorically, that it should've been able to withstand a direct strike. Yet it appeared, at this nascent stage, to be little better than a cardboard box. A pair of socks I'd tossed aside before turning in sailed past on a half inch of water. By the time I stepped outside, I was an island struggling to stay afloat. There was so much rain and wind that it seemed if I didn't hurry, I'd be swept away.

Shoelessly, with sleeping bag bunched underarm and tents cart-wheeling behind me, I splashed to my Subaru Forester. Sodden Bigfooters were trickling out of the woods. I saw their swirling flash-light beams and heard their chorus of "Fuck!" upon discovering the battlefield carnage in camp. I rolled down my window to chat with one of them, an elaborately ponchoed Ohio Bigfooter named Marc DeWerth. With his headlamp aimed at me, he was a disembod-ied voice in the darkness. Marc laughed wearily when I asked how the evening had gone. Probably it was the rain talking, but he said, "There's a lot of deluded people in this. You might decide it's all bullshit. If you decide that, you should write it. Just because others believe it doesn't mean you should."

The wind was frightening now. Marc popped open his van door, the dome light briefly illuminating his rain-beaten face. "Remember to be wise," he hollered and vanished.

I settled in, snugly impervious to the elements. The Forester had been a good call. My wife and I had hemmed and hawed over its purchase. The back seat, I found, reclined nearly flush with the trunk space so that one could lie down in it more or less prone and, stretched out diagonally, unencumbered.

Did I actually detect, carried ever so faintly on the wind, the sound of someone screaming? I couldn't be sure. Sitting up, I located a pair of dry socks, slipped my noise-canceling headphones over my head, and drifted off, lulled by the dulcet ostinatos of Philip Glass as tornado-y gales rocked the Forester like a cradle.

In the morning, a scene of devastation. Tents strewn everywhere, tipped on their sides and wedged under bumpers. Mine, I noticed, was not where I'd left it. At a picnic table on high ground, a dozen of us gathered over oatmeal and coffee: Scott Ward, forty-nine, a drug and alcohol counselor from New Haven, Connecticut; Colby Heffernan, eighteen, a firefighter from Biddeford, Maine; his father, John, fifty-three, an employee of the Maine Turnpike Authority; Francis Culligan, from Guilford, Connecticut, sixtyish; Francis's son, Frank Jr., in his early forties; and Josh Earnest, twenty-eight, a wastewater treatment plant operator from Stockbridge, Massachusetts. Those who'd been out late wore zombified expressions of fatigue. Everyone, Auden famously wrote, "turns away / Quite leisurely from the disaster." But we fixed our gazes on it—on fat squirrels nibbling disemboweled trash bags, on chocolatey trenches our car wheels had dug out of the grass—while trading intel from last night. The tornado had petered out before reaching us here in the Berkshires, someone said. The weather hadn't been that bad, another clarified. He'd seen worse. Get a load of today, noted a third, gazing skyward. The sun was indeed aloft, the sky wiped clean of any trace of what it had borne.

Jonathan Wilk, our expedition leader, waded over. He was fifty-one and wore thin glasses, baggy khakis, midshin Muck Boots, and a gray T-shirt with the words *Entering Squatchachusetts* on a book leaf Massachusetts town sign. Jon was the founder, in 2006, of

"Team Squatchachusetts." He was also an investigator for the BFRO, which hosts a half dozen or so research expeditions every year, costing between $150 and $400, to suspected Bigfoot habitats across the United States. He talked quietly, with a note of wistfulness in his voice, though he was also a practiced speaker: cheerful, funny, expansive.

"That was probably me you heard yelling last night," he chuckled. "I was standing in my tent holding on to the corners, trying to keep the whole thing from blowing away." A shame no one thought to help him.

Jon paused to shoot a missile of phlegm behind him. He had a hacking, late-September, pre-Omicron cough that I knew probably wasn't COVID related. As a paramedic with a FEMA disaster team on 9/11, he had spent forty days inhaling toxic dust at the World Trade Center site. Like tens of thousands of responders, he'd developed respiratory problems, what he called his "World Trade Center cough." I'd had to pry this out of him. He hadn't volunteered it. He never mentioned it again. From time to time, he'd erupt, coughing and wincing, hands on hips, hock a loogie, recover himself, and apologize.

I'd contacted Jon through the Team Squatchachusetts website. He invited me on his Berkshires expedition, a trip, he said, "deep into the heart of Massachusetts Bigfoot country." It was classic western Mass landscape: hills and fields, fields and hills, all orderly and carefully tended. Barns as big as cathedrals. Imposing stone fences sprouting blueweed and briars. The hardest, densest black bread for sale pretty much everywhere. And village "noticeboards" with flyers advertising baby goats and $5,000 credenzas. The Berkshires may be the only place on earth where farm stands outnumber people. I bought monumentally priced eggs on the honor system, eggs I neither wanted nor could refrigerate, squeezing five-dollar bills into a box full of tens and twenties, purely for the pleasure of overpaying for eggs at a farm stand.

Massachusetts's first documented Bigfoot sighting took place in Berkshire County in 1765. The Barrington Beast, as it came to be known, resembled a large bear with a gorilla-like face. It had a habit of breaking into colonists' homes and making off with food and shiny objects. The trespass of private property being a peculiarly American sacrilege, the creature was pursued, captured, transported to Cambridge, and "fixed in a cage" for study, according to one account. The beast had the "appearance of calmness and innocence when observed," it was said, but "boldness and ferocity when thinking itself unseen." Somehow it managed to escape and flee back into the wild. In the summer of 1865, the *North Adams Transcript* published several stories about a "wild man" leaping fences and crossing darkened roads. It was blamed for livestock deaths. "Farmers Terrorized!" screamed a typical headline. Again a posse ran it down. It turned out to be a gorilla, presumably on hiatus from a circus. And on October 18, 1879, the *New York Times* printed an article about two hunters who encountered a wild man in the mountains near Williamstown. It was about five feet tall, they said, "with very wild eyes," walked upright, and was covered in bright red fur. Mistaking it for a bear, one of them shot it. "With fierce cries of pain and rage, it turned on its assailants, driving them before it at high speed." Dropping their guns, the men lit out, vowing never to return. In town, however, there was talk "of making up a party to go in search of this creature."

There's a bunch more. It's hard to know what to make of them. On the one hand, I'm tempted to take such stories at face value, as portents from an unmapped continent. On the other, fake news isn't new. It has been with us since the invention of the printing press . (Objective, fact-based journalism didn't enter the mainstream until the early twentieth century.) Seventeen years after the Barrington Beast, Benjamin Franklin, hoping to stoke revolutionary fervor, published propaganda narratives about rampaging Indians, loyal to the British crown, scalping and torturing American colonists. "102 [scalps] of Farmers...18 marked with a little yellow Flame, to denote their being Prisoners burnt alive, after being scalped, their Nails pulled out by the Roots and other Torments," read one of his fraudulent accounts. In another, he claimed that seven hundred scalps of young boys, girls, and infants had been taken by Indian troops in league with King George. As with the Barrington Beast, some readers would've treated these sensational claims with skepticism. Others would've swallowed them whole. We live in a different world, but sometimes a gap closes between past and present. One wonders how today's ideological bubbles would transmute Franklin's tales.

Curious that no Bigfoot accounts come to us from the Massachusetts Bay Colony or the older Jamestown. We have a 135-year-long interval between 1630 and 1765. Where was Bigfoot? In his 1634 *New England's Prospect*, the earliest record of the region's mammals, William Wood names "Devills or Lyons," and "strong arm'd Beare...large lim'd Mooses," and "ravenous howling Woolfe," but nothing fiercer. Surely the Puritans settlers would've scratched whatever hairy itch the new pagan continent proffered? Cotton Mather, always pinprick sensitive to supernaturalia, warned his contemporaries of "Droves of Devils," "Dragons," "Fiery flying serpents," "rabid and howling Wolves of the Wilderness [which] would make... Havock among you, and not leave the Bones till the morning," plus witches galore and other terrors of the primitive forest. But he had nothing to say of Bigfootish creatures. Despite the unignorable fact that the legends and folktales of local Indigenous tribes did. Maybe it hit too close to home? What was Bigfoot, after all, but a Puritan lost in a howling wilderness?

After breakfast, we convoyed up and drove to the Savoy Mountain State Forest, disembarking near a Civil War graveyard. We were just twenty miles from the Melvilles in Pittsfield, another six from the Hawthornes in Lenox. Straining to be heard over a rain-swollen river, Jon told a story that explained what we were doing there:

It was about 10:30 in the evening, in January 1992. I was a twenty-year-old park ranger on my night rounds when I pulled into this parking lot. Kids used to have keg parties and they'd burn the picnic tables and make a mess, so I'd cruise through now and then. When I pulled in, a creature ran in front of my headlights. I didn't know what it was. But I knew it wasn't a human being and it wasn't a bear. It turned its whole torso and looked right at me. It had long golden flowing hair. I wouldn't call it fur. It looked...groomed. It was pretty. I don't know if that's the right word. But it had amber eyes and was about six feet tall. I call it "the Teenager." What also stood out was its long arms that went down past its knees. And it had no neck, like it was shrugging its shoulders. When I went to get in my truck, there was another creature behind me in the trees, maybe thirty feet away. All I could see was what was lit up by my taillights. But it was much taller. It fell more into the realm of what people describe as a Sasquatch. It let out a scream that would terrify anyone. I'd gotten between it and its offspring, which is not a place you want to be, with them perceiving you as a threat. I froze. Life slowed down. It seemed like I couldn't get in the truck fast enough. You know how in horror movies when someone's trying to close a door on something that's after them? It was like that. I finally got in the truck, slammed the door, and hit the pillar lock. I picked up the mic on the radio to call it in but I thought, "What the hell am I gonna say?" That's when something hit the back of the truck. I don't know if it threw something or what. But I stepped on the gas and didn't let my foot off until I was seven or eight miles down the road. It was a paradigm shift, a glitch in the matrix. One of those life-changing paths we sometimes go down. I don't want to see one here again, not like that. If you're not prepared for it, seeing a Bigfoot is like a horrible car accident. You feel like, "God, I wish I hadn't seen that." Because it did change my whole life. That was the end of my park ranger career. I couldn't come back here. I was too scared. So I quit. Once people find out you've had a crazy encounter like that, they razz you pretty hard. There's a stigma about being a Bigfoot witness. If I hadn't had that experience, I'd be making fun of people like us too. But I got sick of it. There was no internet then, no way of finding others like me. So I just sort of tuned it out.

He found another job, moved, got married, tried to forget what he'd seen. Until an episode of *Finding Bigfoot* rekindled his interest. Jon became obsessed. Not an ideologue. His enthusiasm lacked a presumption of certainty, except for one detail: something was out there. "I try to keep my feet on the ground," he'd told me earlier over the

phone. "There isn't much that can't be explained as natural phenomena. Eyewitnesses are exactly that: eyewitnesses. They've made mistakes
that have sent people to jail under wrongful convictions. But people
are seeing something. *I've* seen something. And I can't unsee it."

We drove on. Up a crooked two-track onto a broad clearing with
dramatic views of a north-south valley lying between zigzagging, sun-
browned hills. An empty fire tower loomed over us with its shutters
open, the latticework bracing reminding me of the Eiffel Tower. The
grass was wet from yesterday's rain. The sun caused some of us to
pinch sweat from our eyes. In the brush, wild turkeys squabbled.

Jon said the hill we were standing on and all the land we
could see had for centuries belonged to the Iroquois—Mohawks
specifically—whose legends accounted for Bigfoot-like creatures. He
didn't elaborate. But in *Giants, Cannibals and Monsters: Bigfoot in
Native Culture*, anthropologist Kathy Moskowitz Strain names three
in particular (taking care to note that when recording traditional
stories, ethnographers have often failed to differentiate between
the Haudenosaunee Confederacy's six tribes: Mohawk, Oneida,
Onondaga, Cayuga, Seneca, and Tuscarora). They are *Ot-ne-yar-
hed* (stonish giant), *Tarhuhyiawahku* (giant monster), and *Genosqwa*
(stone giant), all three truly horrible, dim-witted bastards, conform-
ing to an insatiable indigenous longing for cannibalistic tyrants who
weren't all that bright. One *Ot-ne-yar-hed*, for instance, with its
rock-hard skin impermeable to arrows, ran around the countryside
devouring people on sight while generally acting a fool. Until the
Upholder of the Heavens, *Ta-ren-ya-wa-gon*, lured him and all other
Ot-ne-yar-hed into a cave near Onondaga, in present day New York,
sealing the entrance with a boulder. One managed to escape and flee
the land, seeking "asylum in the regions of the north," Strain wrote.

When we turned to leave, the wild turkeys asserted themselves, squawking maniacally.

Colby Heffernan—he wore a black bomber jacket and had a faint tendril of moustache—thought they weren't wild turkeys at all. For that matter, whatever they were wasn't plural but singular.

"The way it called was more of a high-pitched scream," Colby said.

Jon, sensing the implication, immediately countered, "I think I know most of my wildlife calls, and that sounded like turkeys to me. I'll call 'em up here if you want."

Undeterred, Colby said the noise lacked a turkey's distinctive staccato cluck. "This was more like a whoop. We have wild turkeys in Maine. Turkeys make a lot of noise. But turkeys don't whoop."

His wide-eyed fervor caught on. Other folks seconded him, affirming that the turkeys didn't strike them as remotely turkeyish. A few trotted down the path for a better angle. Some stepped closer to peer into the brush. Had Colby not mentioned it, I wouldn't have bothered to name this particular sound. It was just part of the forest cacophony.

"It could be something else," Colby pleaded. "I just wanna know what."

I thought I knew the feeling—the magnetic tug of hidden things. A few years ago, I went bow hunting for elk in Colorado. It was a couchbound dilettante's heroic fantasy mediated by brawny huntsmen pals who knew what they were doing. For five days, we circumnavigated the White River National Forest, one of the elkiest places in the United States, never once laying eyes on an elk. We heard them bugling. Heard them thrashing in the trees. Found their shit pyramided on paths we'd crossed hours earlier. Twice I was nearly startled into a coronary by mule deer. But no elk. That's how it goes. Elk are full of surprises. They're like Bigfoots, you think, until a herd fifty deep crosses the road behind the Del Taco where you've stopped for lunch. The thrill, needless to say, is in the hunt. But it's also in wilderness's capacity to exceed your imagination, literally and metaphorically. A world that "displays itself in hiding," to borrow John Berger's phrase, contains immensities. "It was not [the tree's] size that now impressed my companions," Jim Hawkins says in *Treasure Island*. "It was the knowledge that seven hundred thousand pounds in gold lay somewhere buried below its spreading shadow. The thought of the money…swallowed up their previous terrors. Their eyes burned in their heads; their feet grew speedier and lighter; their whole soul was bound up in that fortune, that whole lifetime of extravagance and pleasure, that lay waiting there for each of them." It's only a matter of time, surely, before the shadow recedes and the X reveals itself.

We left disappointed, Colby casting wistful, over-the-shoulder glances.

Jon whispered to me. "You can see how the imagination can run wild. It could be something or it could not. But they want it to be what they want it to be. And it's their trip. I'm just here to make sure they don't get lost or eaten by a bear. I suppose it *could* be something. But also, could it? What are the chances of us stumbling on a Bigfoot up here in broad daylight? Pretty slim, I'd say. We've got to remind ourselves that we all have Sasquatch on the brain."

I mentioned something he'd told me earlier about the power Bigfoot can hold over believers. He'd used the word "addictive."

"It can be," he whispered. "Seeing one is like getting a taste. You gotta see more."

Did that mean there was a danger of perceiving Bigfoot in every turkey gobble and snapped twig?

He looked around, sizing up the uncultivated clutter of spiky plants. "I wish I had the answers. If I did, I'd probably have a Bigfoot body. All I have are opinions and unsubstantiated theories. Bigfoot does not let us come to a conclusion."

————

Since we're in his neighborhood, I'll tell you about Charles Hoy Fort. He was from Albany, over the state line. Born in 1874, Fort is often credited with single-handedly inventing our modern notions of the paranormal and supernatural. While Victorians were dabbling in mesmerism and mind reading, Fort was combing through old newspapers in public libraries, clipping whatever bizarre stories struck his fancy (to the profound chagrin of librarians, one imagines)— "damned data," he called them, because they didn't align with scientific orthodoxy—and compiling them into books. He was all over the map: ESP, teleportation, strange disappearances, poltergeists, sea monsters, lights in the sky, flying saucers, alien abductions, reincarnation, stigmata, spontaneous human combustion, mysterious animals, anomalous footprints, "wild men," "wild girls," "wolf children," the Jersey Devil, freak deluges of frogs, rocks, blood, worms, and in one instance, "a thousand tons of butter." Fort speculated that the earth was stationary and surrounded by an invisible "Super-Sargasso Sea," also called "Genesistrine," from which all life originated. Floating somewhere in between were gigantic spongy islands containing dead birds, jellyfish, dinosaurs, mammoths, "hailstones flavored like oranges," odd humans like Kaspar Hauser,[1] and alien life-forms that were in contact via telepathy with secret earthling societies.

Fort didn't take much of this seriously. Like a certain twice-impeached ex-president of ours, he was a troll who liked throwing shit out there just to see what stuck. But his books sold well and were widely reviewed. The *New York Times* referred to one as "so obscured in the mass of words and quagmire of pseudo-science and queer speculation that the average reader will find himself either buried alive or insane before he reaches the end." H. L. Mencken said of Fort, "He seems to be enormously ignorant of elementary science."

Other writers, including Theodore Dreiser, fell under Fort's spell. "To me no one in the world has suggested the underlying depths and mysteries and possibilities as has Fort. To me he is simply stupendous," Dreiser gushed. Another fanboy, the Pulitzer Prize–winning novelist of *Alice Adams* and *The Magnificent Ambersons*, Booth Tarkington, helped found the first Fortean Society in 1931. Screenwriter Ben Hecht (*Wuthering Heights*, *Notorious*), English philosopher and novelist John Cowper Powys (*A Glastonbury Romance*, *The Meaning of Culture*), and the *New Yorker* drama critic Alexander Woollcott were members.

The Greeks, Marina Warner tells us, had a literary tradition called *mirabilia*—collections of "wondrous things." Writer-compilers of mirabilia were known as "paradoxographers." The most famous was a freed slave named Phlegon of Tralles. His second-century *Book of Marvels* described ghosts, ghouls, centaurs, satyrs, zombies, hermaphrodites and sex-changers, offspring of humans and animals,

---

1 A mysterious German teenager who, in 1828, claimed to have spent his entire life imprisoned in a small cell.

enormous skeletons, and other monstrous elements at large in the ancient world. These weren't abstract wonders. They were out there, it was believed, preserved in a living natural history museum. One could, if desired, see "the skeleton of the sea-monster to which Andromeda had been exposed, the hair of Medusa, the skin and the flute of Marsyas...the clay from which Prometheus had fashioned the first humans, Orpheus' lyre, the spear with which Meleager slew the Calydonian boar...Agamemnon's scepter...the Golden Fleece" and so on.

It might be charitably said of Fort that he was a modern paradoxographer, as marvelously and maddeningly discursive as Phlegon of Tralles. But he was motivated by a deep-seated hatred of what he called the "priestcraft" of science. "The monks of science dwell in smuggeries that are walled away from event-jungles," he wrote. "Or some of them do. Nowadays a good many of them are going native." Like Hegel's disciple Paul Feyerabend, Fort abjured any demarcation between fact and fiction, claiming his "data" were no more frivolous than scientific theories. Of course, Fort wasn't a scientist himself and hadn't the faintest idea how scientists test and validate or invalidate theories. But his influence on pseudoscience was huge. "Fort taught the field of pseudoscience that all you need to write a book is a subscription to some newspapers and good sharp scissors," Rory Coker has written. After his death, Fort became a cultish figure, inspiring a generation of science-hating charlatans. Vincent H. Gaddis, inventor of the Bermuda Triangle hoax, was a Fortean. Ditto Charles Berlitz, grandson of the language school founder, whose occult books—one of which *Time* magazine called "a hodgepodge of half-truths, unsubstantiated reports and unsubstantial science"—sold in the millions.

The Scottish biologist and Bigfooter Ivan T. Sanderson was a

Fortean. Unlike Fort, Sanderson claimed to abhor pseudoscience. Like Fort, he was a world-beating bullshitter with contempt for what Forteans called the "wipe"—a gloating, reflexive dismissal by scientists of phenomena that didn't fit established theories. Institutional science had gone stale, Sanderson declared, all "bottle washing and button pushing." Entrenched in their dogmatic and snobbish insularity, scientists were too hidebound to offer much insight into the world at large. Ordinary people, free of such blinders and embodying the true scientific spirit, were better observers of reality. To his credit, Sanderson also championed Native American learning over bookish, a priori knowledge. "I do not share the old British or what seems to be the current American opinion of 'natives' and never have. I would state that I find the so-called 'native' in some respects on the whole more reliable than the foreigner, and the white foreigner in particular."

In the '50s and '60s, Sanderson penned scores of articles for Fortean magazines like *Fate* and *Fantastic Universe* and men's pulp rags *True*, *Saga*, and *Sports Afield*. In one, he proposed that UFOs didn't come from outer space but from the bottom of the ocean, like in the movie *The Abyss*, except that in Sanderson's meaning, it implied a psychological as well as physical abyss. For this he coined the term USOs, or unidentified submarine objects. In another, he attributed unexplained aircraft disappearances, poltergeist activities, and flying saucers to twelve "devil's graveyards," or "vile vortices," like the Bermuda Triangle, "equally spaced areas on the surface of Earth where 'funny things happen.'"

How much of this Sanderson actually believed is questionable. Outré stories paid the rent. The nuttier the better. His biographer Richard Grigonis points out that Sanderson "was always looking for something that would rocket him into stardom." To both ends, his writing pandered to a ravenous appetite for "true" tales that were obviously cut from whole cloth. Like Trumpian relativity, truth was beside the point. It hardly mattered to the mostly white, mostly male readers of *True* if its stories were completely bogus. "Truth in these magazines was not about facts or correspondence with reality," the scholar Joshua Blu Buhs wrote, "but resisting changing values and valorizing an older tradition, when men were men and honored for their skills." The white male utopia was dying. Sanderson's stories massaged the psychic fallout.

Fitting, then, that one of his earliest hornswoggles occurred in the fantasy-rich zone of coastal Florida. In 1948, gigantic three-toed footprints materialized on a beach near Tampa. They measured fourteen inches long and eleven inches wide, had long toes tapering to claws, and were separated by six-foot strides. Sanderson appeared on the scene with his pseudoscientific baggage. After a two-week "investigation," he declared the tracks had been made by a fifteen-foot "vast penguin," a visitor from the southern latitudes. (As Sanderson surely knew, such penguins actually *did* exist some forty to fifty million years ago, in Antarctica, the tallest standing about six and a half feet.) He'd even seen one himself, he swore, while scouting the Suwannee River. It was onyx colored, had massive flippers, and weighed hundreds of pounds. He dubbed it, unoriginally, "Old Three Toes."

Reading animal tracks, according to the cognitive psychologist Steven Pinker, is an ancient part of our circuitry. In his book, *Rationality: What It Is, Why It Seems Scarce, Why It Matters*, he gives the example of the San people, hunter-gatherers of the Kalahari Desert in southern Africa, who track fleeing animals over long distances, following hoofprints, effluvia, and other spoor until the animals drop from fatigue or overheating. Our oldest human ancestors, the San can trace their civilization back twenty thousand years and owe their survival, Pinker says, to a scientific mindset. "They reason their way from fragmentary data to remote conclusions with an intuitive grasp of logic, critical thinking, statistical reasoning, causal inference, and game theory." When finding ambiguous set of tracks, the San assume they're from a commonly known species unless they find definitive evidence the tracks belong to a rarer one. This is the essence of Bayesian reasoning, after the Reverend Thomas Bayes (1701–1761): adjusting one's credence in a hypothesis based on evidence. The San don't need to be told what Bayesian reasoning is. They live it every day, using reason to correct for cognitive shortcomings.

More Old Three Toes tracks were found on the banks of the Suwannee, on Honeymoon Island, and on the Anclote River near Tarpon Springs. They appeared on and off for a decade before drying up in 1958. Sanderson declared, un-San-like, "that any man or body of men could know so much about wild animal life as to make the tracks in just the manner that they appear, but that they also should be able to carry this out time and time again at night without anybody seeing them or giving them away…is frankly incredible." That is, of course, exactly what had happened. In 1988, the *St. Petersburg Times* revealed that Old Three Toes had been a sham, giving Forteanism its first PR disaster. A local mechanic named Tony Signorini and a friend, using tools in their auto repair shop, had made three-toed, cast-iron feet with tennis shoes attached. "Then they rowed just offshore in the middle of the night so Signorini could disembark, wander along the beach, and climb back into the boat, leaving behind mysterious footprints that would often be reported by one of their friends the next morning."

From giant penguins, Sanderson graduated to "wild men," namely Bigfoot. It was the story that most fascinated him. In the fall of 1961, he published *Abominable Snowmen: Legend Come to Life*, an exhaustive five-continent romp dedicated to a Fortean subfield he termed "ABSMery," after "Abominable Snowman." The book is as close to a holy writ as Bigfoot literature gets. Not only did the word "cryptozoology"[2] make its debut (along with the less preening "crypto-esoteric"), but so, in a sense, did Bigfoot. Sanderson "was the first to tell the world about these 'new' hairy beasts of the rain forests of California," Bigfooter Loren Coleman says, referring to giant footprints found near Willow Creek a few years before, educating "a whole new generation of cryptozoologists-in-training," including Coleman himself. *Abominable Snowmen* is also where Native folk tales and iconography of shaggy humanoids first became mashed up with the white man's self-ratifying pseudoscience, fueling a sloppy condensing and transmogrification of Indigenous legends that characterizes much of the Bigfoot canon today (we take what we like, discard the rest).

Abominable Snowmen was the first book to report the strange case of "Jacko," a Bigfooty creature said to have been captured near Yale, British Columbia, in 1884, and interned in the town jail. Initially taken for a "crazy Indian," Jacko (probably slang for monkey) was four and a half feet tall, 127 pounds, with exceptionally long forearms and silky black hair, according to a July 3 *Daily British Colonist* article that Sanderson quoted approvingly: "Since his capture he is very reticent, only occasionally uttering a noise which is half bark and half growl. He is, however, becoming daily more attached to his keeper, Mr. George Telbury, of this place, who proposes shortly starting for London, England, to exhibit him." Sanderson, who was "absolutely sure" of Jacko's existence, failed to mention a follow-up story appearing eight days later in the *British Columbian*, which

---

2 The search for undocumented and legendary species.

reported that the "only wild man visible" at the jail was the jail-keeper, "who completely exhausted his patience" fielding questions from the two hundred people who'd turned up to see a nonexistent Jacko.

Jacko's legend should've petered out there. But Sanderson couldn't help throwing himself into the breech. He was always fighting rear-guard actions against doubters real and imagined. And he loved a good rant. Lamenting that "perhaps the most enigmatic figure ever to appear in the pages of history and potentially one of the most important" (just the *slightest* exaggeration) had vanished without a trace, Sanderson ignored the paltry evidence for Jacko, building his case around Native testimony: "All the Amerinds of southern British Columbia, Washington State, Oregon, parts of Idaho, and the Yuroks and the Huppas [sic] of northern California not only have similar tales to tell but a history of these creatures so complete and extensive that it would take a volume to tell in itself." He went on. "There are traditions and folk-tales spread over an even wider area among these people, but this is another matter. I am here speaking of perfectly straightforward, up-to-date accounts of encounters with such creatures that have been made by them ever since the white man first got to speak with them and which have come in from one source or another annually every year since the capture of Jacko."

You have to admire this about Sanderson, an Etonian *and* a Cantabrigian who took delight in menacing the clannish and bigoted precepts of scientific inquiry and in defending Native traditions long derogated by whites. *Abominable Snowmen* is, to a large measure, a testimony to Indigenous ontology and intelligence. "Don't ever underestimate the Amerind or his knowledge!" Sanderson wrote.

Jacko's story, sad to say, was waifishly thin. No less than John

Green, the eminent Canadian Bigfooter, decided it was probably hogwash, a journalistic hoax spun into folklore. Coleman too thought it was "a local rumor brought to the level of a news story that eventually evolved into a modern fable." But the alternative reality carried Sanderson's imprimatur and became a classic of the genre. Coleman's basic insight was that Jacko was an example of how modern myths find their origin point, acquire narrative gravitas, and get passed down the centuries.

———

Dinner that evening was, as my students might say, Gucci. Jon's term for it was "campfire foil meal." The way it worked was you took two sheets of tinfoil, folded three sides together so you had a big envelope, filled that with sausage and vegetables and McCormick Grill Mate seasoning, stirred, sealed it tight, then tossed the whole thing onto the coals. You then moseyed casually to your car, snuck sips of beer, moseyed back. And voilà: a cowboy pot roast. It was wonderful. Ingenious. Even more wonderfully, it was practically free, as Jon was charging us a pittance for his services. Why do I love eating this way? Out of a bag, in the open air? I prefer it to most Boston restaurants, or New York's for that matter. We ate and drank in silence, a rising breeze tugging deliciously at our clothes and soothing our sunbaked faces and knuckles. I felt happy to be there.

After dark, several of us returned to the state forest: Colby, Scott, Josh, Fran and Frank Jr., two or three others, and Gary Z., a financial services executive from Salem, Massachusetts. (I'm not using Gary's real name. He worried if people in his industry found out he was a Bigfooter, it'd destroy his reputation.) Carrying stacks of wood and a BioLite stove, we climbed steeply up a slippery path, rounding our way to a kind of plateau, where we trod down the ferns and built a fire. Beside us was an enormous boulder, perhaps a story tall, balanced menacingly on one edge, hence its name, Balanced Rock, after the famous sandstone turret outside Moab. Beyond the boulder and encircling us were hundreds of hardy oaks and hemlocks. The hill had been clear-cut twice in the past two hundred years, Jon said, once for a local farm and once for Boston construction, but a few big hardwoods remained. It was a secret, secluded place. With the huge weight of an ancient boulder bearing down on us, the night felt oppressively dim. "As dark as dark is dark," Gary said.

We were expectant, as one is in these out-of-the-way places, more so at night, when they undergo a radical makeover. The nighttime woods are where the uncertainties of myth mingle with the durability of lived experience. How quick the journey is from civilization to its opposite. How absolutely real a world can feel without actually existing in any concrete sense.

The setup, Jon explained, was "a typical bait-type of situation." We'd make a fire and play music—"Beethoven, not Cheap Trick"—alerting Bigfoots to our presence. "If they're around, they'll come take a look." Jon thought there were two up here, including a gray-colored "rogue male" with a black patch on his arm. "You can trace eyewitness reports of him from Maine to Massachusetts." There were also black bears and moose of indeterminate number and ferocity. "Remember," he said. "We're not trying to find Sasquatch. That's not gonna happen. They're gonna find us." He and another team were staking out the fire tower a few miles away.

I scouted around, drawn along game trails through lush vegetation. The air had turned chilly. It was a day past the harvest moon, the first long johns evening of fall, and I thought of Thoreau's comment about summer's end: "I realize what a friend I am losing."

When I came back, guys were scanning the tree line with FLIR thermal imaging cameras. Have you seen these things? They register infrared "heat" signatures in wavy rainbow outlines, like Predator vision. Hunters use them to spot game at night. They're really neat. Neater still was the pair of night vision goggles being passed around, courtesy of a Bigfooter whose name I didn't catch but who bore an uncanny likeness to the actor Jon Bernthal (a lazy description I'm sticking with). Bernthal worked for a federal agency: "I can't tell you which one, but I've got cool toys." The goggles, he mentioned as he helped holster them awkwardly onto my head, cost $10,000. They were the real deal, exactly what the Navy SEALs wear when they kill Osama bin Laden in *Zero Dark Thirty*. The world became a swampy green canvas, both beautiful and sinister.

"Cool, huh?" said Bernthal. "Now I'll take them back."

Assembled around the fire, we gave the lie to Bigfooting's alleged lack of diversity. We were old white guys, young white guys, middle-aged white guys. A representative slice of what Michael Paternini calls "a brand, a typology: Lost White Boy in Search of Enlightenment."

Gary broke out the BioLite and grilled kielbasa, passing wedges around on a paper plate (there's a joke to be made here about a sausage party that's quite frankly beneath me). In *A Walk in the Woods,* Bill Bryson notes the tendency of wilderness to make people in it long for the comforts of civilization. "The whole point…is to remove yourself so thoroughly from the conveniences of everyday life that the most ordinary things—processed cheese, a can of pop gorgeously beaded with condensation—fill you with wonder and gratitude." It's so true! We'd eaten amply an hour ago. Yet I greedily partook of the kielbasa—"inhaled" is an unkind word but perhaps not inaccurate here—savoring every morsel. There are so many things wrong with that sentence I don't even know where to begin. Let's just move on.

Soon enough, we were trading Bigfoot stories. Scott said he'd been kayaking once on a reservoir in upstate New York when something in the trees started lobbing fistfuls of stones. It was near dusk. The place was remote. Who could be throwing rocks? Bigfoot was a blip on his radar. "I'd spent a lot of time in the backcountry and never had an experience that swayed me one way or the other." But something exciting was going on. Red squirrels were chittering away. Songbirds likewise. He beached the kayak at an embankment to take a look when he suddenly fell ill: nauseated, dizzy. The animals went silent. "I started to feel, I don't know, crazy. It was like I'd walked through a veil in some transcendental sense. My ears were congested. I couldn't keep my balance." He skedaddled.

Gary talked about finding a trackway through the hemlock grove over our shoulders. This was a few years ago. Late June. Daytime. Heavy rain. He was with Jon Wilk and others. For no particular reason, Gary whistled. Something whistled back. A wood knock followed. He and Jon heard rustling. Jon saw movement, a dark figure, and walked toward it, into the woods. He found a footprint, then another. Gary joined him. They had the beginnings of a trackway, but the rain was biblical. "I had this feeling like something was hiding from me, watching me," Gary said. "Not hunting, but it didn't feel right. There was a feeling in the air like something was afraid of us." They skedaddled. On the way out, one of their companions started vomiting. Jon too felt off. "Do you guys get the feeling we're being followed?" he asked. Gary, however, was at peace. "It's like when your faith gets altered a little bit and you glimpse a whole new reality. I'd whistled and the forest whistled back. It was a whistle I'd heard five or six times in my life and that I associated with being in the woods. It was calming."

I always liked hearing firsthand Bigfoot stories. Unlike written accounts, you could more easily take their measure; every indentation of the telling was momentarily etched into a single frame, the teller keenly aware of how bonkers they sounded (so it seemed to me) but animated by the kind of details that struck the listener, more often than not, as genuine. You could imagine the confusion, the wonder, the pregnant tension, and almost step through the screen into a world of campfire horror and get close enough to touch the pleasant thrum of danger, for a few minutes at least. Especially if you happened to be sitting at an actual campfire. With the air absolutely still. The trees stretching forth their ghostly limbs.

"This is the fun part," Bernthal said. "But anyone who does this alone is nuts. I've got a fully loaded M4 and I wouldn't be out here alone."

What also caught my attention were the strange echoes between Scott's and Gary's experiences: both were troubling yet epiphanic mysteries to be further explored, the shock of discovery suggesting an entanglement with a sense of validation ("See, I'm not crazy"). The physiological symptoms weren't incidental either: sudden nausea and faintness are common during encounters. And both fed a hunger to fill in narrative gaps and bring reality to bear on whatever they revealed. It's an endearing quality of Bigfooting, the endless inquisitiveness, a rejection of easy answers and the traps they held, constantly seeking and discarding, searching for clarity, for a harbor through the fog, without letup and in the face of inevitable disappointment.

The fire wasn't doing it for me, my ideal temperature being a Swedish sauna in August. Shivering, I yanked my hat down over my ears, shoved my hands into my pockets, and placed my boots practically in the flames, feeling immoderately proud that I wasn't complaining. We each have our peculiar talents and that is mine: complaining. About everything. Always. As Rodin worked in clay and Van Gogh in oils, I work in complaints. A lifetime of memories revolves around them. I can recall with utter clarity petty complaints lodged decades ago. I can see the room, describe everything in it, feel the pleasure of dragging people down to my level... But not tonight. I wasn't in a complaining mood. The Bigfooting spirit had taken hold.

Surprised at my own pluck and fortitude, I hopped to my feet and, borrowing a FLIR from Gary, raked the luxuriant foliage. The effect was captivating. Stones warmed by the sun shone in a sparkling gold and tangerine mosaic. An inert jumble of trees was suddenly ablaze with swirling psychedelia.

"There's something out there waiting for us, and it ain't no man," I said, quoting the late great Sonny Landham in *Predator*. It garnered a single, pitying chortle.

Gary mentioned the woo claim that Bigfoots could sense, and thus dodge, all manner of electronic surveillance, including FLIRs. This led to a discussion of Bigfooting's intimacy with questionably sane beliefs and a larger rejection of scientific norms. Gary said flesh-and-blooders who drifted into woo often did so out of desperation, because it proposed answers to the field's unanswerable questions. Namely why, after all this time, a Bigfoot body or bones or irrefutable video or photographic evidence haven't emerged?

Bernthal: "That's what I don't understand. How can we not have video of an animal that lives in the woods? It doesn't add up."

Gary: "It's always very mysterious, whatever it is. Always blurry and uncertain."

Woo was a way of digging in for the long haul, he said, of explaining the unexplainable. "[Woo'ers] can't figure it out. Actually, neither can I."

Scott: "I can't imagine living in a world where we'd figured everything out."

Bernthal: "We wouldn't be sitting out here if we'd figured it all out."

Josh: "The fact is, nobody has any real idea what Bigfoot is. There's nothing concrete to back it up. And I'm as far over the line into believing in Bigfoot as you can get without actually seeing one."

Colby: "So much depends on what you believe."

On the subject of belief, I mentioned my barberess, Dena,[3] a bright, college-educated woman who runs a thriving independent business and believes absolutely in the power of crystals to promote psychic healing and in bee stings to cure cancer, among other obvious untruths. She had plenty of company. According to recent surveys, more than three-quarters of Americans hold at least one supernatural or paranormal belief: The most common is ghosts and "haunting spirits" (57.7 percent), trailed closely by ancient civilizations like Atlantis (56.9 percent), possession by the devil (42 percent), frequent alien visitation (41.4 percent), extrasensory perception (41 percent), communicating with the dead (29 percent), reincarnation (24 percent), and witches (21 percent). Another common conviction is that "Satan causes most evil in the world" (35.8 percent). That's roughly how many believe, with some certainty, that U.S. officials were complicit in the 9/11 attacks.

Where, I asked, did Bigfoot fit into all this?

---

3 Not her real name.

Gary: "Well, you gotta remember to have a scientific, analytical approach, to rule out everything else first."

Bernthal: "Yeah, the imagination can do crazy things."

Josh: "I try to stay rational. I can't tell you what it is because I don't know."

We chewed on that a minute.

Bernthal: "I just don't understand how they disappear the way they do. If it's a portal, like quantum physics interdimensional stuff, then they must come and go when and where they want. Maybe you only see what they want you to see?"

It's difficult to summarize my feelings about this. We all hold strange beliefs. One could argue that the prevailing ideology of Western civilization is a two-thousand-year-old delusion concocted by sex-starved desert mystics who'd cornered the market on papyrus. "Predispositions in human nature can combine with mythological truthiness to make weird beliefs easy to swallow," wrote Steven Pinker. He's quick to qualify what he means by "beliefs." Drawing on the work of cognitive scientists Hugo Mercier and Dan Sperber, he notes that people tend to divide the world into two distinct zones of belief—what Pinker calls the "reality mindset" and the "mythology mindset." The first comprises the Heideggerian, physical world around us—our desk and chair, our kids, spouses, and coworkers—and the tasks and affairs governing our daily lives. It's what helps us keep gas in the car, money in the bank, beer in the fridge. Helpfully, you can base your behaviors on these beliefs since they're easily discernible as "true" or "false." "People have mostly accurate beliefs about this zone, and they reason rationally with it," Pinker wrote.

The other zone—the "mythology mindset"—is more tenuous.

This is the world beyond the physical: "the distant past, the unknowable future, faraway people and places...the cosmic, the counterfactual, the metaphysical." It's here that we toy with notions and ponder narratives about the world that we may find enlightening, alarming, or entertaining but that we have no way of testing or knowing for certain whether are true or false—truth or falsity being irrelevant in this instance. As Pinker says, "The function of these beliefs is to construct a social reality that binds the tribe or sect and gives it a moral purpose." We tend to keep our mythological beliefs "insulated" (Mercier's term) from our reality mindset. Mostly they float around in the Jell-O between our ears, on a plane apart from the real world and with few behavioral outcomes. Think of your crazy aunt Verna, who believes in her ability to move objects with her mind and that three million people attended Donald Trump's inauguration but who's also a gifted nurse who can diagnose and treat illnesses with precision and care. Her "reality mindset" is running fine. Her "mythology mindset" is a lavishly constructed fantasyland.

In other words, it's possible to hold beliefs that you don't treat as factually true. I believe I'm the finest table tennis player who's ever lived, better than the "Evergreen Tree" Jan-Ove Waldner and "the Dictator" Ma Jong combined and multiplied by one hundred. I also believe that I age imperceptibly faster in my top-floor apartment than the people who live in the basement, as Einstein's relativity theory proposes. But I don't behave as though either of these beliefs has any bearing on reality. Fortunately, most folks are like me. Or they're like the millions of Americans who claimed Hillary Clinton ran a pedophile ring out of a Washington pizzeria and yet never picked up the phone to call the police: we lack the courage of our convictions. Only one conspiracist—poor, deranged Edgar Maddison Welch—took the next step and showed up at Comet Ping Pong with a loaded assault rifle.[4]

Beliefs that aren't just demonstrably false but also potentially deadly corrode the most basic standards of decency and democracy. I thought again of Forteanism and wondered if it were possible to set it alongside the more incendiary extremism of QAnon. Both movements were engaged in asymmetrical wars of belief in which gullibility and a willingness to abjure one's critical faculties—the very criticisms adherents leveled at their establishment adversaries—obtained. But the Balanced Rock crew weren't fringe weirdos. They struck me as curious, honorable guys searching for understanding and connection, parsing idiosyncratic tributaries of faith amid like-minded folks, at times even embracing epistemic caution. Belief for them had as much to do with communal identity as with an animating sense of wonder. That was the heart of it, I thought: pals. Plain are the consolations of solidarity, or in today's parlance, the immunity of the herd.

The night wore on. Around one o'clock, we began getting restless. By "we," I mean "I." But eventually others also talked of packing it in. We had gambled on Balanced Rock and lost.

"I haven't seen tit!" Bernthal moaned. "Can't I at least get hit in the head with an acorn?"

"They call it fishing, not catching," Gary offered.

And then, abruptly, a sighting.

---

4 The point I'm trying to make is that professed "belief" isn't a reliable indicator of real moral conviction. Ask someone if they believe in Bigfoot, chances are you'll get a stock response devoid of real thought: "Sure. Why not? Cool idea." Few active Bigfooters fall into this category, while fewer still have gone Welchian deep. Most instead straddle the gap between Pinker's "reality" and "mythological" mindsets.

Four Bigfooters—Colby, Scott, Fran, and Frank Jr.—had tramped down trail, all the way back to where we'd parked. They were returning along one side of the narrow path when Scott and Frank Jr. heard movement in the trees. Colby and Fran had walked ahead. When Scott and Frank Jr. turned to look, their headlamps scrolled through the leaves and converged. In that split second, Frank Jr. saw something. A head and torso. Standing in the snarled bush. Not a bear. Not a moose. On two legs. Gone. Colby and Fran scrambled over. They all shut off their headlamps to listen. They heard what sounded like footfalls trodding uphill and away. All this Colby and Frank Jr. spat out when they dashed back to the fire.

"On the other side of Balanced Rock!"

"As we were coming back up the trail!"

"Fifty yards away!"

"Standing upright and looking right at us!"

"No, it wasn't a bear!"

The drama of the moment deleted chunks of data.

What I recall is we backtracked to the spot of Frank Jr.'s sighting, found squat, discussed possibilities, walked down a little gorge into a riverbed where a log hung across a rocky torrent, meandered back and forth looking for a better crossing that proved nonexistent, negotiated the log inch by slithering inch, stumbled, fell, got wet, scrambled ashore to much guffawing, walked on, boots squelching, caked in slimy mud, Colby doggedly out ahead of us, urging, trudging along, striking up a gravel path that turned out to be the one we'd followed in, the sight of our cars in the turnout, crowding inside, giddy and exhausted, the luxury of warm air and store-bought chocolate chip cookies, headed out, a sliver of moonlight, the earth traveling around the sun.

———

The following morning, Gary and Colby returned once more to Balanced Rock, hoping to dig up evidence of last night's sighting. An argument was taking place in my head: I'd seen diddly to suggest that Bigfoot resided in the Berkshires. What I'd experienced instead was the intoxicating power of belief, a power that's in all of us. At the same time, one need not be kissed before falling in love. Bigfoot may or may not be real, I thought, but either way, there's something profoundly true about the feelings it evinced.

I said goodbye to the Balanced Rock crew and headed north to Whitehall, New York, at the southern tip of Lake Champlain, for the 2021 Sasquatch Festival and Calling Contest. What a drive, people! Bright sunshine, windows down, shoes off. Through broad valleys of brooding, viridescent fields. Mountains east and west (by "mountains," I mean our bantam class of eastern heights that top out where proper western mountains begin). Across Vermont's southwest corner. Past more untended farm stands with cash-stuffed pickle jars and heirloom tomatoes priced like cocaine, with little to prevent the tomato heist of the century.

I managed to arrive late and had to circle for parking. At the waterfront Skenesborough Park, booths were being disassembled, tchotchkes bubble-wrapped and boxed. The axes at the axe-throwing station stood idle, the bounce house vacant. Of what remained, I saw Bigfoot-themed soap, golf balls, coasters, coffee mugs, earrings, koozies, cheese boards, masks, and water bottles. Parked to one side was a Subaru Outback with "Bigfoot Mobile Command Center" written on its doors. I didn't inquire. A few people wore masks. One man in his late twenties had on a T-shirt that said "Unmasked,

Unmuzzled, Unvaccinated, Unafraid." Not every day do you encounter someone advertising tacit complicity in the deaths of their fellow citizens.

Otherwise, it was a low-key town fair in an opulent setting. Sandwiched between rich agricultural land and the five-thousand-square-mile Adirondack Mountains, with a sparkling arm of Champlain half-hidden on its western flank, Whitehall had the hardscrabble appeal of a New England fishing village. The festival was a testament to local ingenuity, part of a multipronged effort to forestall the economic atomization of flyover country. Besides the festival, there was a Sasquatch Half-Marathon, Sasquatch Saloon (temporarily closed), Bigfoot Wine and Liquor, no shortage of Bigfoot statues (I counted four), and plans for a Bigfoot museum. For good measure, Whitehall had recently declared Bigfoot its "official animal."

The food stalls were open. I bought a carton of mini cinnamon-sugar doughnuts (okay, two cartons of mini cinnamon-sugar doughnuts) and went to watch the calling contest. Perhaps three hundred people filled an outdoor amphitheater, spilling onto shady perimeters. I found a spot in the way back. Bigfooter Steve Kulls, in cargo pants and black polo shirt, emceed. Directly behind the stage, clouds skidded over the surface of the Champlain Canal. Beyond that, a gnarled green knuckle of the Adirondacks, lost in bluish haze, displayed a few scattered homes. Extraordinary to think of all the country between here and the Berkshires. Only two hundred miles from New York City. Looking up at the steep slopes, Bigfoot didn't seem so preposterous.

I only stuck around for the kids' competition. They climbed onstage one at a time to belt out Bigfoot calls, something that moved me unexpectedly. The youngest, a girl of about four with blond pigtails and neon pink cycling shorts, had Bette Midler mezzo chops. Wild applause. Another kid was barely audible through his/her Sasquatch mask. Howls of laughter. This went on for half an hour. The calls ranged from berserker roar to magpie serenade. (Bigfoots were also known to whistle, wail, yelp like coyotes and chimpanzees, and make other, far stranger noises, including what folks described as like a car door slamming, a child crying, "tooth popping," and "samurai chatter.") The winner was a brown-haired boy of about ten. He collected a medal and silver Bigfoot tumbler, neither of which he seemed especially geeked about.

Later, Gary texted to say that he and Colby had found something interesting in the ground behind Balanced Rock: a sixteen-to-seventeen-inch-long footprint. "Let's just say the evidence lined up with the story from that night!" They'd made a plaster cast. Gary sent a photo of it, still wet in the ground. To me, it looked like an oversized shoeprint. But such photos are rarely revealing.

I called Jon to see what he thought. "I have my doubts. I think it's a double-bear print. [This is when a bear's rear foot steps into the lower half of a front paw impression, making it resemble a large bipedal footprint.] But I'm not here to crush anybody's dreams. I want to help people on their journey. You saw something? God bless you."

I called Gary. "The cast looked good when we were pouring it. You could clearly see toes. A bear came up as a thought. But black bears don't weigh much more than we do, and this was thickly rooted hard ground, so whatever this was, it was very heavy. I can maybe see how an expert might look at it and think it's a bear print. But that doesn't discount the fact that a couple of folks heard something, and one person saw something." They'd found other tracks right where

Frank Jr.'s creature would've been standing, suggesting something bipedal. "From that angle, it would've had a direct line of sight to our fire. If something wanted to watch us, that's where they would've done it from." Another impression was found uphill.

He knew Jon was dubious.

"I've experienced enough of these little oddities that the dots connected for me," Gary said. "When you take in the geography of the place, triangulate it the right way, piece all of it together, the evidence adds up. While I can't say it definitely was a Bigfoot, I also can't say it definitely wasn't."

It was impossible to account for it all, and of so many dimensions that one would always struggle to grasp its entirely. Gary spoke again of having a scientific approach.

"I feel like a scientist who says there's a mix of nitrogen and oxygen on a distant celestial body. Even though we've never seen it up close, the evidence suggests it should be there. In the same way, it's fascinating and humbling to think that something like this could be right under our noses. Sort of like UFOs. There's a lot we don't know. I'm open-minded to all of it."

3

HERE THERE
BE MONSTERS

"Scary monsters, super creeps /
Keep me running, running scared."

—DAVID BOWIE

One night when I was eight or nine, I was taken to a patch of woods at the edge of town, a buggy scrubland maybe a mile square with a path running through it that spat you out at the tennis courts behind the Y. It was one of the last remaining tracts of undeveloped land around and in daylight drew joggers and dog walkers, teenagers smoking and drinking and ditching school. A friend's yard backed up to these woods, and as budding pyromaniacs, we spent long hours hiding out in them, lighting shit on fire.

That night there were a bunch of us, a Cub Scout pack with minders, marching single file under a starless sky, light rain drumming the leaves. It soon became clear that someone or something else was out there too, prowling the path's edge, rustling branches, stalking us. Every now and then, it let out an earth-shattering scream that made the entire woods tremble. I'd never felt fear like it, as if the cosmic order had been tipped on its side and we'd suddenly entered a realm where anything was possible. We gripped each other's shoulders as we scurried along, whimpering, flashlights sabering the trees, shadows looming like swollen apparitions, hemming us in. Gradually it dawned on us that the source of the shrieking was one of our pack leaders (we sensed something was afoot when he fell apart laughing). Relieved, we returned his screams with our own, whooping and wailing in prepubescent spasms, stamping madly through puddles, until our lungs and legs gave out. Then we were bundled into station wagons and carted home.

I don't recall what the point of this exercise was except to scare the crap out of us. It was like a coming-of-age ritual undertaken by village elders to carry boys into manhood. But instead of drinking bull's blood, we were cast into darkness, exposed to the threatening forces of nature, and made to understand that it was terrifying. Even an innocuous oval of new-growth shrubbery was a manifestation of a shared if unspoken angst about what lurked under cover of night. No mere borderland between city and country, our woods became sinister and remote, an ever-shifting zone of perception where the real and the imaginary were enchantingly entwined.

Thinking of that night never fails to braille my skin and pucker my asshole. I believe my fear of nature was instilled in me then. Possibly it was there all along, waiting, like an errant nail head, to be hammered home. As exhausted and annoyed as I was by the whole ordeal (I was particularly galled to learn that no merit badge would be forthcoming), I also remember feeling exhilarated by the conceit of it, how the known world could vanish in an instant, our sense of possibility dramatically enlarged, our boring, lily-white, cozy middle-class lives momentarily upturned by mystery and menace. Simply by turning off the lights, adding rocks and leaves, we tapped into an inescapable aspect of what it means to be human: in a nutshell, the Kantian sublime—the "delightful horror" at finding yourself in the teeth of Mother Nature, her molars grinding you down, spilling forth your innermost dregs.

"Childhood is a darkened, fantasy-filled theatre in which, after a long or short while, the houselights are turned back on," Ian Frazier has written. Although for some of us, the lights never really come on. Or they flicker through several cycles, burning and dimming over time. Wilderness has always provided us with a screen on which to project our romantic fantasies and paranoid neuroses. It's a place, us kids knew, where strange beasts ruled and men grew feral. Without anyone having to say "Bigfoot" or "Werewolf" (both *An American Werewolf in London* and *The Howling*, a slinky werewolf horror flick starring Dee Wallace and John Carradine, had just come out) or "ritual child murderer," we understood, deep in our nerve stems, that we could quickly be relegated to the meat aisle. Which was incredible! I mean, as long as there was hot chocolate waiting for us at the end, we were happy, ecstatic even, to briefly inhabit the alternative reality that hovered at the edge of our senses.

———

We are haunted by monsters. Since our very beginnings, we've told each other stories about fearsome man-eating beasts that creep from the shadows to tear flesh from our bones. Some, like Bigfoot, are less threatening, to be both feared and esteemed, perhaps embodying our dread of an ungovernable natural world while reminding us of our mortality as the film critic Leo Braudy has noted. Others are pure evil, like Dracula and Godzilla or, say, Donald Trump, with diabolical plans to take revenge on us and our enlightened pursuit of reason.

Still others have allowed us to harmlessly indulge our fears and anxieties about the scary world out there, a Tolkienesque menagerie of extraordinary creatures roaming the wastes and wilds of the human psyche, invented to help us cope.

Our oldest recorded story is a monster story: the three-thousand-year-old Babylonian *Epic of Gilgamesh*, about the eponymous party boy and warrior-king of Uruk who, with help from his woodsy pal Enkidu, defeats the gigantic ogre Humbaba, saws off his head, builds a raft, and drifts home to glory. Besides being an early template for every buddy-cop movie ever made, *Gilgamesh* blew open the floodgates on a reservoir of mythos. Humbaba's ugly mug—he had "teeth of a dragon" and a tongue stained with human remains—bled into darker and ever more fantastic fever dreams about godless heathens who had to be killed for civilization to march on. It was a short leap from *Gilgamesh* to Perseus battling the sea monster in Ovid's *Metamorphoses*, to Oedipus versus the Sphinx in Sophocles's Theban trilogy, to Dante's Geryon, Saint George the dragon slayer, Heracles, Beowulf, Thor, Siegfried, Ahab, Ripley in *Alien*, Major Alan "Dutch" Schaefer in *Predator*, and so on. It was another short conceptual leap—one could say it required hardly any leap at all—to exciting fictions being consumed as nonfiction.

In his ostensibly factual *Histories*, Herodotus (who Plutarch called the "father of lies") says that in western Libya (a place he'd never set foot in), there lived a race of "dog-headed men and the headless that have eyes in their breasts...besides many other creatures not fabulous." Headless beasts are part of the lingua franca of monster lore. Pliny the Elder, like Herodotus a man with a shaky grasp of facts and geography, described headless men with eyes in their chests called "Blemmyae" living in Ethiopia. Not to be confused with the actual nomadic kingdom of Blemmyes, which ruled Nubia from 600 BC to AD 300, Blemmyae were a phantasm concocted and handed down from antiquity to the Middle Ages and beyond. Callisthenes, a Greek historian who accompanied Alexander the Great on his eastern conquests, wrote of battles with eight-foot-tall cannibalistic giants with faces on headless torsos. The sixteenth century explorer Sir Walter Raleigh called them "Ewaipanoma," swearing they lived in French Guiana (a place he'd never set foot in). Of the many descriptions of Blemmyae in the monster literature, none is more famous, or sadder, than in Shakespeare's *Othello*. Lamenting his Moorish origins, the heroic Othello imagines his homeland as a place with "Cannibals that each other eat...and men whose heads do grow beneath their shoulders."

Dog-headed people—"cynocephali" in Latin—were another familiar bugaboo of the ancient world, appearing again and again in legends and literature. In Egypt, there was Anubis, the jackal-headed god of the dead, famously benign in his association with mummification but also portending bad things, namely death. Around 300 BC, the Greek traveler Megasthenes described a race of "barbarians" in India with dog heads who talked to one another by barking. Marco Polo in his *Travels* meets similar folks with heads "like big mastiff dogs" on remote islands in the Indian Ocean. It became common knowledge in much of Europe that cynocephali were the real deal, to the extent that Christian iconographies depicted the Apostles proselytizing to dog-headed heathens. Some theologians claimed that Saint Christopher had been a kind of dog-man who feasted on human flesh until he was baptized by Christ and became fully human. An eighteenth-century icon called *The Martyrs St. Stephen and Dog-headed St. Christopher*, which shows the latter as a canine warrior in Roman battle dress standing beside his human-noggin'd counterpart, is still revered in the Orthodox church. King Arthur supposedly encountered cynocephali in Scotland. Charlemagne assumed he'd find them in Scandinavia, Columbus in the Americas.[1]

One of the most concise and enigmatic of all entries in the monster literature was written by Isidore of Seville, a polymath who invented the period, comma, and colon. His influential *Etymologiae* encyclopedia, published around AD 630, described several monster races of varying degrees of implausibility. Besides your typical centaurs, satyrs, sirens, Harpies, Cyclopes, unicorns, and griffins, there lived among the eastern tribes the Panotii, whose snakelike "ears spread so wide that they cover their entire body with them." And Sciapodes, or "shade-footed ones," who despite having only one leg were "wonderfully speedy" and could use their foot as an umbrella: "when it is hot they lie on their backs on the ground and are shaded by the great size of their feet." It gets crazier.

We should note that until the sixteenth and seventeenth centuries, European chroniclers often wrote what they thought their audiences wanted to hear rather than what they actually encountered. And for most people, a few hundred miles from home might as well have been the dark side of the moon. But the long and short of it is, Europeans had a propensity to exoticize the East from the get-go, betraying a supremacist worldview that has only marginally faded. To the impressionable Western mind, the outer world often appeared monstrous. Even the usually sober-minded Saint Augustine, writing from present-day Algeria, took monsters of the distant East so seriously that he devoted an entire chapter of his fifth-century *City of*

---

1 Columbus didn't find any cynocephali, but he did report seeing mermaids—presumably manatees—in Haiti.

God to the question of their salvation and to whether "certain monstrous races of men," like cynocephali, were descended from Adam. Answering in the affirmative, he wrote, "It ought not to seem incongruous that, just as there are some monstrosities within the various races of mankind, so within the whole human race there should be certain monstrous peoples."

The impulse to taxonomize monsters reached an apotheosis in *Marvels of the East*, a twelfth-century illustrated manuscript cribbed from an older Latin text called *Liber Monstrorum*, or Book of Monsters. A classic of the genre, *Marvels of the East* is part travelogue, part cautionary fairy tale, part tragicomic hallucinated mindfuck of the kind rarely given expression before LSD came along. It describes thirty-two living, breathing, otherworldly creatures found here on this wild earth, mostly (surprise) in the East: Babylonia, Persia, Egypt, India, and Ethiopia, with the latter two holding the lion's share. (The authors of *Marvels* tended to get Ethiopia and India mixed up, a common muddling that persisted into the Middle Ages.) In India were pygmies, Sciapodes, and unicorns. In Scythia (eastern Iran) were cannibals, griffins, and Hyperboreans, a race of yeti-ish giants who lived for a thousand years. In Ethiopia were fauns, people with long lips and no nostrils, and black-and-red striped ants as big as dogs with grasshopper feet they used to dig up and horde piles of gold. First reported by Herodotus, this critter eluded fortune hunters for twenty-five hundred years, until folks realized he must have been describing the indescribably cute Himalayan marmot. Elsewhere, we're told, roved 150-foot-long dragons; alpaca-like Lertices comprised of donkey's ears, sheep's wool, and bird's feet; fire-breathing dogs with boar's tusks; bearded women who hunted with tigers; half-human/half-donkeys called Homodubii. And my favorite, the fiery chickens of Lentibeisinea:

As you go towards the Red Sea there is a place...where there
are hens born like ours, red in color. If anyone tries to take
or touch them, they immediately burn up all his body. That is
extraordinary magic.

Some of this appears in the Old English poem *Beowulf*, about
a Scandinavian warrior who encounters "healfhunding" (half dogs)
and slays a pair of man-eating monsters from the other side of the
world before he's killed by a dragon. Still more made its way into the
medieval bestseller *The Voyages and Travels of Sir John Mandeville*,
a febrile fantasy dressed up as fact, allegedly written by an English
knight in 1356 and featuring monsters by now so familiar they fail
to impress: Blemmyae, Sciapodes, and Cyclopes, all dwelling on the
pretend island chain of Dondun.

What's extraordinary about *Marvels of the East* is that it was taken
more or less as gospel, encapsulating Western (read: Christian) ideas
about the pagan East for the better part of a millennium. No idle
fancies, such chimerical beasts were "a potent creation of men's imagination," as Tolkien said of *Beowulf*'s dragon, representing the dark
side in an emergent Christian-Muslim divide. They swarmed, slith-
ered, and prowled their way through Western literature, the natural sciences, geography, history, mapmaking, sculpture, and global
politics, a fantasy whirlwind in which Europeans indulged their
utmost xenophobic delusions. Gazing at images of Blemmyae and
Lertices in *Marvels of the East* today is like slipping through a space-
time wormhole, back to a time when direct contact between East
and West was practically nil—North African and Arab Muslims dic-
tated access, through trade, to practically everywhere beyond Europe
until the fifteenth century—and Christian scribes stuck religiously to

classical accounts of the East, subbing actual, observable reality for a nightmarish world of make-believe. One by-product of which was a sweeping psychological underpinning for Europe's idea of itself as the exclusive domain of a single beneficent God.

Speaking of which, I haven't even mentioned the Bible. When it comes to monsters, by God, the Almighty goes big. I'll skip past the obvious horned "beast" of Revelations—Satan—to the runner-up badass of the Old Testament: Leviathan. He appears most memorably in Job 41 as a toothy, fire-breathing serpent, part dragon/part crocodile, with seven heads (give or take) and a double coat of scaly armor that rendered him all but invincible:

> Out of his mouth go burning lamps, and sparks of fire leap out.

> Out of his nostrils goeth smoke, as out of a seething pot or caldron.

> His breath kindleth coals, and a flame goeth out of his mouth...

> His heart is as firm as stone; yea, as hard as a piece of the nether millstone.

> When he raiseth up himself, the mighty are afraid.

Second only to God, Leviathan was the quintessential alpha monster. A gargantuan, swaggering, shirtless spark plug recognizable from the Midwestern keg parties of my youth. He swatted away arrows and javelins like so many math club nerds. He made the sea bubble and boil, gobbled sailors for breakfast. "Upon earth there is not his like, who is made without fear / He beholdeth all high things: he is a king over all the children of pride." Until God, with His infinite strength, squashed Leviathan's writhing heads and distributed the carcass to the hungry. As David Quammen says in *Monster of God: The Man-Eating Predator in the Jungles of History and the Mind*, Leviathan is God's way of reminding Job (and us) that He is not to be fucked with. Stay humble. Lest we forget, "we stand no higher than third on the food chain of power and glory."

All these monsters, of course, preluded Harry (of the Hendersons), and each, in their way, helped light the stage for Bigfoot's twentieth-century debut. Against myths so potent and entrenched, I might venture, reality often struggles.

———

Years ago, I hiked a part of the Appalachian Trail in Maine called the Hundred-Mile Wilderness. It's the longest gauntlet of unbroken forest in the eastern United States, one hundred God's honest miles without a single Arby's. A rare thing, even on the AT, where the average distance between paved roads is a scant seven miles and where mountaintop vistas can encompass turnpikes and travel plazas. Except that it might as well have been Arby's for all the weirdos sidling up to me attempting to make conversation. Dudes, let it be said that the joys of human fellowship can seriously harsh my mellow. And the point of this trip was to avoid conversation generally and small talk specifically so as to enter the crucible of Emersonian self-reliance for which I was wholly unprepared. Such hardship is character building, they say. Take me: I've experienced almost zero hardship in my life and as a result have no character or inner strength to speak of. A single night without flossing and I feel like I've gone totally feral. Intending to change that, I wanted nothing to do with my fellow hikers, cared not a lick for the lunchtime banter at lean-tos or the Burning Man vibe in the campsites at night. To be sure, this thinking is anathema on the AT, where a cultish, hippie-commensal credo obtains. Hikers who just met on the trail that afternoon are tearfully reunited by nightfall as ancient kinsmen. Outside of family holidays, I've never witnessed such cloying and stagy togetherness. Fed by the campfires, it reaches a frenzied crescendo: joints are passed, sarongs donned, trail exploits trotted out, harmonicas strangled to death. It's puzzling. Why trek all the way out here to party with strangers? Fear, namely. The fundamental horse sense of backcountry camaraderie holds that, sooner or later, the hills will exact their tribute. A turned ankle, a torsioned testicle, and you are fucked, Percy Fawcett-like, stranded and left to the mercy of others, subjected to their whims and neuroses and aptitudes for fashioning splints from elm saplings, people who, in lighter moments, might also share their weed. Which, okay. I get how an inhospitable hell like the Hundred-Mile Wilderness might elicit our most hospitable selves. I'll even concede that folks like being neighborly. Just count me out.

As if there weren't enough to occupy me, redoubling my unease was constant trail chatter about hiker deaths and disappearances. More than a few, I was reminded, had vanished from these parts. Just up and poof! Never to be seen again. According to Bigfooter David Paulides, codirector of the *Missing 411* documentaries and founder, in 2011, of the CanAm Missing Project, at least sixteen hundred hikers and wilderness seekers are currently unaccounted for in the

United States, including a few dozen in Maine. The state's Warden Service conducts around twenty-five annual search-and-rescue missions for lost and injured hikers, a disconcerting number of them in and around the Hundred Miles. Most searches, but not all, end happily. In 2013, a woman named Geraldine Largay vanished near Sugarloaf Mountain, having become disoriented after stepping into the woods to pee. Unable to find the trail again, she slowly starved to death. "Freedom is the possibility of isolation," wrote Fernando Pessoa. Tell that to Geraldine Largay.

Although Largay's body was eventually found, it did little to dampen trail rumors about what had really befallen her. At a stream where I'd stopped to refill my water bottles, a hiker who I'll call "Friar Tuck"—a lean, talkative man wearing a graying tonsure and Harley Davidson T-shirt with a flaming eagle on it—offered this (totally unsolicited) theory: contrary to the bunk I'd been fed by "the media," Largay, as any clear-thinking person could see, had in fact been abducted, held captive, and starved to death by, you guessed it, Bigfoot. I didn't realize it then, as it predated my Bigfoot crusade, but his account betrayed a deep crypto schooling. Otherwise devoid of meaning, random events became, in his telling, freighted with narrative. A strange glee rising in him, Friar Tuck went on:

"Probably it meant to eat her but got scared off by humans. There's accounts going back to the late 1800s. French trappers camping around Moosehead Lake… Two of 'em left and came back and found their friend dead. He was all et up."

"Why would they starve her before eating her?" I ventured.

"You heard of Jessie Albertine Hoover?" he said, unmoved. "Dropped off the map around Abol Bridge in 1983. Neither hide nor hair."

He continued like this for six or seven minutes, his stories rolling by like grainy newsreel footage, the richness of his horrors ranging into the Hitchcockian register and shot through with kindred psychosexual currents. (Bigfoot, I immediately wanted to unlearn, more or less invented polyamory.) Before long, I drifted off.

Behind us, Mount Katahdin lay hidden in dark, lumpy clouds. In the opposite direction, I could see, through a gap in the trees, a long curve of hills climbing to the horizon and breaking up into open country, where several more days of hiking with dwindling cell reception awaited me. I'd been reading about plans to reintroduce gray wolves to Maine. The animals had thrived here for five hundred thousand years until—shocker—Europeans arrived. Although they were extirpated from the state by 1890, wolves continued to pop up on trail cameras now and again. Two were killed in the mid-1990s, including one outside Bangor. Conservationists had been lobbying for a recovery plan in New England similar to what existed out west. Like Bigfoot, wolf sightings were common currency on the AT. There was even a hotline to call if you saw a wolf or thought you heard one howling.

At a glance, the Maine woods seemed Edenically nice. It was easy to forget they were also a place of disorientation, where the trees drew close and bearings got lost. Bill Bryson writes memorably of his profound unease here in *A Walk in the Woods*, about his failed attempt to hike the AT from start to finish. By the time he reached Maine, he'd logged eight hundred miles. He was so miserable in the Pine Tree State that he quit after just one day, but not before his hiking partner, Stephen Katz, got lost. "And once you were lost in these immense woods," Bryson wrote, "you would die. It was as simple as that." (Katz eventually resurfaced.)

A crow or raven screeched into view. Ditto a pair of mink, whether frolicking playfully or engaged in mortal combat, it was hard to tell. The place suddenly roiled with an awesome power and gravity, putting me in mind of Thoreau's judgment of it in *The Maine Woods*: "a deep and intricate wilderness...savage and dreary...everywhere wet and miry." Maine soured the budding naturalist on unfettered nature. Wolves haunting the edges of his campsites at night especially unnerved him. Compared with his bucolic Walden Pond, a breezy three miles from Concord, where his mother did his laundry for him, Maine was *too* wild: "Vast, Titanic, inhuman."

I'd grown acclimatized to trail clingers like Friar Tuck. They trended toward tragic case studies, harmless sad sacks, and off-center strivers for...what, exactly? Unclear. In his instance, judging from some fresh-looking tattoos, a spiritual rebirth of sorts, or existential oblivion, or front-row seats to the Rapture, or all of the above. Whichever, he appeared relieved to have unburdened himself.

"Avoid the East Branch lean-to!" he hollered as he puttered off, trekking poles scissoring metronomically. "Some eerie shit!"

Yes, my friend could've been screwing with my head, plying me with troublesome nuggets to gnaw on as I trudged into the encircling gloom, pursuing my evening's campsite. Little about him suggested this. He seemed, instead, like a wayfaring priest. Sincere, devout, consumed by an irrepressible desire to believe.

———

As antiquity graduated to the Middle Ages, monsters moved closer to Europe. Lurid and sensationalist accounts of "wild men"—godless cannibals who lived in remote, forested regions—exploded in the monster literature. Bigfootesque, the wild man was often depicted covered in thick fur matted with dirt, or "black like a Moor, large and hideous, sitting on a tree stump and holding a large club in his hands," as one account put it. These "frightful monsters," said another, "with split teeth and crooked hands, roam the night on the rooftops, descending into the houses down the chimney, uttering mournful howls." Its speech was "a soft murmur and confused sound / Of senseless words, which nature did him teach," according to Edmund Spenser's *The Faerie Queene*. A shape-shifter and wielder of devilish magic, he could suddenly triple in size until he towered over the forest. Making his home in caves, tree hollows, burrows, and rocky redoubts, wild men shunned civilization but were known to kidnap human children and replace them with "changelings." Misbehaving kids could be frightened into obedience by the specter of wild folk coming to snatch them away. In the Tyrolean Alps, there was said to dwell a huge female ogre called "Faengge" with an awful stench and flapjack breasts so large she had to toss them over her shoulders as she ran through the woods and who'd kidnap and devour children raw. (I plan to immediately start using this on my own kids.)

Early medieval nature was no sylvan utopia but a gaping hell mouth patrolled by the Prince of Darkness himself. Living in uneasy proximity to the inferno drove people batty, to the point where nearly all of life became twisted by religious superstition into a virulent and free-range crackpottery. To an eleventh-century peasant, the wild man materialized like a herald bearing news of imminent damnation. He also signified a boatload of repressed desires and anxieties. What set him apart from other familiar monsters is that he was, at root, us. "Sublimated in the wild man were the preeminent phobias of medieval society—chaos, insanity, and ungodliness," the scholar Timothy Husband wrote. A remnant of our pagan past, the wild man was a living symbol of our innate wantonness and hardened nature, of what could happen if you strayed from God.

Like vampires of Eastern Europe, wild men were blamed for unexplained calamities. Sudden deaths, crop failures, stillborn children, disease, pestilence, bad weather, murder, suicide, impotence, constipation, migraines, mental illness, you name it, all were thought to be their dirty work. Tacitly endorsed by the church, such beliefs snowballed, growing in ferocity and hype. Things got so out of hand that hunting parties, not unlike witch hunts, were organized to ferret out culprits: in most cases, folks living at the social fringes—the insane, destitute, those who'd committed or had merely been accused of a crime, or old trouts or curmudgeons who'd taken to the woods—people who today we might call homeless.

Monsters are rarely static. They're in a state of constant renewal and rejuvenation, updated to fit the times. By the fifteenth century, the God-abandoned wild man in league with Satan was falling out of fashion. As feudal Europe collapsed and gave rise to a decadent urban middle class, the wild man acquired a bohemian, Bear Grylls vibe. Now an itinerant bon vivant, closer in spirit to Tolkien's Badger-folk, he lived in harmony with Mother Nature, indulging his impulses guiltlessly in an unspoiled woodland idyll. Reflecting changed attitudes toward wilderness, the image of "winsome, elfin creatures merrily tilling the soil" suddenly appealed "to an urban bourgeoisie with no conception of the realities of rural life," wrote Husband, embodying for man "the possibilities of a free existence if he broke the shackles of convention placed upon him."

The rest of the world is just as monster crazy as the West, arguably more so. (We are all dreaming the same dream, Schopenhauer wrote.) Chinese folklore is probably nuttier and denser with monsters than anyone's, awash with shape-shifting dragons and giant sea turtles. Stories of man-eating demons haunting the Ganges River and the Himalayas form the bedrock of Hindu cosmology. Similar beliefs and traditions, from Inuit child-snatchers to Brazilian "Mula-Sem-Cabeça" (headless mule), from the "Mokèlé-mbèmbé" (water dragon) of the Congo River to the legendary Nue, or Mononoke, of feudal Japan, to thousands of other gauzy tales, have shaped the human imagination for millennia. But I'm getting ahead of myself.

Our worldwide monster obsessions are understandable. Joseph Campbell said such myths are deeply woven into our unconscious. Designed to help us understand and accept the mysterious—birth, growth, decay, death—they give meaning to an otherwise meaningless existence. "Psychologically, the dragon is one's own binding to one's ego. We're captured in our own dragon cage," Campbell said. "The ultimate dragon is within you; it is your ego clamping you down." Even Mr. Big Dick himself, Beowulf, succumbs to the all-powerful dragon and to the same inescapable fate of us all. The dragon too must eventually die, as in Wagner's *Siegfried*, and surrender his hoarded treasure.

The philosopher Paul Shepard thought our penchant for imaginary beasts must be a chromosomal thing, a holdover from our primate ancestors, "whose tribes were pruned by horrors whose shadows continue to elicit our monkey screams in dark theaters." How else to explain the "huge, make-believe fauna of monsters, prodigies, and wonders" that have no exact equivalent in nature, "as though the natural world were somehow deficient"? Although most of us, fortunately, no longer contend with the blood-soaked world of our

Paleolithic forebears, we come preprogrammed with the same fear and trembling. Campbell thought we inherited from the first humans in East Africa an "inward darkness," which we encounter whenever we enter a shadowy path or step onto a desolate savannah, like finding a message in a bottle on the shores of consciousness. "Memories of their animal envoys still must sleep, somehow, within us, for they wake a little and stir when we venture into wilderness. They wake in terror to thunder."

———

Looking back, what's striking about Friar Tuck's yarn was how unremarkable, how familiar, it was. A grab bag of cryptozoological lore, I can see now, and a testament to our fondness for recognizable narratives, with shades of Albert Ostman, the Canadian lumberjack who claimed in 1924 to have been kidnapped and held captive by a Bigfoot family for a week before escaping. Further shades of the 1980 film *Night of the Demon*, in which Bigfoot terrorizes campers in rural California, ritually disemboweling them and tearing off the penis of a motorcyclist. And the Bobcat Goldthwait-directed *Willow Creek* (2013), where we see a hapless documentarian, Kelly, taken by Bigfoot as a "forest bride." A number of such stories, following similar patterns, occupy an oddly discordant category in recent monster lore, standing beside a larger category that draws nearer to Harry from *Harry and the Hendersons*. Friar Tuck didn't discriminate. His was an easy, unselfconscious mongrelization of all these versions, light and dark, good and evil. Far from inhabiting a secret world unreachable by you and me, Bigfoot could be found—about this Friar Tuck had no doubt—in its shifting, hidden locales.

Lying awake in Maine at night, the film I found myself thinking of was *Predator*. It'd be impossible to overstate the spell it cast on me when it came out in 1987. Major Alan "Dutch" Schaefer, Arnold Schwarzenegger's most perfectly achieved role (excepting *Kindergarten Cop*, perhaps), pandered to my insatiable fourteen-year-old appetite for heavy weaponry and camouflaged valor. Whereas John Rambo and Chuck Norris's Colonel Braddock were outgunned yet laughably invincible, Dutch was more vulnerable, more futile, which is to say more warlike and (in contrast to his alien adversary) authentically human. In naked disregard for international law, Dutch leads a for-hire special-ops team into an unnamed Central American jungle, with tagalong CIA operative Dillon (Carl Weathers, fresh off reprising Apollo Creed for the third time in *Rocky IV*) representing the moral abyss of U.S. warmongering. The soldiers, tracking hostages in rebel-held territory, soon learn the tables have been turned. A transmogrifying alien (played by seven-footer Kevin Peter Hall, who was also Harry in *Harry and the Hendersons*) hunts the men for sport, bagging them one by one in a deliberately choreographed slaughter, all but mounting their heads in a trophy room before melting back into the foliage. They're easy prey, succumbing to the jungle itself, penance for America's Cold War meddling.[2] Predator *is* the jungle. The soldiers are caught in its literal and figurative quagmire. When Dutch overpowers Predator, it self-destructs, blowing the jungle to smithereens, as if to explode our sentimental notions of benign, unsullied nature. An ancient drama of sin and redemption played

---

2 The film appeared a year after a U.S. Coast Guard plane was shot down over Nicaragua, exposing Reagan's Iran-Contra hustle, in which his administration peddled arms to our archenemy Iran to underwrite an anticommunist insurgency trying to overthrow the Sandinistas, then lied about it to Congress.

out on a biblical stage with doomed warriors battling an elusive monster from the infinite darkness of space, *Predator* is something Joseph Conrad might've written had he been born one hundred years later and huffed mescaline with Philip K. Dick. It shows us not only the ultimate chaos of nature but—and this is its genius—how randomly its phantoms materialize.

Maybe such stories satisfy us so deeply because they remind us, all too chillingly, of what it means to be hunted. An instinctual fear of predation, and of nature's corollary as a dark, pernicious space, is an important part of monster lore. It's not the sauntering specter of Bigfoot that terrifies so much as the possibilities contained in wilderness. The unseen, the strange noise in the shadows, the suffering hidden by beauty, is what gets our blood up. We feel it taking shape inside us, a sinking feeling, like Predator sawing into Dillon's chest cavity, which sends us scrambling for a flashlight and makeshift truncheon. (Hiking Maine's outback was an object lesson in the miracle of electricity; with a 350-lumen LED headlamp, we can finally, after three hundred thousand years in the dark, turn night into day.) "The principal task of civilization, its actual raison d'être," Freud wrote, "is to defend us against nature." A laughably porous defense, *Predator* reminds us, when extravagantly weaponized commandos fail at defending even themselves.

Freud, paradoxically, seemed unconscious of the larger picture. Try as we might, we can't estrange ourselves from Mother Nature, not really. It's a weirdly codependent relationship, one that cuts deeper than we might think. This resonates with me because I know the feeling—the exotic experienced safely. I *liked* being a scared-shitless Cub Scout in Michigan, gnawing my shirtsleeve to rags while nearly pissing myself. (From such a distance, the experience itself bleeds into myth.) Grown men inciting our worst fears, drumming up our insecurities merely for a goof, the very definition of a sadistic personality disorder, you say? Probably. But that was when it clicked for me: I was missing out. From then on, I resolved to shorten the distance between myself and our nocturnal woods. I thought if I spent more time in them, they might reveal something to me. What, I hadn't the foggiest idea. But that was how, in a roundabout way, I found myself in buttfuck Maine thirty years later being stalk-talked by Friar Tuck in a tomb of whirring insects, sans carbonated beverages, central air, ESPN highlights, or dry socks, and with little idea of where I was headed or why, yet fairly certain that *this, yeah, this right here, was living.*

Our "negative liking" of nature, Kant wanted us to understand—its irresistibly frightening beauty, simultaneously attractive and repellant—reveals irreconcilable truths about us, truths we nevertheless struggle to reconcile. On the one hand, we understand the natural environment as a part of who we are, inseparable from our raw material. Some of us wannabe Lord Byrons even seem to require it, passing eccentric stretches in nature's bosom to recharge our muses. On the other hand, we feel fundamentally cowed by nature, awed by its destructive power and, more to the point, humbled by its elusive night stalkers. A mismatch that's the price of being human. So we build our teeming postmodern monoliths, alter whole ecosystems, dredging and dynamiting critical wetlands, felling thousand-year-old redwoods for roofing shingles, terraforming the globe to accommodate our office parks and car dealerships, Walmarts and Home Depots, Pep Boys and Steak 'n Shakes. And in twenty-five years, we tear it all down to rebuild it anew.

Or worse. We vomit up monstrosities like "Walden Monterey,"

for my money the most priceless iteration of the Babel we've made for ourselves. Part of a trend of "agrihood" among "high-end residential real estate developers prizing nature" and "a certain polished rusticity," its ad copy says, Walden Monterey is an idealized nature colony for the filthy rich plopped down within commuting distance of Silicon Valley, designed to obscure the tensions between the civilized and the wild, but not, apparently, between the one percent and the rest of us. "Think of it as Thoreau's cabin 2.0," where "some of the world's biggest execs" commune with nature in "Zen meditation gardens," partake of a sunrise yoga platform, attend "TED-like discussion series," and dine on the ova of foreign fish at an "outdoor communal farm table commissioned by a local artist." Its twenty-two lots start at $5 million.

Welcome to Barfsville, Pop. 22.

Anyway, maybe we're drawn to Bigfoot stories because they represent our hope that not every square inch of this continent has been slash-burned and subdivided into a homogenous glop or cordoned off by the rich to indulge their exclusive pathologies. Here, in this very forest, Friar Tuck might've been saying, could still dwell creatures not yet decimated by the onslaught of human progress. Humbaba, after all, was appointed by the Sumerian deity Enlil to guard the forests of Cedar Mountain and attacked Gilgamesh because that fucking asshole was chopping down all the trees, for no reason except to prove he could do it. A victorious Gilgamesh then shaved the landscape bare, launching civilization on a four-thousand-year-long course of destruction.

"It's simply a better world if Bigfoot is real," Lynne S. McNeill, a folklorist at Utah State University, told me. "It says something positive about our wilderness spaces. It says we haven't totally destroyed our planet, that there are enough wild places left that a creature like Bigfoot can live undetected."

In her late forties, with light gray-green eyes and dark hair, McNeill grew up in northern California. As a girl, she was drawn to all manner of folklore, from ghosts to cryptids to UFOs, eventually turning it into a career. In addition to publishing in flagship journals, she has appeared as the voice of reason on the TV shows *Paranormal Caught on Camera* and *In Search of Monsters*. When I mentioned Friar Tuck, she walked me back from dismissing him out of hand. "People articulating something that seems crazy or irrational might actually be onto something," she said. "On a very fundamental level, we need there to be some mystery in the world. Those mysteries can be frightening, or they can be enlightening. Bigfoot is about mystery and about possibility, not about certainty. It's about what might still be possible in this world of ours. For your friend Friar Tuck, the mere possibility of Bigfoot existing might be a psychological necessity, because it means we haven't totally ruined this place."

Fair enough. Bigfoot is a reckoning of sorts: with a disenchanted world, with our estrangement from nature, with the spectacular mess we've made of things, and with what remains. Like gray wolves, Bigfoot—both, depending on who you ask, ruthless killers or fiercely intelligent survivors—could be viewed as a portent of our earthly transgressions, a stand-in for our grief, in the Aldo Leopoldian sense, over our squandered bounty and what we might do about it. Substitute for wolves the ivory-billed woodpecker, Florida panther, California condor, Bryde's whale, Nevada pupfish, leopard frog, passenger pigeon, monarch butterfly, American crocodile, and other species going or gone. Friar Tuck, in his gruff way, while being painfully alive to all that's dead and dying in this world, allowed himself hope, a hope devoid of tree hugger schmaltz or sentimentality. By this logic, a goony cartoon Bigfoot slapped on a microbrew speaks to a wish to put our imaginary Eden back in the bottle, to indulge our nostalgia for an "undefiled, green republic, a quiet land of forests, villages, and farms dedicated to the pursuit of happiness" that no longer exists and probably never did, as the critic Leo Marx observed, but which retains a mythic power over our imaginations.

To baldly plagiarize David Quammen, perhaps our eagerness to forge a psychological connection between imaginary monsters and the real beasts who prowl or once prowled our landscapes reflects a longing for the "beautiful harshness" of the old legends, when heroes fought and died in a war against nature and when the firewall separating us from it wasn't so formidable. Nowadays, the landscapes that evoked our original terrors have, on the whole, gone under the plow. Even the Hundred-Mile Wilderness, for all its majesty, has been ransacked many times over, its ancient stands of white pines reduced by the cold calculus of "woodland management" into yet another tradeable commodity. When you think of it that way, there's something heartbreakingly sad about Bigfoot. The idea of unspoiled nature and the monsters it contains is so far-fetched that it's intoxicating to those who choose to believe in it.

And there's the nut. We want to believe. So badly do we want to believe in something that we're willing to believe in almost anything, against much evidence to the contrary. Being hardwired for narrative, we ascribe meaning to things when there isn't any, invent mythological systems that render abstractions as concrete realities. "Ontologically, we're driven to categorize our experiences, to fit them into current knowledge," McNeill said. "When our institutions lack knowledge to explain our experiences, we turn to folklore."

Sometimes, then, in trying to make sense of events that defy comprehension and thus seem subject to the realm of magic, we grasp at straws. According to McNeill, that might actually be a good thing. "Bigfoot scratches an itch that religion often scratches," she said, "but there's a wonderful secular-ness to Bigfoot that allows you to question and challenge orthodoxy, to articulate the kind of doubt that in church would border on apostasy. With Bigfoot, doubt is part and parcel of the tradition."

To my ear, this sounds dangerously close to "fake news." Some Bigfooters, like devout Trumpists, hard-core woksters, and religious fanatics, have a way of spinning belief into an ever-widening web that entangles and devours everything in its path. But we all do this on some level: bend reality to be what we want it to be. We interpret events based on our convictions rather than on evidence, leap from rational to nonrational assumptions when it suits us, especially when we're protecting our pet ideas, and cling to false beliefs in the face of facts. Another way of putting it is our brains aren't great at discerning the truth. They're good at telling stories, stories that attempt to resolve or give context to our uncertainty, fear, and confusion, stories we want to believe are true. Psychologists call this "narrative fallacy"—recasting events as compelling and meaningful anecdotes with logical chains of cause and effect, with us at the center of the action, the star of the show. The problem with stories, of course, is that they're just stories. And certain kinds of stories negatively affect how we think.

The single most pervasive cognitive deficit we all suffer from is confirmation bias. Say you've told yourself a certain story—about a stolen election, a haunted house, your cat understanding conversational Mandarin—chances are you'll find evidence for it everywhere.

Even the most counterfactual, contrary evidence won't dissuade you from your belief.[3] The psychologist Leon Festinger coined the phrase "cognitive dissonance" to describe the discomfort we feel when our dearly held beliefs are confronted with such evidence. These tendencies can lead us astray, especially when we're emotionally invested in our subjects, as Bigfooters can be. "Once you *really believe*," Kurt Andersen wrote, "you can always find new evidence to support your beliefs."

A dogged persistence in the maintenance of belief, although nothing new, feels like the crisis of our times. But is faith in Bigfoot really just religion without the pious packaging, as McNeill said, an unshakeable faith that *something* is out there, even if we can't see it with our own eyes? Maybe. But not to the Bigfooters I know. "Belief is for something where there's no evidence," Cliff Barackman, the enigmatic cohost of *Finding Bigfoot*, told me. "Bigfoot isn't a matter of belief. It's a matter of evidence, and the evidence is real." Barackman is just shy of stocky, with short gray hair and a neat beard. He chanced into the *Finding Bigfoot* gig after years of scouring western backcountry for Bigfoot and came to the show convinced that the creatures were real, a conviction based largely on conversations with eyewitnesses. "I've spoken to thousands of people over the years who've seen Bigfoot," he said. "Thousands. Police officers, military people, clergy, professors. Are all of them lying? With so much eyewitness evidence, belief is sort of beside the point." We'll get to the eyewitness evidence later. For now—at the risk of entering a semantic blind alley—let me say that believing in evidence still counts as belief, and preexisting belief makes it easier to overlook details that contradict your preferred hypothesis and to see your quarry in every shadow and silhouette.

---

3 Research suggests that we experience a dopamine rush when processing information that supports our beliefs.

But McNeill said something else. "Bigfoot can represent a very libertarian set of values, which is self-sufficient, in tune with nature, and unobstructed by government. It's 'There are things out there that don't have a rational, contemporary, scientific answer. We haven't broken down everything into their composite parts and understood their mechanisms.' To that way of thinking, Bigfoot is a success story of independence and freedom." In our modern context, when truth is often ordained by institutional consensus—by mainstream science and medicine in particular—people can feel disempowered. Bigfoot is a means of staking a claim, McNeill said, of saying, "You scientists don't know everything. I don't need to trust your institutions. I can trust my own instincts and my own beliefs."

Even demonstrably batshit belief—in headless cannibals, in Jesus rising from the dead, in the COVID-19 pandemic being a global hoax orchestrated by the CDC and Zoom to prevent the Tangerine Tornado from being reelected—can make you feel as if you've pierced the Baudrillardian veil to see the world as it truly is. Not so long ago, perfectly reasonable people thought exposure to moonlight could get a girl pregnant. Or that rainwater found on tombstones removed freckles. Or that 7,409,127 demons worked for Lucifer, overseen by seventy-nine devil princes and helped by countless witches who multiplied faster than they could be burned alive. "I believe *because* it is absurd," went the credo of third-century Christian theologian Tertullian. In many ways, our lives remain influenced by beliefs that were set in place when we crucified people on the regular.

Thankfully, Americans aren't alone. More than half of Icelanders believe in an ancient elf people called Huldufólk who inhabit a world parallel to our own, to the extent that construction projects are changed so that the rocks where Huldufólk are thought to live remain undisturbed. Mention Bigfoot in Quito, Nairobi, Okayama, Moscow, Guangzhou, Sitka, Manaus, Alice Springs, not only will folks know exactly what you're talking about, many will have stories to tell about their own brushes with similar beasts: the Chinese Yeren, Kenyan Chimiset, Brazilian Mapinguari, Japanese Higabon, Vietnamese Nguoi Rung, Australian Yowie, Tlingit Kushtaka, Indonesian Orang Pendek, Russian Almas. Extraordinary bipedal creatures living at civilization's edge are hardly novelties. Rather, they're a universal mainstay, a combination of myth and anthropological gimcrack that has been with us throughout recorded history.

There is, however, something singularly American about the intensity of our belief. Monsters, according to Adam Gopnik, have "supplied our only reliable, weatherproof American mythology, one sturdy enough to sustain and resist debunking or revisionism." I'm messing around! He actually said *mobsters*. What's one consonant? Point is, whatever mythic yearning monsters fulfill, we're jonesing hard. Sixty-six million of us, according to a recent survey, profess to believe in just one: Bigfoot. Sixty-six million! As these numbers suggest, it's not only crackpots who believe. There may be no more sacred expression of American exceptionalism than faith in a monster we've adapted to fit our peculiar view of history, unfalsifiable by facts proffered by science or qualified experts, and suggesting a medieval belief in the raw and violent power of nature. Perhaps we all need Bigfoot in our lives, whether we realize it or not.

4

ALL KINDS OF MYSTERIOUS CRAZINESS

"It is only that which is under your nose
which seems inexplicable."

—WILLIAM CARLOS WILLIAMS

Seventy miles past Whitesville, two hours west of the Old Frankfort Pike, roundabout the joint end of the chicken leg of the fifteenth state to enter the Union, I crossed into the thirty-seven parallel's most hallowed Squatchin' ground. The sky was a disappointment—low, gridlocked clouds, their edges drooping like an overhanging roof, and just past the county line, a wall of rain—but the road was flat, straight, plain sailing. I'd come here because Charlie Raymond, founder of the Kentucky Bigfoot Research Organization (KBRO), had asked if I wanted to join his fall expedition. A bunch of us would be camping out, taking long hikes through the woods, and comparing notes. I'd reached out to Charlie and explained how I hoped to chronicle Bigfooters in my third favorite state. He was keen to have me along, he said, given one proviso: any true Bigfooter, like any true fisherman, had proprietary feelings for the loci of his former success. "It's like a fishing hole," another Bigfooter had told me. "Once you find a place you like, why go anywhere else? Otherwise, you'll wind up chasing unicorns and gnomes." So to protect what Charlie called his "research area," I'd withhold the exact location. I can tell you it was reminiscent, at first, of Kalamazoo, Michigan, in the 1980s: fallow fields bordered by goldenrod and autumn olive; mile after mile of wood fencing and rangy roadside weeds; pickup trucks of indeterminate vintage; a derelict gas station with broken fluorescent lightbulbs and Swisher butts and plastic Schnapps bottles strewn around the parking area, and above the toilet in a fetid men's room, a handwritten sign: "C'mon, Guys.—the Mgmt."

Probably most folks wouldn't peg Kentucky as a Bigfoot hotbed. Until pretty recently, neither did Bigfooters. With the exception of John Green's totemic *Sasquatch: The Apes Among Us*, Kentucky hadn't been cited in any of the books I'd read. Green mentions it only in passing. But as Charlie Raymond liked to point out, this was merely an oversight. In a state with twelve million forested acres and a population density comparable to Washington's, why not here? Intending to put the subject on the table, Charlie founded the KBRO in 1997 as a "non-kill research group which seeks to prove the existence of, and protect of [sic], these magnificent creatures," according to its website. Sightings multiplied. Charlie, a web designer by trade, became a local expert, guide, investigator, and Bigfoot booster, despite never having seen one himself in three decades of searching ("I'm a believer, not a knower," he'd told me). Of all the Bigfooters I'd met, Charlie was the most devout. It was largely because of him that Kentucky was now ranked fourteenth in the BFRO's national sightings database, with 114 since 1995.

On the phone, Charlie exhibited what I'd come to know as a characteristic wit and irreverence. About his entry into Bigfooting, he'd said, "There were just too many people in gorilla suits crossing the highway to ignore." I admired his good cheer, the way he seemed to find humor in almost everything, a sense of humor in Bigfooting being an elusive species. "Laughing and having fun," he'd said, "that's what attracts Bigfoot." I also liked his backdoor conservationist credo: "We have to protect Bigfoots. In Kentucky they'll be extinct in the next hundred years if we don't protect their habitat and keep decimating our forests. It's getting harder and harder to go very far without hitting another shopping center." Even this had his affirming, can-do-it ring, as if suburban/industrial sprawl were a problem to be hashed out by lunch.

Bearing west, the landscape changed utterly. I went spinning down a river valley, over dams and along hogback hills. Leaves were just beginning to yellow. As I closed in on Charlie's base camp, a red pickup swung into the road ahead of me, its quad duallys spitting a plume of shoulder gravel. The suspension was a good two feet off the ground, and the truck was festooned from bumper to bumper with confederate flags and Trump flags (talk about sore losers), that yellow Gadsden flag with a coiled rattlesnake above the words "Don't Tread On Me," and other peckerwood shibboleths. It was like a MAGA version of Immortan Joe's Gigahorse from *Mad Max: Fury Road.* Among some acquaintances in my hometown of Kalamazoo, such excessive sloganeering, while not quite so aggro, wasn't unprecedented. But then it happened again. Different truck. Same imaginary parade. I trailed it for a half mile before it fishtailed away.

I'd seen the voter maps. I knew Trump had won this county by nearly 80 percent in the past two elections and that Biden had taken just a pair of the state's 120 counties, the blue islands encompassing Louisville and Lexington. I also knew it was a bad time to be a Kentuckian and had been for a while. The state ranked near the bottom in almost every livability metric: health care quality and outcomes, median income and fiscal stability, education level, life expectancy, and air and water quality. It had the nation's highest cancer death rate and was dead last in jobs. According to a 2019 index of the worst twenty-five counties in the United States to live in, based on average life expectancy at birth, education, and employment, ten were in Kentucky. Manufacturing had evaporated. Coal was on life support. Even thoroughbred racing was in decline. That, of course, was before the pandemic. The hope that someone had noticed and had not dismissed Kentuckians' grievances as the petty resentments of a "privileged" underclass appeared to be visceral and all consuming. Even if that someone was a self-mythologizing male gorgon of the lowest order who himself never wanted for anything. That a bigoted, narcissistic, morally and fiscally bankrupt, lying sponger had channeled the legitimate anxieties of Kentuckians into a narrative of righteous indignation, though it charred my mutton, also made a twisted kind of sense. Myths, as someone once said, are as important as reality.

The rain let up. I found the campground and parked. I'd been told the site itself was lovely, and it was. Potentially memorable, I remember thinking. A floating mist encircled the trunks of young oaks and black walnuts and a few tulip trees. It was warm but not too warm, with birdsong being piped in from offstage and late-summer light adding a burgundy substratum. Two-, three-, and four-person tents, some with elaborate nylon porches and sunscreens, others attached to pimped-out mini trailers and campers, filled up the dewy grass between the road and a forest that grew down to the river.

As I was assembling my tent, I was nearly brained by a falling walnut. All weekend, black walnuts, acorns, and hickory nuts rained down around us, sailing past our heads, bouncing off tents, catching a few folks plumb on the noggin. The walnuts were a special menace. They were the size of tennis balls but as hard as apples. The meagerest rustle of wind sent them flying and bursting apart on the road or on the hoods of our Dodge Rams and F-250s, where they left egg-size dents. Every so often, someone would holler "Watch it!" and we'd cower with our hands over our heads until the danger passed.

There were about thirty-five of us, including a dozen women. Many were friends from previous expeditions. Except for an African American man from Georgia named Mike Gamble, everyone was white. We sat around a firepit chatting and drinking pop. Almost every man present was named Mike or John. Still, we wore name tags on lanyards clipped to our clothing, which injected an air of unearned intimacy. A Michigander, for instance, might find himself subjected to ribbings about his accent and a long-suffering NFL franchise. The vibe was slaphappy, pregame. "There are a lot of nuts out here, and not just us," someone said, making everybody laugh. As the sun set, we ate supper by lantern light.

Charlie Raymond materialized. He was a powerfully built man, about five eleven, fiftyish, with a short dark beard and bright, canny eyes. He delivered a brief lecture on the history of Bigfoot sightings in the area. They went all the way back to the Woodland Indians who'd lived here five thousand years ago, he said, and came forward to the present, to as recently as last night, in fact, when some early arrivers had spotted a Bigfoot strolling past the restrooms not thirty yards from where we sat. It was large and hairy and vanished into the tall grass that ran through the middle of the campground. A few expeditions ago, a white-gray-colored Bigfoot had been seen crossing the road and entering the same grassy median. "This place is red-hot," Charlie said, his fingers laced before him. Two or three Bigfoot couples, plus two juveniles, lived in these woods, of that he was certain. "I've had many, many amazing experiences out here. I'm a researcher. This is where I research."

He explained that we'd split into three teams, fanning out in pursuit of nighttime encounters. "Please respect peoples' experiences," Charlie said. "Respect their research." I took this to mean that if you had reason to doubt somebody's claims of a sighting, don't miss the opportunity to shut up. Sound advice for any occasion.

By now it was pitch-black. We all clumped together, our headlamp beams roaming about like searchlights, throwing *Blair Witch* shadows among the trees. It reminded me of a line from *Walden* that has always stuck with me: "I believe that men are generally still a little afraid of the dark, though the witches are all hung, and Christianity and candles have been introduced." James Attlee, in his memoir-cum-history *Nocturne: A Journey in Search of Moonlight*, elaborates on Thoreau: "This fear, this shunning of the night, is by no means a new phenomenon. It is possible that man evolved the habit of sleeping in safe, secluded places as a response to the danger of attack from wild animals… In Jewish and Christian theology, God separated light from darkness shortly after creation and human beings have been attempting to extend light's dominion ever since." It also comes in handy when you drop your car keys in the grass.

A last word of caution from Charlie—"Watch out for snakes! Copperheads have been spotted all over the roads!"—and we were off. I joined a team with Charlie, his wife, Lyndsey, and their terrier Chihuahua mix, Whiskey Rose. We were also Marge Gates, fifty-six, an events coordinator from suburban Chicago; her friend

Barbara Mueller, a retired sheriff from Illinois in her early seventies; Jason Grainger, forty-one, an ex-Marine who managed a Lowe's in Willisburg; Victoria Haydon, Jason's girlfriend, a real estate agent, also in her forties; and Mason, a burly and bearded Kentuckian about whom I could learn nothing else.

Leaves rustled underfoot. With our headlamps switched off for stealth, it was so dark that if you stopped without warning, the person behind would walk right into you. I got to talking with Lyndsey Raymond. She was a sweet blond woman from Yorkshire, England, in her forties. A retired police officer, she wore a white T-shirt with gray pants and carried a cotton sack like a mailbag for Whiskey Rose to rest in when she got tired. Lyndsey had recently left the force to devote more time to Bigfooting. She helped run a motel in Clay City that she and Charlie had just bought and planned to turn into a Bigfoot Inn & Museum. Lyndsey's accent stood out even more than mine. Speaking to her, I felt suddenly that my own English was rather coarse and nasally, that my flattened vowels were especially offensive to the ear. In England, she said, there wasn't much Bigfoot culture to speak of, owing to a lack of Bigfoots, and that if you expressed an interest in it, people thought you were insane.

We reached a trail junction Charlie called "the Crossroads." The wind was up. Acorns and walnuts were dropping everywhere. People leaned against trees or sat on the ground. Charlie asked if someone would play music on their phone, music being a Bigfoot attractant. I fetched mine from my pocket and put on Jim Croce's "I've Got A Name." No one seemed impressed. I tried again with "Fork" by 2 Chainz but was politely voted down. Someone then played an unlistenable dance track. Musically, we never recovered.

From his backpack, Charlie produced a wooden club resembling an axe handle, like what Clint Eastwood thrashes the prospectors with in *Pale Rider* ("There's nothing like a nice piece of hickory!"). Lots of Bigfooters carry these, not for self-defense but for "wood knocks." The idea, Charlie explained, was to draw out Bigfoots by knocking on trees—their preferred style of communication during nocturnal hunts. "Sometimes they'll think you're another Squatch and they'll knock back," he said.

Charlie found a tree and beat it three times with his club. Leaves rained down around us. "Three knocks are best," he said. "Squatches use one knock to call to each other, two or three to echolocate."

We waited for a reply. Acorns plonked and kerplunked. Bigfooting, like deer hunting, requires patience. Much of your time is spent waiting around in undistinguished stretches of wood, twirling your thumbs.

"It's rare to get a knock back," Charlie whispered. Just then, three knocks came back to us—Knock! Knock! Knock! Everybody froze. If it's possible for something unseen to make a dramatic entrance, that was what happened. The atmosphere became electric. Our headlamp beams skittered across the brush, extending for ten feet or so, illuminating the fracture lines of tree bark and little else. Had I been alone, the knocks probably would've passed without notice. The impression I had was of falling acorns or walnuts. But there was no way to say for sure what it was. Which, I supposed, was the point.

Charlie radioed another team positioned a few miles away. "Did you guys just do three knocks?"

"Negative."

Silence.

"They like watching us," someone offered. "We're their TV."

And for a moment it was like a scene in a movie or an H. P.

Lovecraft story, a scene in which we were active participants rather than passive viewers. In this way, Bigfooting was a little like wilderness LARPing, pursued in often abstract terms, with an endgame that was hardly more real than Quidditch.

Charlie knocked three more times. Nothing.

"What I'm trying to figure out is if it was acorns falling," he said. "My gut tells me it was three acorns."

Earlier, Charlie had mentioned that Bigfoots can become aggressive. "We've had them bluff charge us, breaking branches and grunting. What else does that? What else knocks and whistles and bluff charges you?"

I had in my bag a sheet of folded laminate called "Sasquatch Field Guide: Identifying, Tracking and Sighting North America's Relict Hominoid," by Jeff Meldrum. Designed to look like a pocket naturalist guide, it included primers on Bigfoot habitat and distribution, language, and diet and how-tos on casting tracks, recording vocalizations, and handling scat for DNA analysis ("Use a stick or wear gloves"). It was a clever stroke of Bigfoot monetizing by Meldrum that also neatly summarized his thinking. It came with a warning: "While there have been no substantiated reports of unprovoked attacks on humans, sasquatch are nevertheless large and very powerful creatures demonstrating feats of considerable strength and should be accorded the same caution as a bear, moose, or any other potentially dangerous wild animal."

Lyndsey heard movement in the trees. "There's something out there," she said.

Mason heard it too. "Sounded like someone trying to move quietly, taking *two* steps."

Then a whoop like a police siren reached us from far away. I thought it was a blackbird or a barred owl, the latter being liberally distributed here, though a part of me struggled to grasp exactly what we were hearing. Coyotes too, Charlie pointed out, made similar cries.

"You just don't know if it's a Bigfoot or a coyote," he said.

With everyone on edge—except for Whiskey Rose, who was asleep, or pretending to sleep, in her sack—three of us volunteered to push farther into the dark. A recon mission of sorts, the point of which I didn't grasp but had something to do with triangulating the noise being made—by us, by Bigfoots, by falling acorns, and/or by the other team—while flushing a Squatch in the process. Jason, the ex-Marine, walked point with Mason close behind, while I brought up the rear.

We walked for an eternity, my alliterative companions and I, into the shapeless night. Actually it was probably five minutes, but five minutes marked by confusion and awe at finding ourselves in subterranean gloom. The woods were all around, teeming with possibility. Our headlamps were basically useless, reflecting the dimmest impressions back to us.

"Man, I love this!" Jason announced. "It's so exciting. It seems like something we shouldn't be allowed to do." The comment was striking coming from someone who'd served four tours in Iraq. He said it so sweetly, with a big grin, that I felt compelled to reply. "Yeah, man!" I said stupidly.

Jason had faded blue eyes and a graying buzz cut, and he smoked a lot. He'd told me earlier he didn't care much for Bigfoot. He was here on account of Victoria, who did. But he'd thrown himself into the spirit of it. And I had to confess, it *was* exciting. This was what Bigfooters love: the collateral kick of adrenaline that comes from doing what feels mischievous but is, in fact, good wholesome fun, excitement at a higher rate of return than life normally offered.

Unless, of course, you'd served four tours in Iraq, in which case, well, it was still exciting, just absent IEDs and ambush points.

Mason, it seemed, was in a graver mood. With the acorns going completely bananas, crashing fore and aft, his head was on a swivel. He clutched tightly at the Louisville Slugger he carried for wood knocks. When I pointed out the staggering abundance of acorns, he growled, "That's not fucking acorns!"

We came upon a pile of saplings lying across the trail. Jason thought they'd been placed there to block our progress. By Bigfoot? He didn't say. "All I know is trees don't fall that way." Next, we found impressions in the mud resembling hoofprints. We had a long look at them. You couldn't really make out what they were. I guessed they were horse prints and said as much. Neither Jason nor Mason was convinced. Next, we caught a whiff of cucumber, though slightly sweeter, like a Pimm's Cup...

"Copperheads," Jason announced. The snakes emitted a cucumber-y odor when cornered, he said. This explained the nebulous rustling in the ferns. Though usually diurnal, Jason went on, copperheads love nothing more than a warm, humid Kentucky eve such as this. And in case we were wondering, why yes, copperheads *are* venomous. Very much so. They also happened to be at the end of their birthing season, meaning not only were there venomous copperheads out here, but venomous *baby* copperheads. Lots of venomous baby copperheads. And the venomous baby copperheads slithering trailside? They're more dangerous than adult copperheads because they lack "bite control" and therefore tend to excrete more venom. (I didn't know it then, but this last part turns out not to be true.)

"If you don't get an antivenom fast enough, you can die," Jason finished. (This part, however, is true.)

We decided to hurry back to the Crossroads. But not before a few wood knocks. Jason radioed Charlie a heads-up. Mason located a defenseless oak, positioned his Louisville Slugger along its trunk, and swung for the bleachers. Three massive blows ricocheted up and away. The ensuing quiet was tremendous. A feeling of communal magic tightened its grip. Jason, taking a drag from his cigarette, smiled and said, "All kinds of mysterious craziness."

———

The following day, I went fishing with Bigfooters Leila Karge and her fiancé, David Boehmker, who'd driven down from Indianapolis, and their friend Mike Gamble, from outside Columbus, Georgia. This was their first Bigfoot expedition. They were old army pals. Each was also a current or former police officer; I partly lost track of who was what. We chose a river renowned for bass and catfish of prehistoric girth. Leila, thirty-two, had just returned from a year stationed in Kuwait. She had a pretty face, red-dyed hair, and tattoos along her shoulders and calves. David, thirty-four, a tank officer who'd served in Iraq, had chiseled features and a full head of dark hair under a ragged Cincinnati Reds cap. Sergeant First Class Mike Gamble, in his thirties, was built like a wrestler, or rather a couple of wrestlers, with a tapered torso filling out a T-shirt with an image of Bigfoot carrying a fishing rod above the word "Bassquatch." (The reader may be wondering about the number of military and police on this expedition. Both demographics are overrepresented in Bigfooting. About a third of attendees in Kentucky, I guessed, fell into at least one category.)

The sun shone brightly. David loaned me a rod and some flies from a well-appointed box. I tied on a pumpkin-orange woolly bugger because I liked how the color popped against the river's matcha green. The banks were steep and slick and knotted with brambles that came up past my chest. I worried about ticks. Mostly I worried about slipping and snapping David's fly rod.

After Mike staked out a primo spot near the boat launch, I wandered downstream to where a big oak hung horizontally over the river. I inched my way onto the trunk until I was a good ways out. It was a precarious spot, but one with casting room. The river was like a slowly moving mud puddle, completely eddyless, with swirls and sworls gathered around a few sagging limbs. I cast and got instantly snagged on the tree I was standing on, broke off, retied, and got snagged again. In about as much time as it took me to free my line, both Mike and David fell into the river. I couldn't see either of them, but from what I gathered, Mike had managed to pull himself out while David had not. I scrambled over to where he was. Leila, struggling to extricate him, was making little progress. The problem was the mud, which wasn't like ordinary mud at all but a kind of polyurethane-coated Teflon. Try as we might, we couldn't gain purchase on it. David, with one knee sliding off the bank and fly rod clenched between his teeth, nearly dragged us both in. When we finally hauled him out, he stood on the bank panting, streaked with mud from the waist down.

"You're soaked!" Leila said.

We decided to pack it in. On the drive back, we talked Bigfoot. I was curious about where they sat on the continuum of belief, whether they were "believers" or "knowers," as Charlie had put it. I also wondered how Mike felt being the lone African American in the Bigfoot cracker barrel, but I couldn't very well ask him that. He mostly stayed quiet.[1] David, with Leila nodding along, said the two of them were 60–70 percent convinced that Bigfoot was real, based on amateur films and footprint casts. I asked about the remaining 30–40 percent of uncertainty. On this subject, Leila was the most talkative.

The issue, as always, was one of interpretation. While the "wood knocks," she agreed, could've been acorns or walnuts, and the "whoops" coyotes, what occupied her more were eyewitness reports. She'd been trained as a cop to take witness testimony with a grain of salt and to consider the fallibility and biased nature of memory.

"Legally, eyewitness testimony is the least reliable evidence there is," she said. "It's just a piece of the puzzle, not the whole thing." Investigators, in their search for accuracy, had to entertain the possibility that a witness to a crime, even a credible witness, one who strived to tell the truth about what they saw, might be wrong in their recollections. Sometimes what we "see," Leila said (I'm paraphrasing her), isn't a reflection of objective reality but a by-product of our psychological predispositions. What's more, witnesses are influenced by their circumstances and other people around them. "At an event like this," she said, "with people telling and listening to a lot of the same stories, they're susceptible to suggestion."

It's an old story: that we're primed to have certain kinds of experiences, that each of us, according to the psychologist Daniel Kahneman, is not only "blind to the obvious" but "blind to our blindness," our judgments springing not so much from mental clarity and reason as a stew of deceptive emotions, dingy memories, and

---

1 I eventually caught up with Mike on the phone: "Nobody said anything odd about race to me in Kentucky," he said. "I grew up around white people, so it wasn't an unusual environment for me to be in. It was my first time Squatchin' though. I expected to find a bunch of people wearing tinfoil hats and talking about UFOs. But they were the nicest, most normal people." With one other exception, Mike was the only person of color I met in a year of Bigfooting.

the biases and forecasting of our unique cognitive loads. We are, in other words, apt to get carried away. Knowing what we know about the human brain, Leila was saying, required asking some uncomfortable questions. "Are you seeing what's really there?" she said. "Or are you seeing what you want to see?"

———

In her book *How Emotions Are Made: The Secret Life of the Brain*, psychologist Lisa Feldman Barrett says that humans are hardwired for certain kinds of delusions. That's because our brains construct virtually everything we perceive, filtering sense data and relying on stored knowledge to make predictions about the world around us. Rather than merely *reacting* to events as they occur, our brains *predict* what's going to happen, then test the results against what they already know. "Through continual prediction, you experience a world of your own creation that is held in check by the sensory world," Barrett wrote. "Once your predictions are correct enough, they not only create your perception and action but also explain the meaning of your sensations."

Prediction is your brain's way of dealing with information overload. Baseball is a classic example. Aroldis Chapman, a pitcher for the New York Yankees (barf), once threw a fastball at 105.1 miles per hour, the fastest ever recorded. While most pitchers top out in the mid-90s (even Dwight Gooden's fastest pitch was 100 miles per hour. Pathetic!), that still leaves batters only a half second or less to see the ball, judge its approximate speed and trajectory, decide whether to swing at it and, if so, where and when, and execute the swing. The only way this works is because a batter's brain predicts the entire process from beginning to end, allowing them to react to a pitch well before they're aware of their intent to do so.

In the same way, we're all constantly making predictions that determine how we perceive, make sense of, and act on incoming data. Our entire conceptual system is, at root, anticipatory. We imagine the future before it happens. This is our default setting and an energy-saving device, like a Nest Learning Thermostat. Without it, we'd feel "experientially blind," in Barrett's words—that is, permanently hungover: drained, confused, and a little ashamed. (I made that last part up.)

Despite its flaws, the human visual system is also extraordinarily good—"one of the wonders of the world," wrote Steven Pinker, "a precision instrument that can detect a single photon, recognize thousands of shapes, and negotiate rocky trails and high-speed autobahns." But sometimes even precision instruments malfunction. In its struggle to keep us alive and fully functioning, the brain cuts a lot of corners. One way it does this is by something psychologists call "affective realism," also known as "unconscious affect"—the idea that our feelings color our perceptions, quite literally determining what we see, often without us realizing it. As Barrett puts it elsewhere, "feeling is believing." Without explicitly mentioning this phenomenon, Jeff Meldrum has conceded as much, acknowledging a "hazard for misidentification" in the field, especially given the resemblance of Bigfoots to bears standing on their hind legs.

Until pretty recently, scientists thought that the visual field worked like a camera, capturing and constructing a more or less accurate, photograph-like image of reality. Today we know that's hardly the case. Far from being passive recorders of experience, our brains, Barrett tells us, are conjurers of reality, constantly "reassembling the past in the present," causing us to perceive what we already believe. Everything we discern about our physical environment—sight, sound, smell, taste, touch—is influenced by our past experiences and memories, by cultural and social cues, including "perceptual contagion" from other brains around us and by input from the heart, lungs, metabolism, and immune system. Stress and anxiety also shape our perceptions. "Neuroscientists like to say that your day-to-day experience is a carefully controlled hallucination, constrained by the world and your body but ultimately constructed by your brain," Barrett wrote in her 2020 book, *Seven and a Half Lessons About the Brain*. "It's an everyday kind of hallucination that creates all of your experiences and guides all your actions."

This means there's sometimes a considerable gap between perception and reality. The stakes can be much higher than mistaking an acorn for a Bigfoot. In a courtroom, witness testimony often plays a crucial role in determining the outcomes of criminal trials. But as any competent jurist or investigator like Leila Karge will tell you, eyewitness reports are often unreliable. They are a record not of unvarnished reality but of events filtered through a witness's inherently distorted perceptions. According to the Innocence Project, mistaken eyewitness identifications contributed to 70 percent of the more than 365 wrongful convictions in the United States that were eventually overturned by DNA evidence. Nearly a third of those cases involved *multiple misidentifications* of the defendant by their accuser. This means that at least 245 people have gone to prison in recent years—many lingering there for decades, some on death row—for crimes they didn't commit based on the testimony of eyewitnesses, a number of whom proved to be wrong not once but time and time again. The Innocence Project estimates that between twenty thousand and one hundred thousand people are currently imprisoned in the United States for crimes they didn't commit.

These numbers get even worse when defendants are Black. African Americans make up roughly 12.5 percent of the U.S. population but account for almost 50 percent of the nearly two thousand people who have been wrongly convicted and exonerated, according to a 2017 report by the National Registry of Exonerations. Of all convictions overturned by DNA testing, at least 42 percent were based on "cross-racial eyewitness identification," a polite way of saying that a white person randomly picked a Black or brown suspect out of a police lineup. Unfortunately, jurors tend to believe a witness's misidentifications, especially when the suspect is Black. As I was writing this, Alice Sebold, author of *The Lovely Bones*, publicly apologized to a man who was wrongly convicted of raping her when she was eighteen. Anthony J. Broadwater spent sixteen years in prison after Sebold, who wrote a memoir about the experience called *Lucky*, misidentified him in court as her attacker. Sebold is white. Broadwater is Black.

"Eyewitness identification thus presents the legal system with a challenge unlike any other," Judge Jed S. Rakoff of the federal district court in Manhattan wrote in an essay titled "Our Lying Eyes." "Modern science suggests that much of such testimony is inherently suspect—but not in ways that jurors can readily evaluate from their own experience. The result, alas, is a likelihood of wrongful convictions."

Setting aside systemic racism and a criminal justice system that myopically targets poor people of color, part of the problem of misidentification is that we're just really bad at remembering things. "In talking about the past, we lie with every breath we draw," William

Maxwell wrote in his novel *So Long, See You Tomorrow*. Decades of research, most notably by the psychologist Elizabeth Loftus, a professor at UC Irvine, suggest pretty much the same thing. According to Loftus, our memories are not permanent, pristine records of the past that we retrieve and replay on demand like a movie but murky blends of fact and fiction that are under constant revision and are highly vulnerable to suggestion.

"Truth and reality, when seen through the filter of our memories, are not objective facts but subjective," Loftus has written. "We interpret the past, correcting ourselves, adding bits and pieces, deleting uncomplimentary or disturbing recollections, sweeping, dusting, tidying things up. Thus our representation of the past takes on a living, shifting reality; it is not fixed and immutable, not a place way back there that is preserved in stone, but a living thing that changes shape, expands, shrinks, and expands again, an amoeba-like creature with powers to make us laugh, and cry, and clench our fists. Enormous powers—powers even to make us believe in something that never happened."

Memories, put simply, are distortions of actual events. They dim over time, but they also develop. In Loftus's terms, they're "reconstructed," altered by what we're told by others, by ideas and suggestions plucked out of the ether, by a new context or telling, and by our own later experiences. Sometimes we come to believe in a fantasy of our own creation. (This is close in sentiment to Kant's view of reality, which, the philosopher felt, wasn't a static reflection of the way things are but rather part of an ongoing creative process of organizing knowledge that's rife with "mirages.")

The point isn't that all memories are kaleidoscopic illusions. For the most part, Loftus says, our memories serve us reasonably well, mainly because their details don't usually matter much. (It's when someone's on trial for a crime they didn't commit that the "flimsy curtain that separates our imagination and our memory" becomes a life-or-death issue.) In my extended family, for instance, I'm known for having a memory of Swiss cheese. I don't mean a nice aged Gruyère from the Wine & Cheese Cask. I mean deli Swiss, second rate and full of holes. At holiday gatherings, I'll occasionally find myself recounting a vivid childhood memory to a tableful of family—these tend to be character assassinations of my parents disguised as light comedy—after which someone, usually my twin sister, Erin ("the smart one"), will offer a correction. "That's an arresting story," she'll say, casually swirling the wine in her glass. "But everything you just described happened to *me*, not to you." "All autobiographies are lies," is the advisory George Bernard Shaw appended to his autobiography, perhaps overstating things a tad. "I do not mean unconscious, unintentional lies. I mean deliberate lies."

In Bigfooting, a witness's memory and testimony are generally taken on faith. The KBRO and BFRO are exceptions. Their investigators follow up on reports to try and determine their veracity, sometimes traveling to sighting locations to collect and corroborate evidence, casting tracks and taking hair and scat samples for DNA analysis. An honest attempt is made to balance personal anecdotes with physical facts. For obvious reasons though, they're still beholden to eyewitnesses, from whom the vast bulk of Bigfoot evidence derives. The BFRO website transparently endorses eyewitness reliability: "Every day in courtrooms across America, legal conclusions are handed down based solely upon witness testimony, and often upon the testimony of a single witness." To their credit, when questioning witnesses, BFRO investigators, conscious of the potential for misidentification and misremembering, attempt to wheedle out inconsistencies while reckoning with the circumstances of an event, such as a driving-down-a-turnpike-in-the-middle-of-the-night sighting, as Matt Moneymaker calls it. "A given witness might be very credible, but could have honestly misinterpreted something that was seen, found, or heard," their website says. But Loftus's research reveals that the questions themselves can provoke false memories and associations, "overwriting" an original memory with a completely new one. "You can plant entire events into the minds of otherwise ordinary, healthy people," she has said, adding that someone being urged to remember more about an event might simply fill in the blanks with a guess, which can start to feel emotionally true. "The emotion is no guarantee that you are dealing with an authentic memory."

The power of suggestion, intentional or not, can be a potent distorter of reality, as Loftus's colleague Gary Wells has argued. A distinguished professor of psychology at Iowa State, Wells has spent decades documenting eyewitness mistakes. In one study, he chronicled in chilling detail how, when given misleading information under questioning, people "remembered" entirely fictitious events, in some instances believing they'd been hospitalized, attacked by animals as children, or had witnessed demonic possession. An eyewitness's "certainty," Wells wrote, has little bearing on the accuracy of their claimed experience.

We can, in other words, conjure Bigfoot out of thin air. "You don't have to see a hairy monster to be able to remember seeing one," David J. Daegling, an anthropologist at the University of Florida, wrote in *Bigfoot Exposed: An Anthropologist Examines America's Enduring Legend*. It goes without saying, but Daegling says it anyway: "This has no bearing on the person's moral character or sincerity; the mere act of interpretation distorts reality."

More research has shown that we're often unable to detect large and seemingly obvious visual changes in our environment, that we're bad at weighing evidence against our prior convictions, and that we make huge leaps from correlation to causation. "Event factors," such as whether it's light or dark out, the duration or trauma of an experience, can also make perception go awry, as can our expectations, which are warped by television, movies,[2] and other external data, such as being told we're in a Bigfoot hot zone. Even our biases have biases. The social psychologist Emily Pronin has found that a large majority of us rate ourselves as less susceptible to biases than the average person, while virtually none of us considers ourselves more biased than anyone else. "We excel at noticing the flaws of friends," Pronin wrote, but have an "inability to spot those same mistakes in ourselves." This "bias blind spot," she says, is more pronounced in people with higher intelligence, attesting to a phenomenon that most of us have encountered at one point or another: smart people aren't as smart as they think.

But we're all in the psychology textbook somewhere. And nobody, especially yours truly, likes being told they didn't see what they say they saw or that their memory is like one of those reality-bending M. C. Escher stairways where the normal modes of discernment don't apply. But any quest to understand Bigfoot involves detours into the nature of perception. The research done by Barrett, Loftus, and others complicates the statement often heard from eyewitnesses: "I know what I saw." Very often, as Leila had told me, we see what we want to see, which is what we already believe is there. Even when what we see is a close approximation of reality, it eventually gets reshaped and supplanted by memories that may be no more real than our dreams.

---

2 One of my favorite factoids ever is that between 2001 and 2015, when *The X-Files* was at the height of its popularity, UFO sightings in the United States increased by 241 percent.

Which, Barrett notes, raises some heady epistemological questions about free will and how much we can ever know about ourselves (let alone about Bigfoot). If we're all effectively slaves to our internally biased hardwiring, our judgments and actions arising from a precooked, hallucinatory casserole, then not only are objectivity and fairness bogus concepts, but we humans can be said to lack control over what we do. It upends some pretty fundamental ideas about personal agency and autonomy, suggesting that we may at times inhabit an imaginative world so saturated with self-delusion that reason itself evaporates entirely.

To some extent, Barrett says, it's possible to break our cognitive chains and cultivate a mind that perceives reality in slightly sharper focus. In a way that's not so dissimilar from what Buddhists call *deconstructing the self*, we can tweak our predictive brains, rethink the essential fictions that make us who we are, and become less gullible, less prone to believing in our own inventions, and perhaps, I'd add, even better Bigfooters. But I'm afraid you'll have to read her books to find out how!

———

At base camp, meanwhile, there was a palpable deficit of beer. Expeditions tend to be dry affairs. I'd heard rumors of past debauches, of mini kegs and pint bottles stashed away in the trees, of ham-sandwiched Bigfooters face-planting midtrail. As is so often the case, a bunch of sousers had spoiled it for the rest of us. So officially, alcohol was prohibited on BFRO expeditions (although the KBRO was Charlie's gig, he was also a BFRO investigator). Unofficially, I had a six-pack in my car. I felt bad about this. But not so bad that, après fish, I didn't quietly guzzle one down and distribute others among my river rat cronies.

As I sat on my bumper in the darkening twilight, an older gentleman came over to talk. He had a thin white moustache, wore a faded Yellowstone National Park T-shirt, and spoke in the pleasing, loping drawl I've learned to expect from North Carolinians. His name was Jeff C. He said he didn't want his full name to appear in any Bigfoot book. About Bigfoot, though, he had some opinions. "Eighty percent of it is bullshit," Jeff said. "People are misidentifying things. Overinterpreting coincidences. It's dark out. They're excited. Or afraid. You've heard of confirmation bias?" This is our universal weakness for evidence that corroborates a preexisting belief and our disinterest in evidence that refutes it. I said I had but didn't see how that could account for tens of thousands of eyewitness reports from across the continent. "Oh, Bigfoot's real," Jeff said. "I've seem 'em. Twice. But they're rare." To hear him tell it, Bigfoot was like the American cowboy, an endlessly elaborated trope that bore only passing resemblance to reality and whose actual numbers were minuscule.

My own thinking had a lot in common with Jeff's and attempted to reconcile some oppositions about human rationality and the madness of crowds. Sometimes I thought of Bigfoot obsession as not unlike the messianic exaltation that struck supporters at a Trump rally; that is, an expression of white anxiety and fear mixed with nostalgia for an imagined American past. "Here was a creature that…could live without civilization, that was self-reliant and strong," Joshua Blu Buhs has written, and that, to Bigfoot's demographic—largely male, conservative, working-class whites whose lives were shackled to Hobbesian market forces—"was authentic and genuine, a repudiation of the society around them, a society that very often did not value them or their opinions."

Among the countless imponderables of Trump's ascent, he routinely polled as the most "authentic" candidate, even when voters thought he was also a "lying demagogue." His lies were justified, in their minds, as a form of "symbolic protest"—a middle finger extended to the liberal aristocracy. Not incidentally, the era that Trump often cites as the acme of American greatness—an Eisenhowerian niche of economic expansion, rising wages, and efflorescent white supremacy—happens to be when the modern Bigfoot strolled onstage in northern California. Perhaps for some Bigfooters, the beast's telltale effluvium carried the scent trace of that bygone era?

The previous evening's firepit throwdown had occasioned some hard words about Biden/Harris.[3] But I confess I hadn't encountered much overt Trumpism. No red-hatted MAGA howlers or red-faced paranoiacs ranting and raving about Mexican rapists. Hardly an errant star and stripe presented itself. Everyone I spoke with struck me as perfectly decent and sane. They just happened to have an oddball hobby and a quibble or two about gun control and "kneelers." Their reasons for being there were myriad and not discernibly political or easily pigeonholed. I often wondered what opinion they had of me, with my Moleskin and digital voice recorder and spotless $150 hiking shoes, parachuting in from Cambridge to cast my imperious gaze at them. I continued to worry, in a Janet Malcolm-y way, about my own interest in Bigfoot and whether it reflected voyeurism or exploitation, or worse: an inbred disdain for flatlanders you encounter on the Boston cocktail circuit. The situation was further complicated by the obvious fact that whatever value this book has comes on account of the people who've opened themselves up

---

3 Bigfooters typically don't discuss politics, an unwritten rule intended to keep the peace at gatherings like this. But sometimes things get said.

to me and my dissections and whose kindnesses are impossible to repay.

That night, a dozen of us piled into trucks and drove to an old cemetery down a winding gravel road. I shared a back seat with John Baranchok, a psychologist from Rome, Georgia. We talked about the predictive brain, how stress can trigger delusions and impair memory, and how fantasies sometimes provide relief from loneliness and anxiety. Baranchok was about to publish a book with the Defoean title *Psychological Horizons in Scientific Bigfoot Research: Using Fight-Flight Reconditioning Techniques, Psychological Knowledge, and Scientific Research Processes to Enhance the Scientific Validity of No-Kill Bigfoot Fieldwork*. He said its aim was to familiarize Bigfooters with baseline psychological deficits that impede rationality so they could minimize errors during encounters. He was familiar with Lisa Feldman Barrett's work. Perceptive failures, he conceded, marred many firsthand Bigfoot accounts. But it didn't have to be that way. "Scientifically objective data is crucial to understanding and preserving this species," he said.

At the cemetery, I sat with my back against a tree and shut my eyes. It turned out I'd set up my tent directly next door to a double-bass, Richter-scale snorer and had slept poorly. I dozed off. When I awoke, Lyndsey was telling a story about a night she'd spent alone in a rural hotel somewhere; the door handle to her room rattled intermittently, as if someone were trying to get in, but every time she got up to check, no one was there.

The mood was mellower than the previous night. Charlie was eating potato chips on a blanket with Whiskey Rose curled at his feet. After Lyndsey's story, talk hovered around ghosts and the paranormal. Lori Russell, a retired helicopter pilot and mechanic from

Ohio, had brought along a Mel-8704 meter, a gadget popular with ghost hunters. "It picks up things we can't hear," she explained, "like changes in the electromagnetic field and sudden shifts in temperature." Both could be signs of an invisible presence, she said. Lori was in her midsixties, I guessed. She had a wrinkled face framed by chin-length, salt-and-pepper hair, mostly pepper. Despite her Jeep's prominent Ohio State Buckeyes flag, which gave me more shudders and shivers than Lyndsey's ghost story, I liked her a lot.

A footnote regarding the Mel-8704 meter: its inventor is Gary Galka, an electrical engineer from East Granby, Connecticut. "Mel" stands for his daughter, Melissa, who was killed in a car crash at age seventeen ("8704" is the year she was born and the year she died). Galka and his family have said they began receiving after-death communications (ADCs) from Melissa shortly after she died. She'd ring the doorbell, change TV channels, tap them on their shoulders, call their names, and kiss them on their foreheads. To try to communicate with her, Galka developed the Mel-8704 and other "electromagnetic detection devices." He claimed to have recorded Melissa saying, "Hi, Daddy, I love you."

Charlie didn't truck with such stuff. As a flesh-and-blooder, he considered the paranormal an investigative hamster wheel. Just more grist for the woo's mill. "You can't prove any of it," he said. Lori glanced at me and shrugged. "If nothing else, it's an excuse to spend time in the woods," she said.

Large and stately trees encircled us. The cemetery had about a hundred gravesites, most dating from the late nineteenth and early twentieth century. Only a few headstones had legible inscriptions; prominent names were Cox, Davis, Kerr, and Logsdon. The remaining graves were marked by plain fieldstone slabs. The place was so cool that we decided to stay a while. Charlie made a fire. Those who'd been smart enough to bring a camp chair—everyone except me—lolled cozily in them. High above us, a screech owl started losing its mind. "Sounds like a damn horse in a tree," Marge said. That's a totally accurate description of a screech owl. Now and then, Whiskey Rose popped up to growl at the brush and the tension would rise. But these incidents passed, and we'd resume our fireside chatter.

In 2020, Charlie self-published a compendium of local lore and reports called *Bluegrass Bigfoot: Encounters with The Kentucky Wildman, Vol. 1.* It mentions how Daniel Boone, the famous frontiersman and settler of what became Kentucky, bragged about killing a ten-foot-tall hairy "Yahoo" near the town of Alvaton in 1771. Yahoos are the depraved, humanoid beasts that Gulliver encounters in Boone's favorite book, *Gulliver's Travels*: "Their heads and breasts were covered with a thick hair, some frizzled, and others lank; they had beards like goats, and a long ridge of hair down their backs," Gulliver said. "They climbed high trees as nimbly as a squirrel, for they had strong extended claws before and behind, terminating in sharp points, and hooked. They would often spring, and bound, and leap, with prodigious agility." Boone's biographer, John Mack Faragher, said Boone's story was a type familiar to American pioneers: "It was a tall tale that Boone repeated to a number of people during his last year, and one such as he would have told in a winter camp." Folklorists have wondered whether Boone's Yahoo—by way of Jonathan Swift—and other frontier "creature tales" could be an origin point of Bigfoot stories in North America. "There is no real reason why Bigfoot cannot have come to life from the pages of Jonathan Swift's book and made the rounds of the camps of deer hunters and trappers of the frontier," wrote Hugh H. Trotti. "Various pranks, hoaxes, and more tall tales would add to the legend, and such a potentially fearsome creature's existence could lend awe and romance to wild areas far from most people's daily lives." Unlike Faragher, Trotti allows that Boone's story could also be true—evidence of a Bigfoot-like animal driven into the wilderness and eventually to extinction by westward expansion. Whichever, it fulfills a key function of folklore: to mark the boundaries between nature and civilization and define what it means to be human.

Around midnight, two guys from our group moseyed down the road and soon came jogging back, spooked by a strange noise. Charlie, Lyndsey, and I went to investigate. Again a coffin-like darkness fell over us. With my headlamp off, I couldn't see my shoes. The smell of cucumber was strong, but we kept going. After a few hundred yards, we stopped to listen. I was going to say it was quiet, but coyotes yipped and yapped. The birds were raising a racket. I heard a whip-poor-will, then a nightjar cooing in a pile of thick snag. And from all points of the compass, barred owls beckoned in a fitful carnival chorus: *Who cooks for you? Who cooks for you all?* Teetering with exhaustion, I had a feeling of being elsewhere. I usually hear barred owls only in Vermont, where they occupy the woods around the cabin my family and I rent in summer. Some nights they call so loudly and so repeatedly that they keep me awake for long stretches. It occurred to me that in almost twenty summers at the cabin, I'd never actually *seen* a barred owl, so expert they are at hiding themselves.

Then something weird happened. Charlie's handheld radio died at the same moment that his FLIR zonked out. Both were fully charged. He fiddled with them, sighing mightily. The next minute, my headlamp quit. There was no cell service, so we were technologically blind, save for Charlie's and Lyndsey's headlamps. Such tech crashes are customary among Bigfooters, who tend to regard them as benign, woo-like episodes that help account for the lack of photo/video evidence. Charlie made nothing of it, even when, a half hour later, both his radio and FLIR came back on simultaneously and fully charged. The spookiest thing of all? My poor headlamp never recovered.

When we returned to base camp, incredible news. Someone in another group had seen a Bigfoot! It was Jason, the ex-Marine. He'd been at the front of his team near the campground when he'd heard shuffling leaves and deep grunts ahead of him. As acorns started hitting the ground, an eerie feeling came over him.

"All of a sudden, I saw this spider monkey type thing crawling on its stomach in the dead center of the road," he said. "It was huge, alligator size, maybe seventy-five feet away. And it was flying. I saw it for just a split second, it was so fast. I've never been so scared in my life."

He was trembling as he told me this. Victoria reminded me that Jason had spent forty-eight months on wartime active duty. She'd never seen him so shaken. What Jason described sounded to me like a wall-scaling Jeff Goldblum in *The Fly*. Charlie called it a "stomach crawler."

"Adult Squatches don't really crawl like that," he said, "but juvies do. And that's what we think we've got out here, a couple of juveniles. Now there's no doubt."

"I believe it," Jason said, his road to Damascus conversion lacking only a name change. "I've seen all I need to see."

In the end, there was a mystery, something leftover that remained unexplained. Bigfoot stories are like Greek myths in that way. They almost always take oblique and fragmentary form. What defines them are the questions that arise from irresolvable claims: How do you separate the credible from the crackpot, a "genuine sighting" from a full-bore sensory illusion with no anchor in reality? Is an experience like Jason's explicable in terms of misperception, trauma, confusion, or some other enchantment rendered in corporeal form? Does it reflect a deep-seated nostalgia for a lost world? Or is all that beside the point? Is the point of the story merely that it concerns common allegories that span civilizations and have a meaty narrative hook—one as old as storytelling itself—that leaves everything open ended?

5

THE LEGEND OF
BAYOU DE VIEW

"I knew that the best things were hidden."

—DAVID BERMAN

For seventy-odd years, sightings accumulated all over the South. In 1950, Allan Cruickshank spied one crossing Highway 29 in Florida's Collier County, on the western edge of Big Cypress National Preserve. Five years later, John Terres and his wife startled a pair south of Homosassa Springs, near Tampa, but were so leery of being ridiculed they kept it secret. Old Man Stoddard swore on three positive IDs, in '51 and '53, all in Georgia, the first two along Ward's Creek, the third while flying over the Altamaha River outside Mount Pleasant. Olga Hooks Lloyd (April '66) and John Dennis (December '66 and February '68) reported sightings in east Texas's Big Thicket. George Lowry Jr. of Louisiana State University observed two in the Atchafalaya Swamp, west of Baton Rouge, in late '71. Twenty-eight years on, an LSU undergraduate named David Kulivan came to within fifteen feet of an adult male and female on the Pearl River near New Orleans. Kulivan watched as the amorous couple knocked on trees, chipping away chunks of bark. "They vocalized continuously, making a sound he'd never heard before," one chronicler wrote. From 2005 to 2008, Auburn University professor Geoffrey Hill and a team of researchers recorded thirteen encounters along the Choctawhatchee River on the Florida-Alabama border. More recently, a pig hunter in Florida caught eerie sounds on his iPhone, and a group of Louisianans revealed intriguing videos and photographs.

Witnesses included scientists and academic researchers, some of whom published their accounts in books and scholarly journals. But none of the sightings, or dozens more like them, came with definitive proof. What photos and videos did exist, a believer confessed, had a "Bigfoot/Loch Ness monster fuzziness." People who thought seriously about such things mostly dismissed the sightings out of hand, attributing them to misidentification, bad science, and wishful thinking. "A sighting is just an eyewitness account," the skeptic David Allen Sibley said. "Just like eyewitness testimony in court, it's inherently unreliable. You need harder evidence."

The astute reader will have guessed I'm not talking about Bigfoot. The above reports refer to the ivory-billed woodpecker (*Campephilus principalis*), a magnificent, chromatic-black and tusk-white bird with a shark-fin crest. Sometimes called the "Lord God" bird, on account of what folks said after seeing one, the ivory-bill was largely eradicated from this country's river forests in the early twentieth century. The last universally accepted sighting, by wildlife artist Don Eckelberry, was in 1944. Long before then, most serious birders considered it already extinct. Nearly all its hardwood bottomland domain, including twenty million acres in the Lower Mississippi River Valley, had been logged, dammed, channelized, and drained. When people reported seeing an ivory-bill, they were treated skeptically at best. It was the

Snuffleupagus of woodpeckers, always sauntering offstage before the audience arrived. That it also closely resembled the common pileated woodpecker, with which it shared habitat, didn't help. "Unless the person reporting was a well-respected ornithologist, he or she might be branded a fool, a liar, or a kook—a situation that, sadly, is even truer today than it was in the early years of the last century," wrote Tim Gallagher in his 2005 book, *The Grail Bird: The Rediscovery of the Ivory-billed Woodpecker*.

Gallagher, an ornithologist, spent five years searching for ivory-bills in the southeast United States. When he started out, he wasn't sure whether he believed the bird still existed. "I was agnostic about it," he told me. "I thought it was a beautiful animal and it'd be an interesting project." He soon became infatuated. "I talked to people who'd had actual sightings of ivory-bills: John Dennis, who I interviewed on his deathbed. Nancy Tanner, the wife of [celebrated ornithologist] James Tanner. Then I started hearing about all of these other people who claimed even more recent sightings, hunters and fishermen and so on, and I followed up on those." Birders often fall on such eyewitness reports like hyenas on a zebra. "There's almost an unwritten law in birding that any ivory-bill sighting after Eckelberry's in '44 is immediately thrown out, or at least highly suspect. It doesn't matter who saw it. Even John Dennis, who'd photographed a nesting ivory-bill pair in Cuba in '48 and wrote an article about it, when he saw them again in Texas in the '60s, people didn't believe him. I thought, Huh?"

Based on his interviews with eyewitnesses, Gallagher decided there was a good chance a few remnant ivory-bill populations survived in the South. "What an amazing thought," he wrote of a rare environmental success story in the age of climate cataclysm. "I didn't want to give up on that dream. I didn't want to accept that the ivory-bill was gone forever."

At 1:30 p.m. on February 27, 2004, Gallagher, his friend Bobby Harrison, and a local outdoorsman named Gene Sparling were paddling a remote swamp in eastern Arkansas called Bayou De View. The bayou occupies a privileged place in the Cache River National Wildlife Refuge, which contains some of the last contiguous bottomland hardwood forest in the country and is, according to Gallagher, "perfect for woodpeckers, with lots of food and dead trunks and limbs in which to forage and dig roost and nest holes." It was their second day there. They'd already seen a promising woodpecker lineup: red-bellied, red-headed, downy, yellow-bellied sapsuckers, and dozens of pileated. The implausibility of their ivory-bill search, however, was never far from their minds.

"We're talking about a bird that's in really, really, extremely low numbers," Gallagher said. "Even a hundred years ago, it was in extremely low numbers. They're hard to see, let alone photograph. A random bird cruising through a vast swamp, not even stopping but just moving through, what are the odds you're gonna see it, identify it, and get a picture? I mean, seeing it and identifying it are themselves two different things. Then, 'Oh, wow! I've gotta get a photo!' But by then it's too late. And while you're out there paddling around, you're always looking for cottonmouths, which will try to get into your canoe. There's dense foliage, and in some places, alligators—not in Arkansas, but in more southerly states—and it's really wild. Even in spots that're populous with people, you've got a river and swamp to contend with. It gets dangerous."

With a camcorder mounted in the bow of their canoe, Gallagher and Harrison trailed Sparling, who scouted ahead in a kayak.

"And then it happened," Gallagher wrote. "Less than eighty feet away, a large black-and-white bird that had been flying toward us from a side channel of the bayou to the right came out into the sunshine and flew across the open stretch of water directly in front of us. It started to bank, giving us a superb view of its back and both wings for a moment as it pulled up, as if it were going to land on a tree trunk." Simultaneously, Gallagher and Harrison hollered, "Ivory-bill!"

It vanished as quickly as it appeared. But Gallagher caught another glimpse, then another, mentally ticking through the bird's field marks—large, crested, coal black, with white on the trailing edges of the wings—as it finally dipped out of sight. They hadn't had time to reach for a camera. Reviewing what they'd seen, Gallagher and Harrison asked themselves whether they could've mistaken a pileated for an ivory-bill. "No way," they determined. "The bird we saw was a different animal." They were absolutely convinced. "No knowledgeable person could have misidentified it."

If correct, it was the greatest ornithological rediscovery of the past half century. One with the potential to redraw conservation maps in the South and drive tourism dollars to Monroe County, one of the poorest places in Arkansas. For that reason, Gallagher and Harrison decided to sit on it a while, at least until "positive proof" in the form of roost holes or photographs emerged. Proof was precisely what they didn't have. Without it, Gallagher fretted over his professional reputation. "Claiming you've seen an ivory-bill could ruin your career," he said. You'd get lumped in with the "Bigfoot chasers," as he called them, the crackpots, charlatans, clairvoyants, and "woodpecker-whisperers" he'd encountered during his years in the field. He didn't even tell his wife.

An exception was made for John W. Fitzpatrick, head of the Cornell Lab of Ornithology in Ithaca, New York, where Gallagher then worked. Fitzpatrick, an ivory-bill optimist, believed Gallagher's story. Cornell staff soon mounted a massive search of the Cache and White River National Wildlife Refuge, sixty miles to the south. Sworn to secrecy, they recorded more than a dozen ivory-bill sightings between 2004 and 2005. Around the same time, an engineering professor from Little Rock named David Luneau captured a brief and blurry video of a purported ivory-bill in Bayou De View, not far from Gallagher and Harrison's sighting. Together, the evidence was published in 2005 in the journal *Science*. "Ivory-billed Woodpecker (*Campephilus principalis*) Persists in Continental North America," written by Fitzpatrick, affirmed the existence of at least one male ivory-bill in eastern Arkansas. "This is confirmed. This is dead solid confirmed," Fitzpatrick declared at a press conference.

Delighted by the news, David Sibley, the ornithologist and illustrator of *The Sibley Guide to Birds*, rushed to Arkansas. "Initially I had no question about it. I figured it's the Cornell Lab. They've got video. It's gotta be there," he told me. But after ten days in the Cache and White River refuges, having failed to find any ivory-bills, he started to wonder. "Every day I met people in the woods—fishermen, hikers, canoers, horseback riders—and when they saw my binoculars, they said, 'Oh, you're looking for that woodpecker. Me too. I've been out here every day and I've got my camera and I'm ready to take a photo.' The publicity around [the Cornell Lab's announcement] was so intense that every single person who went outdoors in the southeast knew about it and knew they could be famous by getting a photograph of an ivory-bill. And still nothing more turned up."

The following year, Sibley and three colleagues published a

critical review of the Cornell paper, claiming the features of the bird in Luneau's video were consistent not with an ivory-bill but with a pileated woodpecker. Gallagher and Harrison, Luneau and Fitzpatrick, and the lab's other team members with their numerous positive sightings were, Sibley suspected, sorely mistaken. Fitzpatrick issued a counterresponse, standing by the lab's evidence and asserting it was Sibley et al. whose analysis was flawed. Ornithologists Jerome Jackson, Rick Prum, Mark Robbins, Kenn Kaufman, Martin Collinson, among others, eventually weighed in against Cornell.

The crux of their beef was that, given the dearth of verifiable evidence and the fickleness of eyewitness testimony, Cornell should've been more cautious about their claims. "They had this very blurry video," Sibley said, "and a handful of sightings, every single one of them a brief glimpse of a bird flying away or across a lake. A lot of the people didn't even have time to raise their binoculars. And yet they came out saying, 'This is incontrovertible proof that ivory-billed woodpeckers are still there.' They got way, way out in front of the evidence."

David Luneau, who'd captured the four-second ivory-bill video, summed up how a lot of birders felt: "The arrogance of telling someone they didn't see what they saw doesn't sit well with me. Sibley himself was biased. He's supposed to be an expert birder, and he was out there for days and didn't see anything. Therefore, you know, ivory-bills can't exist."

Gallagher, for his part, had no hard feelings (Sibley even wrote a carefully worded blurb for *The Grail Bird*.) "We've been told all our lives that the ivory-bill's extinct, so it can be tough to swallow," Gallagher said. "With a rare bird, even a semi-rare bird that's not seen very often, big-name birders want confirmation before they accept it. That's a blanket response." In an essay for *Audubon* magazine, Gallagher even admitted that if their roles had been reversed, he could see himself in Sibley's shoes. "I often wonder: If other people had made the sighting, instead of Bobby and me, would I have believed them?"

————

Some stories, at their roots, are universal. I wanted to see for myself how the search for ivory-bills compared with that for Bigfoot and how the purported existence or extinction of a famously elusive, never-common animal was vetted by scientists. Gallagher thought ivory-bills were still out there, that two videos not yet made public showed them alive and well in southern swamps. Indeed, on the eve of my trip, scientists from Pittsburgh's National Aviary announced they'd captured images and sound recordings of ivory-bills living in Louisiana marshes. "Our findings, and the inferences drawn from them," they wrote, "suggest an increasingly hopeful future for the ivory-billed woodpecker."

So I set out for Bayou De View, just about dead center on the map between Little Rock and Memphis. I'd done practically zero research, thinking I'd simply be able to rent a kayak nearby. No sirree Bob. The closest outfitter I could find was two hundred miles away. There was an Ivory Billed Hunting Lodge & Guide Service and Outdoor Gun Range outside the town of Brinkley, with an Ivory Billed Firearms Training Center and, in June, a "Guns & Ivory Ladies Retreat." But no kayaks or canoes for rent.

It being the South, a work-around was quickly arrived at. My old pal Dacus, as luck would have it, hails from Searcy, Arkansas, an hour's drive from Bayou De View. In a matter of minutes, he put me in touch with his father, Bobby T., who put me in touch with a fishing buddy, Jimmy Behel, who put me in touch with a ten-foot kayak. I met Jimmy in his Searcy driveway. A retired statistics and business administration professor at Harding University, Jimmy is a self-possessed, garrulous man of seventy-two with soft features and deeply expressive, searching brown eyes. He wore a long-sleeve Carhartt T-shirt, dark-brown work pants of the type with a hammer loop, and slip-on shoes. Originally from Florence, Alabama, Jimmy had one of the most colorful accents I'd ever heard (that's saying a lot considering where I come from), with gently flowing r's and multidirectional vowels. An expansive talker and thinker, he wore his intelligence lightly and had a tendency to end sentences with a noncommittal, "But anyway."

Jimmy offered to accompany me to Bayou De View and help launch the kayak. We rolled out of Searcy with him leading the way in his pickup while I followed with the kayak strapped to mine. Large American flags fluttered from modest single-family homes and ranch houses. We quickly entered table-flat farmland, driving along-side dust-colored fields with idle center-pivot irrigation sprinklers, past auto-repair shops and grain elevators and Family Dollars and Dollar Generals, into the throbbing lumbermill town of Des Arc, where green timber lay chained in huge piles beside the highway, and over the near motionless White River, bending southeasterly across a blankly umber vista. For much of the drive, we chatted via speaker-phone, with Jimmy again leading the way.

"You're basically in delta from here all the way to the Mississippi River. It's mostly wetlands. Bayou De View is a tributary of the Cache River. The Cache is a tributary that joins the White River from the north. The White then heads on up to the Mississippi. Virtually all of Bayou De View runs through private land. A lot of it's soybean farms. Plus corn. And cotton. You seen that cotton gin? It's almost brand new. Rice too. Arkansas is a leading rice producer in the country... I remember when all of this was still largely forested. Then in the early 1970s, soybeans became a big money crop. The price went from about three dollars a bushel to six or seven dollars a bushel. That was the impetus for clear-cutting a lot of the hardwood trees here. I witnessed it myself. I know of situations where people tried to lobby to preserve some of the land, but I don't know what folks could've done to save it even it if they'd wanted to. It was private land, after all, and no management policy was in place back then to give people an incentive to do differently. Most of 'em cleared it for soybeans or sold it. Big ventures bought up a lot and cut all the timber. They proved to be pretty successful. But family farms? You've heard Willie Nelson sing about family farms? Remember this is wetlands. It floods every spring. People found out pretty quickly they couldn't get their crops planted and harvested fast enough before the flooding started. They spent a lot of money trying to drain the land. But it just didn't work. Hardly anybody could see the futility of what they'd done before it was too late. But anyway."

Hardwood bottomland forest once dominated southern landscapes. Tens of millions of virgin acres, hundreds of miles wide in places, stretched from Memphis all the way to the Gulf of Mexico. In the early twentieth century, steel companies began strip-mining it for coal. Henry Ford laid waste to many thousands of acres for his Model-T's wood-spoke wheels. The Singer Sewing Machine Company of Chicago hauled out tens of thousands more for its sewing cabinets. When the soybean craze hit, only a tiny percentage remained. Rather ironically, a major driver of that craze, according to historian Matthew

Roth, was the hippie counterculture's embrace of tofu in the '60s and '70s as a politically conscious vegetarian food. Then again in the '80s, health-obsessed hippies-turned-yuppies touted soy as a cruelty- and cholesterol-free meat and milk alternative. The boon for their arteries was a further catastrophe for Arkansas's bottomland forests. "Some terrible things had been done to the pristine lands of the south," Gallagher wrote, "…and an amazing number of people are still angry about it almost a century and a half later."

Jimmy went on. "There have been federal programs to reclaim some bottom timberland and plant it with hardwoods. But that's a long-term investment. Hardwood aren't like pines. They take a long time to grow and cover real acreage. Like those pecan trees we saw a ways back? You're planting those for your grandchildren… Even a lot of the hardwoods that're here now are dying because the water's staying on them longer and longer every year. Bottomland gets flooded in winter and usually dries out by May. The last three years, though, it hasn't dried out till June or July. I know that because I fish in this area. Timber can tolerate being under water for a while but not that long. So a lot of the trees you'll see are either dead or dying. I don't know if you can say it's related to climate change. Maybe it is. But anyway."

The woods became denser the farther south we drove. A red-tailed or Cooper's hawk sat atop just about every other telephone pole, while kestrels hung on the wires. When they weren't bunched up in threes and fours over roadkill, kite-like buzzards sailed constantly. I asked Jimmy if he remembered the to-do around Tim Gallagher's ivory-bill sighting.

"Oh yes. I remember it well. As a matter of fact, I was all over this area during that time, mainly to fish. We had an unusually dry fall, and the Cache was running so low you could wade clear across it."

Following Gallagher's sighting, the Nature Conservancy offered a $50,000 reward for information leading to the discovery of an ivory-bill's roost or nest. That's top dollar in Monroe County.

"I made sure I always had a camera with me," Jimmy said. "Nearly everybody around here did."

By the time we reached the put-in at U.S. 17, the sun was high over the trees. On the White Refuge, most access roads were flooded. Here on the Cache, the water was up, but not as up as it had been. Beneath the overpass, an African American man was tightlining for catfish. He had three, maybe four, lines out, baited with earthworms, he said. The rods sat in PVC holders wrenched into the mud, like what folks use for surf casting, but without bells to indicate a strike. The lines glittered like spiderwebs in the sun. Tall, heavily built, in his late forties, and with an Igloo cooler at his feet, he leaned back in a lawn chair, smiling while staring at the sky. A fine way to pass a morning, Jimmy and I agreed.[1]

A sign next to the launch mentioned barred owls, herons, bald eagles, rare prothonotary warblers, and red-headed and pileated woodpeckers but said nothing about ivory-bills. As trucks rumbled over the bridge, I set the kayak in the water and slipped on my life vest. Jimmy handed me a cord to cinch the vest to my paddle in case I dropped the latter. Eyeing me with fatherly concern, he said gravely but in a cordial, southern way, "You know, folks have gotten lost in there. Once you get in among those tupelo and cypress, it all looks the same. You sure you'll be all right?"

"I think so?"

---

1 I'm embarrassed to say I was hesitant at first to ask Jimmy whether he believed in Bigfoot. I assumed he didn't, since it hadn't come up. Finally, I asked: Negative. "In all of my outdoors jaunts, I have not seen one." he said.

"Well, better text me when you return to the truck."

A current ferried me downstream. In no time at all, I found myself ducking under low-hanging branches and glancing off football-shaped cypress knees. The color of the water was exactly how I take my coffee—peanut butter—not a shade lighter or darker. Trees 100 and 150 feet high threw shadows across the surface. They were a mix of overcup, water, and Nuttall oak, sweetgums, and cypress. Some of the cypress, I'd read, were a thousand years old. A few had cavities big enough to park a kayak in. As the din from the road faded, the din from the wind picked up and whistled through the boat hatch. I didn't expect to actually see an ivory-bill, any more than I expected to see a Bigfoot. But I wanted to get a feel for their territory. I paused to watch a red-bellied woodpecker bound spastically up a tree and circumnavigate its trunk. Even with the branches bare of leaves, I had a terrible time locating it with my binoculars. As soon as I did, the current swept me off.

Bayou De View wanders like a shoelace through eighty-three miles of the Cache Refuge, crosses the Dagmar Wildlife Management Area, then hooks back up with the Cache. Fifteen miles of it is designated water trail, blazed every fifty yards or so. It'd be hard to get lost. But if you did, finding your bearings would be harder. I didn't see any cottonmouths. I did see lots of woodpeckers though: downy, hairy, more red-bellied. Also titmice, nuthatches, and some kind of yellowish warbler. Mallards and wood ducks. A paper wasp's nest. Three whitetails in the shallows. And staring at me from a cypress trunk, a thickly whiskered river otter, eyes glittering brilliantly, front paws dangling like a wrestler's.

Following its dust-up with Sibley, the Cornell Lab undertook another, vaster search for ivory-bills from 2006 to 2010. Its staff and volunteers walked and canoed some five hundred thousand acres of promising habitat in eight states, including Arkansas, Florida, Georgia, Louisiana, Mississippi, South Carolina, Tennessee, and Texas. Their remote cameras and sound recording units yielded two thousand hours of audio and 7.8 million images. The Arkansas team searched 44,523 acres by foot and 152,877 acres by helicopter, mapping 215 tree cavities and capturing one million photos. In the woodpecker-rich forests of Bayou De View, searchers logged three thousand man-hours. There, as elsewhere, the official report acknowledged, "no definitive evidence for the persistence of Ivorybilled Woodpeckers (IBWOs) was obtained."

I could appreciate how daunting the search must've been. After only a couple of miles, I was ready to turn around. Kayaks and canoes quickly date middle-aged guys like me. Old soccer injuries announce themselves. Migraines blossom. I got out to stretch at a leafy embankment that I imagined was a proper hill when the river ran low. For the first time that morning, I heard not a sound. A chest freezer missing a door lay in some weeds next to a mangled oil drum. Beer cans, a plastic milk carton, an oven cleanser cylinder, twelve- and twentygauge shell casings, a blue dishrag, and a single red Uno card, either left behind by visitors or deposited by the river, were strewn about. If it weren't for the sun, it'd have seemed dreadfully gloomy, perfect for a cold open of *Law & Order: SVU*. Still, I have a weakness for places like this. A nowhere place, spooky and provisional, that only birders and duck hunters and film scouts appreciate. I like reminders of the everyday flow of things. I like the quiet, imperceptible drama and knowing the world is always changing underfoot, that the river will eventually rise and obliterate evidence of human trespass.

Somewhere off to my left, a pileated woodpecker shattered my reverie. *Cuk cuk cuk cuk cuk!* Their call is shiver inducing, like a criminally deranged robin. It lifts your eyes immediately to locate the source. The ivory-bill's call, by contrast, was a sweet, old-fashioned, "nasal tooting *kent* often described as the sound of a 'tin trumpet' or of blowing on a clarinet mouthpiece," per the Cornell Lab.[2] There were other differences between the birds. At more than twenty inches long and with a thirty-one-inch wingspan, the ivory-bill was the largest woodpecker in North America. It weighed nearly twice that of pileateds, which are generally shorter winged. Another difference is coloring. While a pileated woodpecker's back and wings are mostly black, save for white flashes visible in flight, ivory-bills had extensive white wing patches noticeable when perched or flying. Females wore black crests versus the pileated's red. Ivory-bills were altogether more magpie-ish, I'd say, whereas pileateds lean crow-ish. And of course there was the ivory-bill's unmistakable, shiny white bill, which in profile resembled a letter opener.

The pileated multiplied, calling from all directions at once, repeating its urgent spiel over and over. It echoed around the huge old trees. *Cuk cuk cuk cuk cuk! Cuk cuk cuk cuk cuk!* Rarely do I get a chance to see them. City living doesn't suit such shy birds. In Vermont, we'll see one, maybe two, per summer, if we're lucky. A year will pass before we'll see another. In hot pursuit, I dashed along shore, picking my way over downed trunks, tripping over vines, zigzagging through puddles of battleship gray, until a net of water oaks stopped me. Backpedaling, I tried another direction, only to stop and backpedal again. The light was now garish and unpromising. A fungal stench invaded my nostrils. Alas, the calls stopped. It's amazing how often it happens. This

---

2 You can listen to it on their website.

very morning, I stood at our bathroom window, scrutinizing a maple for a bird whose song I couldn't place. Probably an eastern phoebe, an early migrant. I wanted to be sure. It couldn't have been more than twenty feet away. Ten minutes passed. Nothin'.

"Failure to find the birds in a given area is no proof that they are not there," Arthur Allen, the Cornell ornithologist (not to be confused with the Zodiac Killer) wrote of ivory-bills in 1937. Scouring Louisiana's Singer Tract, Allen and his team managed the impossible and found an ivory-bill nest. They even took photos and film of a mating pair. Camped within a football field of the nest, they seldom heard or saw the birds. "We had great difficulty in following them through the woods to learn their feeding habits even after becoming very familiar with their notes," Allen wrote. "The senior author at one time stood under a giant oak and caught in his hand chips of bark and wood that an Ivorybill was scaling from a dead branch high in the tree without either one being able to see the other. We had hunted for three days for this particular pair of birds without ever seeing them." Change a few keywords and Allen's lament is the same as that of countless Bigfooters.

The return trip upriver was uneventful. At the launch, I wrenched the kayak out of the water with the requisite bashing of shins. The fisherman had skedaddled, the holes from his rod holders the only sign that he'd been there. After texting Jimmy that I'd made it out in one piece, I drove farther south to Apple Lake, in the Dagmar WMA, where I could approach the spot of Gallagher's sighting from the opposite direction. On foot.

This time, the sign at the entrance was explicit: "These trails offer access to habitat near the area where the ivory-billed woodpecker was sighted." Following one, I startled a pair of barred owls, or rather they startled me, two dark silhouettes springing raucously from waterside brush. I stopped and held my breath. I'm always thrilled to see owls. Such improbable, secretive creatures, they really do seem the stuff of legend. Largely invisible to us, they inspire a sense that something extraordinary is afoot. Bernd Heinrich said that owls, once seen, vanish like ghosts. So you stare admiringly as long as possible, sponging up the moment. To me, barred owls were next level. I said in the last chapter that I'd never seen one before. Now I had two—two!—circled in my binoculars, thirty yards distant, regarding me with their depthless eyes. The whole trip took on new meaning. Here was something real, an accomplishment of sorts, to help explain to my wife what I was doing so far from home. I felt acutely then, as I often did out Bigfooting, how a teensy nugget of success will momentarily dispel the failure of an otherwise fruitless search. I stood for a long time, my heart beating violently. It was a powerful incentive, I thought, to clutch to slippery "evidence" like falling acorns and indistinct impressions in the mud, without which, it seemed to me, Bigfooting would feel like a permanently rained-out picnic.

I walked until I reached the bottom of the lake, or what I thought was the bottom. It was impossible to tell. The trail was so overgrown that I rarely caught sight of a big body of water. Through waving branches, something appeared that resembled my idea of a coastal marsh but with pockets of cypress spread about. Before it gained WMA status in 1952, most of the Dagmar was logged. These open areas, or "lakes," are what got left behind. Offshore, a rusted barge, like from the film *Atchafalaya Houseboat*, listed glumly to starboard. Staring at it through my binoculars, I felt a stirring at my feet and looked down to see a garter snake sliding past. A few paces on, I

nearly stepped on a painted turtle sunning itself midtrail. An arma-
dillo, supernaturally pink, scampered through sagging brush.

The saddest story of the ivory-bill's demise occurred in Louisiana's
Singer Tract, the bird's last-known hideaway. Owned by the Singer
Sewing Machine Company, which to its credit had never logged
the eighty-one-thousand-acre demesne, it held patches of ancient
bottomland where panthers, bobcats, bears, and wolves roamed.
Theodore Roosevelt, hunting bear there in 1907, counted three
ivory-bills: "They seemed to me to set off the wildness of the swamp
as much as any of the beasts of the chase." The trees, particularly the
cypresses, he wrote, were of "towering majesty...unsurpassed by any
trees of our eastern forests; lordlier kings of the green-leaved world
are not to be found until we reach the sequoias and redwoods of the
Sierras." In 1937, Singer sold the land to a wooden-box manufac-
turer, Chicago Mill and Lumber Company, which wasted little time
gassing up its chainsaws.

Everyone knew that logging the Singer Tract would spell the end
of the ivory-billed woodpecker. John Baker, president of the National
Audubon Society, tried to intervene. He enlisted the support of
President Franklin D. Roosevelt, the U.S. Forest Service, the U.S.
Fish and Wildlife Service, and the governors of Arkansas, Louisiana,
Tennessee, and Mississippi. Louisiana ponied up $200,000 for an
ivory-bill preserve. There was talk of turning the Singer Tract into a
national park. No dice. Chicago Mill refused to bargain. The com-
pany reportedly sped up cutting in response to Baker's entreaties.
"We are just money grubbers. We are not concerned, as are you
folks, with ethical considerations," admitted its chairman, James F.
Griswold. With Louisiana's woodcutters away for the war, German
POWs cut the timber. In April '44, as saws buzzed and belched,

twenty-three-year-old Don Eckelberry, an Audubon artist, sketched a lone female ivory-bill roosting in what remained of the tract. The German loggers, Eckelberry noted, were appalled by the destruction. "They were incredulous at the waste—only the best wood was taken, the rest left to wreckage." No one ever saw an ivory-bill again. At least officially.

Perhaps owing to this catastrophe, I returned to my truck in a funk. The ivory-bill's absence hung heavily in Bayou De View, nowhere more so than in this deforested "lake." I remembered a passage from Gallagher's book when he and Harrison beheld a flattened field that had once been part of the Singer Tract, both "depressed as hell." In the end, not an acre was saved for the bird's survival, there or anywhere else. The ivory-bill wasn't the only loss. Wolves. Panthers. Trees older than Chartres Cathedral. Wildness itself was pushed off the map. "Even though we had never before stood in this place, our sense of loss and grief over the things that no longer existed here was profound," Gallagher wrote. "We knew we would never be able to experience a primeval bottomland swamp forest."

One commonly enacted fantasy is that when we enter a forest, we're entering a primitive zone, an unsullied Whitmanian redoubt against the wrecking ball of progress, when really we're doing nothing of the sort. We are touring ruins. With rare exception, all forested scenery is new scenery. The pattern is the same everywhere. Of the approximate 1.04 billion acres of virgin forest that formerly existed in the United States, more than 96 percent of it has been cut down. Almost nothing older than two hundred years old remains anywhere. Our vast country is, by and large, a seedy patchwork of cutover lands and housing tracts and Piggly Wiggly's interspersed with second-, third-, and fourth-growth intimations of our dying world.

I'm often prone to gloom over this. But I was beginning to suffer from a greater loss of purpose that, looking back, I see now was only indirectly related to ivory-bills. The day before, Russia had bombed a maternity hospital in Mariupol, Ukraine, killing two adults and a child. Russian officials claimed, QAnon-like, that the incident was staged and that a bloodied pregnant woman photographed at the scene wasn't a victim but a "crisis actor" playing one. Identical things had once been uttered by Alex Jones, the right-wing radio host and conspiracy nut, about the parents of first graders killed in Sandy Hook, who, he said in his shrill and bilious cant, were pretenders in a sinister government plot to upend gun owners' rights. Walking through Bayou De View, a landscape layered with human malfeasance, it dawned on me that Bigfoot perhaps had more in common with such nefarious twisting of reality than I'd been prepared to allow.

I tried to push the thought away, but the truth is, I couldn't shake the idea of Bigfoot as a symptom of mass cultural delusion, part of the "fantasy cascade," in Kurt Andersen's terms, of metastasizing paranoia and believe-whatever-you-want fictions "in which millions of bedoozled Americans surfed and swam." Not by a long shot is epistemological failure uniquely American. We're just proud overachievers in it, uncontested heavyweights of hooey. But I'd wanted to give Bigfoot a pass. Born of necessity and heartache at the savagery visited upon America's wilds, of desire to brook our inner chaos and loneliness, I understood its appeal. For the better part of a year, I'd thought of Bigfooting as mostly harmless fun. Never was there a more companionable, passionately eclectic, inventively foul-mouthed subculture of odd fellows than Bigfooters, some of whom I'd come to think of as my people. But wanting something to be true doesn't make it so. Entertaining possibilities is one thing; staunch infidelity to reason is another. What worried me now was a potentially corrosive lie at the heart of Bigfooting—a minor tributary lie of a mighty Trumpian river of distortion, but a lie nonetheless—one blithely indulged by some adherents who, with few guardrails on their beliefs, risked further abusing what James Baldwin called "that battered word, truth."

———

Every state lays claim to at least one Bigfoot-like legend: Dover Demon, Jersey Devil, Florida Skunk Ape, Michigan Dogman, Ohio Grassman, Maryland Goatman, Louisiana Rougarou, Van Meter Monster, Montauk Monster, Mogollon Monster, Pope Lick Monster, Tennessee Wildman, Northfield Pigman, Alabama White Thang, Connecticut Melon Head (I'm not making this up), Beast of Bray Road, and of course the Lizard Man of Scape Ore Swamp, to name a few. That's leaving aside the numerous Loch Ness-y leviathans like Sink Hole Sam, Tahoe Tessie, Carolina Sewer Monster, Champ the Lake Champlain Monster, and the Monster Turtle of Big Blue.

Arkansas shares with Oklahoma and Missouri the ursine Ozark Howler but claims as its own the Heber Springs Water Panther, an amphibious Bigfoot mountain lion mash-up. Better known is the Fouke Monster, an inhabitant of Boggy Creek, a river swamp much like Bayou De View, in the state's southwest corner. The Fouke Monster has been described as between seven and ten feet tall, with apish arms, red eyes, and a putrid smell. In *The Beast of Boggy Creek: The True Story of the Fouke Monster*, Lyle Blackburn wrote, "the monster reeks of Southern swagger, occasionally letting out a bellow from the dark corner of the forested backwoods. There's no well-groomed, well-fed California Bigfoot here. No, the beast of Fouke is lithe, lean, and covered in long matted fur." If ever there was a working-class hero—isolated, unglamorous, hirsute, bearing an armor of sadness—the Fouke Monster is it. All that's missing is a stalled marriage and rebuilt T-top Camaro.

If people outside Arkansas have heard of the Fouke Monster, it's likely thanks to Charles B. Pierce, the filmmaker behind cult classic *The Legend of Boggy Creek*. Pierce, who died in 2010, grew up in Hampton, Arkansas, near the White River Refuge. After working as a weatherman in Shreveport, he moved to Texarkana, over the state line from Fouke, where he ran an advertising agency while moonlighting as a character named Mayor Chuckles on a children's TV show. With a borrowed 16-mm camera, he also shot commercials for local businesses. That led to his first film, *Boggy Creek*, made in 1972 on a shoestring budget. It was a breakout hit, grossing $25,000,000, or about $135,000,000 in today's dollars. Pierce was hailed as the George Romero of the South.[3]

More than *Harry and the Hendersons*, perhaps even more than the Patterson-Gimlin film,[4] *Boggy Creek* is *the* pop-cultural touchstone for Bigfooters, most of whom came of age in the late '60s and early '70s and recall seeing it at drive-ins when it first came out or later in friends' rec rooms on pirated VHS tapes and feeling strangely throttled by its gloominess. They looked for signs in it of the horror cinema they knew then and found nothing to compare it to. The film unwittingly launched a monster mania in Fouke, where moviegoers, confused by *Boggy Creek*'s shadowy, fact-versus-fiction aura, flocked to see the creature for themselves. As with the ivory-bill woodpecker,

---

3 *The Blair Witch Project* (1999) directors Daniel Myrick and Eduardo Sánchez, among others, have cited *Boggy Creek*'s faux-documentary style as an early influence.

4 Keep reading.

the Fouke Monster "ignited a sense of public curiosity that could not be easily doused," wrote Blackburn. "The story had already gone viral, and it would become clear that no efforts to debunk or calm the situation would be entertained."[5]

Pierce got the idea for *Boggy Creek* from a series of 1971 newspaper articles about a three-toed swamp monster terrorizing the good people of Fouke. The first victims, Bobby and Elizabeth Ford, told the sheriff's department they were attacked in their home one night by a creature that stuck a paw through a window and kicked in their back door. Officers found strange tracks nearby and claw marks on the Fords' porch. More sightings, and more tracks, followed.

A lover of both Arkansas and horror, Pierce smelled a genre-busting riff on a local mystery. After convincing Fouke residents of his honorable intentions, he cast many of them in his film, which he based on their eyewitness accounts, and hired nine Texarkana high school students as his crew. The result is a dramatized oral history that's halfway between tasteless and tolerable. Devoid of plot, characterization, backstory, or even much dialogue, *Boggy Creek* leans immeasurably on the dreariness of its Southern Gothic swamp-scape, on the pallid, harrowed visages of its amateur ensemble cast, on its portentous sermonizing, and on our evolutionary fear of the dark and the monsters that once hunted us. Pierce cut budgetary corners with his ape suit, which looks as though it was papier-mâchéd by a six-year-old using a Costco sheepskin rug. But there's the faintest

---

5 Pierce went on to direct twelve more largely forgotten feature films, including an unfortunate sequel, *Boggy Creek II: And the Legend Continues* (1985), and *The Town That Dreaded Sundown* (1976), another low-budget, high-grossing "true story" horror flick, about a masked serial killer that beat by two years John Carpenter's *Halloween* (1978). With writing partner Earl E. Smith, Pierce is credited for the fourth and penultimate Dirty Harry installment, *Sudden Impact* (1983), with its famous line, "Go ahead, make my day."

trace of life—or rather, life imbued with fear of death—in the Ford family as they do battle with the monster, particularly in the ingénue Mrs. Ford, played with cosmic angst by Bunny Dees, whose brow no doubt required surgical unknotting once filming wrapped. Her confusion is our own confusion when life turns more beastly than we'd imagined and when guns don't help. The men, with their ineffectual weapons, are as hapless and helpless as the women and children, perhaps more so. They cower, unmanned and disarmed, in their ill-lit home, and there ain't a hoot and holler Charlton Heston can do about it.

Impossible to ignore is the fact that *Boggy Creek* is indescribably bad. But the film speaks loudly to the folkloric roots of our neurotic relationship to nature. It's about myth and dread and deliverance from the things that pursue us. The tremor of apprehension we feel at night—Poe's "raven-winged hours"—and out alienation from the natural world, are its defining features. Even after all the terror and wanton pig mutilation we've witnessed, when the Fouke Monster retreats into the swamp, roaring and baying as he goes, the narrator laments its passing: "I'd almost like to hear that terrible cry again, just to be reminded that there is still a bit of wilderness left, and that there are still mysteries which remain unsolved, and strange, unexplained noises in the night."

————

I've drifted. One day I headed over to the Cache Refuge headquarters, near the town of Cotton Plant, to meet Richard Crossett, a biologist with the U.S. Fish and Wildlife Service. Crossett, sixty, is a genial and wide-shouldered man with a short gray beard and blue-gray eyes that betray decades of squinting under delta suns. He wore black-framed glasses, faded FWS-issued khaki, and knee-high rubber boots. On the wall beside his office door was an unflattering photo of Donald Trump's face x-ed out in black marker. On the walls inside were pelts of black bear, red fox, and coyotes and photos of Crossett on a bear hunt in Alaska.

When I asked about ivory-bills, he sighed heartily.

"I have to be careful about what I say. It's a sensitive topic," he said.

I hadn't realized this. The ivory-bill, apparently, was politically loaded, and word of my visit had reached Crossett's minders in Washington, DC. On the subject of ivory-bills, he'd been apprized, so it appeared, to zip it. What the issue boiled down to, I discovered, was bureaucratic and budgetary cross-purposes.

Back in 2007, the FWS proposed a $27.7 million windfall—long overdue, many felt—for ivory-bill conservation. It amounted to roughly 5 percent of the Endangered Species Act's total annual budget. These well-intentioned efforts quickly turned to grief for the FWS, which in a good year struggles to cover basic administrative costs, let alone implement a massive recovery plan for an endangered species. Spending so much public money on an unconfirmed bird, when many of the then fourteen hundred threatened and endangered species in the United States—a fraction of the one million globally at risk of extinction—received less than $10,000 a year, some less than $1,000, struck others as unfair. What of the bog turtle, black-footed ferret, roseate tern, streaked horned lark, or rusty patched bumblebee? At the time, the northern long-eared bat, a Cache resident facing extinction from white-nose syndrome, an invasive fungal disease that has killed more than 90 percent of North America's hibernating bats in the last decade, had no recovery plan at all. "The U. S. Fish and Wildlife Service is charged to pro-mote the conservation and recovery of *all* threatened and endan-gered species, not just this one," David Sibley wrote on his website. "Making the Ivory-billed such a high priority inevitably diverts resources from other species."

When searches turned up no indisputable proof of ivory-bills after Gallagher's sighting, the FWS ate what's known in official-dom as "a fat one." In early 2021, with its ivory-bill conservation plan amounting to bubkis, the agency removed the birds from the endangered species list, effectively declaring it extinct while wiping its hands of the whole mess.

With ivory-bills off the table, Crossett and I quickly ran out of things to talk about. We hopped in his truck and cruised through the refuge, stopping to observe northern pintails and gadwalls bobbing in flooded fields. A half-million migratory birds pass through the Cache each spring and fall. Mallards, green-winged teals, northern shovelers, American widgeons, lesser scaups, canvasbacks, Mississippi kites, wood storks, and neotropical migrants like hooded, cerulean, Swainson's, and prothonotary warblers. Red-tailed, red-shouldered, broad-winged hawks, and bald eagles roost year round. Crossett pointed out a forma-tion of white fronts and snow geese flocking overhead.

As we drove, Crossett expertly parried my ivory-bill questions. Mostly I wanted to know how another ivory-bill sighting might impact the refuge's management plan. Would money surge again from Washington's coffers? Crossett, like Babe in *Marathon Man*, couldn't be broken, partly because, like Babe, he didn't have the answers. He merely seconded what Jimmy had said about hardwood mortality: "Seems like the dry periods keep getting dryer and the wet wetter." Ditto southern deforestation: "You know the old saying that a squirrel could've traveled from the Atlantic coast all the way to the delta without ever leaving the trees because there was so much continuous forest? It wasn't quite like that, but close."

The road descended through brown rectangles of fallow fields, past long avenues of sycamores and river birch, over some hills and across more fields (rice and cotton) and around waterfowl impoundments. We saw few other cars. The Cache is a patchwork refuge, with blocks of intermittently connected land, like a jigsaw puzzle in progress. At one point, we exited and entered Cotton Plant, pop. 960, a town of empty lots and boarded-up one-story structures. An uncollared Lab lay in the shade of a brick building that was missing a roof. The guitarist and gospel singer Sister Rosetta Tharpe was born in Cotton Plant in 1915, when it was a proper agricultural center with sawmills, woodworking factories, an opera house. I saw only bareness, perhaps another reason for Crossett's silence.

The bird's ostensible rediscovery fueled hopes of economic U-turn in Monroe County. Brinkley, eleven miles south of Cotton Plant, sprouted a small tourism industry, drawing birders and ornithologists. One resident, responding to a *Washington Post* article about ivory-bills, wrote, "Arkansas normally gets nothing but bad press, but for a magical period in the mid-2000s we were proudly the home of the ivory-billed woodpecker." After a few short years, birders stopped coming.

Many Cotton Plant homes looked abandoned, with paneless windows and dingy yards that had recliners and bed springs and bike tires in them. Not that you could tell, but some ten thousand people lived within a dozen miles of here. I'm embarrassed by my hackneyed vista of decline: the failed little hub, worn-out farms, abandoned factories. The unhappy South. More bad press the man spoke about.

Disaster porn. My wife knows it well, having seen its silly aesthetic applied to her beloved Detroit. Yet I can't ignore what's here and what had been.

"You get a sense of what that bird might've meant to the folks of Monroe County," I said as we puttered out of town, a place that reminded me of many Squatch towns I'd visited, where you could almost feel the outside world's disinterest.

Unexpectedly, Crossett volunteered his first and final thoughts on ivory-bills. "Yeah, I guess it would've been a big deal," he said. "Like seeing Elvis."

———

David Allen Sibley was born and reared on birds. When he was seven, his father, a Yale ornithologist studying California condors, set him on his life's path, wittingly or not. A self-taught artist with an organic curiosity about nature, Sibley began sketching and observing birds and, overcome with devotion, never quit. After a year at Cornell, he dropped out to travel and chase birds full time. His first book, *The Sibley Guide to Birds*, for which he painted every image himself, took twelve years to finish and earned comparisons to the great Roger Tory Peterson's work. A second edition came out in 2014. If you own a birding book, there's a good chance it's a *Sibley Guide*. Renowned for their beauty and infallible concision, more than two million are in print. Sibley has been birding, thinking about birds, sketching birds, and painting birds for most of his six decades.

The widespread assumption about Sibley is that he's an ornithological pugilist and killjoy. When I reached him at his home in Greenfield, Massachusetts, his voice was gentle, steady, its volume never ticking above monastery quiet. Like most birders, he was initially charmed by the ivory-bill's apparent resurgence and what it might mean for American ecology. But during our talk, he underscored the distinction ornithologists must make between evidence and belief, between good science and bad, a distinction, he felt, that Gallagher and the Cornell Lab had muddled, granting legitimacy where none was warranted.

Earlier that month, a rare Steller's sea eagle had been sighted in Dighton, Massachusetts, near the Taunton River. Native to Russia, Korea, and Japan, where they winter in coastal ranges, it was the only Steller's sea eagle ever recorded in North America. Likely blown off course by a storm, it was first spotted in interior Alaska, then in Chaleur Bay, New Brunswick, Quebec, and then Nova Scotia before alighting within commuting distance of Boston. A local birder, not sure what he was looking at, passed a photo on to the state's Division of Fisheries and Wildlife, which posted it to Facebook. Birders and ornithologists, as birders and ornithologists are wont to do, flipped out. A Steller's sea eagle craze ensued. In pursuit of this rarest of raptors, with its pineapple-yellow beak and eight-foot wingspan, birders swooned en masse to Dighton, found the bird, adored it, photographed it, posted it, and departed. Two weeks later, it turned up in Booth Bay, Maine, where it lingered for more than a week and was seen almost every day.

Herein lies Exhibit A in Sibley's case against ivory-bills (one that, I'll hazard, we might also extend to Bigfoot). Forget about photos and videos for a second. Birding, he said, requires redundancy. Sightings, even of rare birds, *especially* of rare birds, must be duplicable, with repeat observations recorded by several witnesses.

"If somebody actually found an ivory-billed," Sibley said, "it shouldn't be hard to find again. They're resident. They don't migrate.

They spend their whole lives in a few square miles of forest. They're big and noisy. After the [Gallagher] story came out in '05, if an ivory-billed was there, it would've been found within the first month of the sighting."

Exhibit B: On his second day in Arkansas, Sibley was walking through a clearing when a large woodpecker flew in front of him. "Just in that flash, in a couple of wingbeats, I saw bright big streaks of white. I thought, 'Oh my God, that's it! I just saw an ivory-bill woodpecker!' And then it landed. It flew into a big tree in the middle of the clearing. I was so convinced that what I'd seen was not a pileated that I dismissed that idea immediately. I walked up to the tree, circled it, and out flew a pileated woodpecker. Several more times over the next eight or so days, I saw pileated woodpeckers banking and turning so that the sun caught the white on the underside of their wings, with that momentary flash that makes it look really different from the typical view of a pileated. But by then, I was onto the illusion."

Addressing the issue of illusions, Sibley, sounding like an amalgam of Lisa Feldman Barrett and Elizabeth Loftus, was unapologetic.

"Eyewitness accounts are unreliable. People tend to find what they're looking for. You see it happen all the time in birding. Anyone is capable of turning anything into anything else. That's why I don't trust sight records alone. And I put all of my own sightings in the same category. It's too easy to make a mistake. That doesn't mean [Gallagher and Harrison] are bad observers or were deliberately misleading. It just means we get excited, we catch a quick glimpse of a pileated woodpecker turning and the light striking it, and we think there's a lot more white than there actually is. They're big black-and-white woodpeckers, just like ivory-bills. Of course, nobody alive has actually seen an ivory-bill. Probably their flight style and shape were really different, but we don't know. So we're looking for a pileated with more white in the wings. Then your brain goes to work and turns the memory into something like an ivory-billed woodpecker. Most of the time, you don't even know you've made a mistake."

Our thinking on this was closely aligned. But I understood the response of people like David Luneau, who felt personally attacked by Sibley and buffaloed by the suggestion that field observations by so many reputable birders and ornithologists could be universally skewed. Didn't such repeat sightings qualify as redundancy? Not quite, said Sibley. The ivory-bill, on account of its rareness, required a multiform dose of incredulity.

"One of the questions I heard a lot was, 'What are the odds that all of these different people would make the same mistake?' To me, the answer was so obvious that it wasn't a serious question. As soon as one person makes a mistake and says there's an ivory-billed wood-pecker, every single person that goes to look for it is much more likely to twist a glimpse of something into an ivory-bill. All of the reports Cornell promoted in their paper, except for the first one by Tim Gallagher, were by people paid by Cornell to search for ivory-billed woodpeckers. They're in the woods explicitly with that purpose. If you go out with the intention of finding a certain species, then you've got that search image in your mind, and anything, a clump of leaves, can turn into that species."

When he emerged as an ivory-bill skeptic, Sibley became, in his words, persona non grata among certain birders. They didn't understand that it wasn't criticism for its own sake but a responsibility Sibley felt to address what others would not, without hedging or pandering to baseless optimism.

"I knew it wasn't going to be a popular position. It's always delicate when you challenge someone's identification of a bird. A lot's riding on it—reputation, expertise—and who are you to tell me what I saw? In this case, I wasn't just saying, 'I think you might've made a mistake.' I was saying, 'I think you might've made a mistake *and* the feel-good birding story of the year might be wrong.' But people's lives were changing based on that story. In Arkansas towns, there was investment in tourism related to ivory-bills. The tourists never showed up. And I know for a fact there were other endangered species, endangered birds, that didn't get the resources that were requested because the money was diverted by the Fish and Wildlife Service to ivory-billed woodpeckers. All of this was happening for a mirage."

Exhibit C: According to James T. Tanner, the inestimable ornithologist who studied ivory-bills extensively in the 1930s, wood-boring beetle larvae comprised most of the bird's diet. With its hard, chisel-pointed bill and extensible tongue, the ivory-bill was uniquely suited for peeling back the bark from dead and dying trees to spear larvae underneath. Such wood-borers have a thing for bottomland hardwoods, namely oaks, sweetgum, and hackberry, in which old-growth southeastern forests once abounded. Because of its strength, the ivory-bill dispensed with heavy bark that even a pileated can't loosen, leaving behind five-inch-deep conical holes as wide as a man's hand. An ivory-bill's range would presumably be littered with such pock-marked deadfall. In the Cache and White refuges, Sibley found none.

Exhibit D: To the question of photographs, Sibley, like Carl Sagan, might say, extraordinary claims require extraordinary evidence. "Let's imagine that I saw a golden eagle fly over my house today. It would be rare but within established patterns. If I said I saw

Steller's sea eagle fly over my house today, it would be like, 'Whoa, the one in Maine must've come back down here.' But if I said I saw a white-tailed eagle, a European species that has never been seen in Massachusetts, it would be, 'Well, wait a minute. How do you know? Where's the photograph? Let's see if someone else can find it.' Without that, there's only opinion and belief."

Ornithologists, Sibley said, must weigh their judgments conscientiously, free of prevailing pieties, as scientists. His own judgments angered so many partly because they required us to consider cognitive errors in ways that don't bode well for humans as well as issues of plausibility, rareness, redundancy, and the likelihood of a species in a given time and place that don't bode well for ivory-bills. More dishearteningly, they forced us to reckon with the health of our forests and with our hope for an animal's survival versus the long odds of logic and reason.

In a sense, though, it's possible that both Sibley and Gallagher are mistaken. Obviously, subjective assertions about rare (or in Bigfoot's case, unproven) species stake no claims on the truth—without incontrovertible evidence, they're little better than myths—but neither do objective, science-based counter claims, which naturally allow that rock-bottom certainty is almost always beyond reach. It's an epistemological war of attrition in which science and myth give little ground. Until a breakthrough occurs that upends scientific dogma, legends will endure, ubiquitous but invisible.

6

GLOOSKAP AND THE FOREST WALKERS

"It is the absurd ideas which are the clearest ideas,
and the most absurd ideas are the most important."

—THOMAS BERNHARD

I recall reading somewhere that the Appalachians are connected by magmatic umbilical to the Scandinavian Mountains. Until about three hundred million years ago, both were part of the Caledonides Range on the ancient supercontinent Pangaea, a Frankenstein creation of all the earth's landmass stitched together. Heading north on Maine's Route 1, I could see a common variant of glaciated fjords and piney uplands, of distant whitecaps and battered fishing trawlers plunging up and down. I've skied in the Scandinavian Mountains, which is the most pretentious thing I've ever admitted. They have that lonely, windswept, Scandinavian seriousness. Maine, if you ask me, got the better end of the deal.

Halfway into my Bigfoot walkabout, I decided to return to Maine. Despite a measly twenty official sightings in the BFRO's database, I knew it to be a center of East Coast Bigfoot action. Driving, my mind strayed. I thought of my last time here, a decade ago, when I hiked the Hundred-Mile Wilderness. Every morning, I was up before sunrise, massaging Badger Foot Balm into my cracked and swollen, Twizzler-red toes. Leaving a sleeping bag in the cold dark is a unique form of masochism. But my feet would've been barking all night. And there was no point in delaying the inevitable. After instant coffee and oatmeal, the stowing of camp gear—bag and bedroll, stove and trail bars, tattered tent and rain fly—I'd sit for a while, anticipating the day ahead. Then I'd rise and press on to the south, toward the village of Monson, my finish line.

It was hard going. I had trekked to a point on the map where I didn't belong. The trail was mostly unpeopled but much disturbed by mountains. A Mainer named Myron Avery, the principal architect of the Appalachian Trail in the 1930s, is mostly to blame. His famously thorny personality matched the Dantean void he designed. In the '70s, another tireless Mainer, Lester C. Kenway, then president of the Maine Appalachian Trail Club (MATC), plucked the baton from Avery's clutches and elaborated on his scheme to drive ATers to despair. It was Kenway who invented a hand-winch system called a Griphoist that could move otherwise immovable hillside impediments, such as boulders and downed trees, to unscalable heights, allowing trails to go where they'd never gone before. Under Kenway's direction, the MATC relocated about 170 miles of the AT from lower elevations onto the peaks. These so-called ridge-top trails, intended to furnish hikers with commanding views of Maine's choicest real estate, were an ingenious bit of advertising, if also maniacally cruel. Looking at a map, you see that every opportunity Kenway had to go *around* a mountain, he opted to go *over* it instead, often by the steepest route available.

Mountains often have sacred meaning in Indigenous cultures. New Hampshire's Mount Washington, called Agiocochook by the

Pennacook-Abenaki people—loosely translated it means "Home of the Storm Spirit"—is a divine realm never to be summitted. It'd be like free soloing the Temple Mount. The Mescalero Apache homeland lies within four sacred peaks: Guadalupe, Sierra Blanca, Three Sisters, and Oscura. For the Blackfeet, it's Nínaiistáko, or Chief Mountain, in Glacier National Park, home of a primordial deity called Ksiistsikomm. Blackfeet only climb Nínaiistáko for rare ceremonies. Maine's Mount Katahdin is a sacred Wabanaki landmark. In one story, the griffin-like spirit Pamola was dispatched there by Glooskap, the transformer hero, to guard it against trespassers (today the summit is called Pamola Peak). In 1845, a Penobscot Indian named John Neptune bumped into Pamola while camped near Katahdin. He described it as "a great beast, with mighty wings that dragged on the ground, with a head as large as four horses, and with horrible beak and claws."

My suspicion is that Lester Kenway knew all this, fancied himself a modern embodiment of Pamola, and rearranged Maine's AT as divine punishment, with Katahdin its Seventh Terrace. Long before Kenway got his nefarious hands on it, Thoreau hiked much of this country. He even thought to warn us about it in *The Maine Woods*, published in 1864, two years after his death: "This was that Earth of which we have heard, made out of Chaos and Old Night. Here was no man's garden, but the unhandselled globe. It was not lawn, nor pasture, nor mead, nor woodland, nor lea, nor arable, nor wasteland... Man was not to be associated with it." This was after failing to summit Katahdin, an experience that impressed upon Thoreau how "tame and cheap" was his native Concord's ordered farmland. Maine, by contrast, was "treacherous and porous," Katahdin fit only for "daring and insolent men... Simple races, as savages, do not climb mountains—their tops are sacred and mysterious tracts never visited by them. Pamola is always angry with those who climb to the summit of Ktaadn." (I love Thoreau on Maine, but as you see, even this benevolent soul harbored condescending views toward Indigenous people, though his attitude softened over time.) Thoreau was guided to Katahdin by a Penobscot man who skipped the summit attempt, suggesting to Thoreau that he leave a bottle of rum on top to appease Pamola. "He had planted [a] good many," Thoreau wrote, "and when he looked again, the rum was all gone." Returning from this doomed ascent, Thoreau mused, "This ground is not prepared for you."

The difference today being that the ground *is* prepared for you, quite meticulously, by Lester Kenway and his cabal of ridge-top sadists. If no longer "unhandselled" (unused, pure), the Hundred-Mile Wilderness is inarguably—and *intentionally*—chaotic. Still, it's nice enough.

One morning, I surprised a moose. I'd just set off when it crashed over the trail behind me, high-stepping and tumbling through chest-high ferns while trailing a cloud of black flies. I imagined it too had just gotten out of bed when it heard my approach. A remarkable sight. Pure slapstick. There's a line attributed to Aristotle: "In every animal there is a measure of noble life and beauty." Well, Aristotle never laid eyes on a moose. This was Bullwinkle, graceless and knobby kneed, with a long, tawny snout and lachrymose eyes, a camelish muzzle and waddly dewlap dangling from its jaw. It crashed noisily down a sharp hill, slipping and skidding all the way.

In Wabanaki legend, the first moose was an enormous monster that trampled everything in its path, people included, until Glooskap slew it and refashioned the animal into the more reasonable size and shape we have today. Canadians sometimes refer to moose as "rubber

-nosed swamp donkeys," and I could see why. By all appearances, it was totally ill suited for the wild.

————

There's a scene in the 1972 film *Jeremiah Johnson* in which the mountain man Del Gue, reflecting on the virtues of a wilderness life, calls the Rockies "the marrow of the world," extolling their dearth of lawmen, asylums, and priests. "Ain't this something?" he says to the eponymous Johnson, played by Robert Redford, meaning the cable of western peaks stretched before them. "These here is God's finest sculpturings!" Johnson gazes back at Gue. Despite having lost his family to vengeful Crow, he agrees. The landscape was why he'd gone there in the first place, why he'd endured such hardship. Like Ishmael's sea, it's where man and the natural world become one.

Gue and Johnson fit the classic mold of rugged individualists, which is to say, white boys going where they're not wanted, living out a fantasy of freedom that is exactly that, a fantasy. As Gue so memorably expresses, they prefer to think of the mountains as otherwise uninhabited. There's an obvious problem with this, which Johnson is slow to grasp, until Flathead Indians force him to marry one of their own, volunteering him for a domesticity he thought he'd left behind. Director Sydney Pollack has said that Johnson "turns his back on civilization because he wants to find a place where it's totally unnecessary for him to conform to a code of ethics not his own." He soon realizes there's no such place, that the idea is played out. Besides, the Indians have their own code of ethics. After Johnson trespasses on a Crow burial ground and they kill his wife and adopted son, he has nothing left, including the metaphors and similes of wilderness salvation. Crazed by grief, he tracks down the responsible parties, exacting his vengeance with a *Kill Bill* efficiency. The life of a monster hunter, "the hairy-chested adventurer, the plain, straight-talking ordinary guy…that fellow so beloved in American folklore, and so rare as to probably be mythical himself," as the writer Daniel Cohen puts it, has become, in Pollack's telling, an unqualified disaster. "I'm as much a victim of the romantic myth of 'getting away' as anyone else," said Pollack, who treats us to long shots of Johnson riding forlornly through empty passes. "My head tells me it's myth, but I don't want to believe it is."

Pollack might claim the opposite intention, but *Jeremiah Johnson* is part of the common repertory of old Hollywood Westerns, from *Apache* to *Stagecoach*, with predictably moronic depictions of Native Americans. Clad in beads and buckskins, with pained and painted faces, they're utterly devoid of intelligence, their presence accentuated either by silence or war yelps, their daughters impulsively offloaded onto passing whites. Again, we take what's convenient and ignore the rest. The film hits on two fundamental truths: first, reverent and uplifting views of wilderness are a dangerous myth but an endlessly attractive one, and second, even well-meaning white depictions of Native life stray wide of the mark.

———

For twelve thousand years before the white man, Algonquian-speaking people lived in what's now called Maine. The Wabanaki, or "People of the Dawnland," comprised five main bands—the Mi'kmaq, Maliseet, Passamaquoddy, Penobscot, and Abenaki—whose homeland ranged south from Maine through New Hampshire to Massachusetts, north to Newfoundland and the Maritimes, and west to Quebec. They were among the first to encounter the advance guard of European explorers and soldiers of fortune, to die in successive waves of typhus, smallpox, yellow fever, cholera, and bubonic plague and by aggressive settlement, enslavement, and wars of extermination. Precontact, some ten thousand Penobscot lived in Maine. By 1800, only five hundred remained. Disease killed three-quarters of the Passamaquoddy and Pennacook, close kin to the Abenaki. It's estimated that a 1616 epidemic decimated 75 percent of New England's Indigenous people. In Massachusetts, the English colonist Thomas Morton described "a new-found Golgotha," where Indians "died on heapes, as they lay in their houses." Colonists were generally pleased by this development. The Puritan minister Increase Mather, father of Cotton, captured the sentiment of the day by claiming that smallpox was God's punishment for Indians encroaching on land they'd "sold" to the English. By the same logic, both he and his son owned Black and Indian slaves.

According to Frederick Matthew Wiseman's *The Voice of the Dawn: An Autohistory of the Abenaki Nation*, some Indians worried that Glooskap, their protector, abandoned them when Europeans arrived. In the past, Glooskap (there are more than two dozen spellings of his name) vanquished forest monsters and made the earth cozy and inhabitable, allowing people to flourish. In some stories, he kept his lodge at Katahdin. Until the "Black Robes" with their "cold and alien" crosses brought evil to the dawnland. Glooskap departed, saying, "I await the changing of the days." Others believed that he'd only withdrawn to a hidden island to fashion arrowheads for eventual slaughter of the intruders. Still others said he hadn't really left but had merely gone quiet, and that anyone seeking Glooskap could find him if their heart was true.

Joseph Bruchac, an Abenaki writer and elder, told me there are many stories about Glooskap and that when they're recounted, it's as if the early days, the time before the white man came, were only yesterday. One of my favorites is retold in Bruchac's book *The Wind Eagle and Other Abenaki Stories*. Aglebemu, the frog monster, has dammed up a river, hoarding the water for himself. People are going thirsty. Glooskap picks up Aglebemu and squeezes him so hard that his eyes pop out and he starts to croak like a bullfrog. Glooskap likes the result, so he keeps squeezing until Aglebemu is reshaped into a little green frog. Most Glooskap stories are about righting a wrong, reaffirming nature's power while asserting some human control over it.

Bruchac said the Abenaki also have traditional tales about Bigfoot—I'd made the mistake of calling them "myths," and he corrected me. "The old ones are in our Abenaki culture too," he said, "and not as myth. No one I know in any of our different tribes in the U.S. or Canada refer to Bigfoot as a myth." These "forest people" or "forest walkers," as he called them, "who've been dubbed Bigfoot by white folks," were "shy, reclusive, very powerful, but usually not threatening and never an aggressive or dangerous being. Sometimes [they're] also seen as a helper or a protector of the people."

Among the Nulhegan Band of the Coosuk Abenaki in Vermont, to which Bruchac belongs, the word *Ktsi Awas*, meaning "big animal," sometimes refers to forest walkers. They're neither inventions of the past, Bruchac said, nor unique to the Abenaki. "I've been told stories about encounters, first-person accounts in the present day—by Native friends from several of our different cultural traditions around the continent. Some friends in the Canadian Abenaki community of Odanak told me that when the forest walker was seen by some people there a decade or so ago, it was viewed as a very good sign."

Other Wabanaki creatures are less cuddly. Kiwakw (or Giwakwa), known to Abenaki, Maliseet, Passamaquoddy, and Penobscot, is a cannibal giant with glowing eyes and a heart of ice who can rip trees from the ground. It's said that a Kiwakw is encircled by the souls of its victims, that each new soul gives a Kiwakw more power. Among the Mi'kmaq, a Chenoo or "devil cannibal," is a half man/half beast from the north with a wolf's eyes and lips gnawed away in hunger. "Kiwakw and Chenoo refer to a monster like a windigo, as Cree and other more western Algonquin people call him or her," Bruchac said, "who was once a human but turned into a giant cannibal monster."

Mel Skahan, a member of the Yakama Nation in central Washington, told me that as a boy, he heard Bigfoot stories from his great-great-grandfather. In these tales, Bigfoot was usually an allusive, nonliteral figure, one possessed of clairvoyant and telepathic powers. It sometimes warned humans of approaching illness or danger; a friend of Mel's family, days before she died, was advised by a Bigfoot she never saw to prepare for her own death. "I took these stories as a passing along of symbolic tales," Mel said. "My great-great-grandfather never admitted to having an actual sighting. We figured they were also meant to keep us from wandering off, because of bears and cougars. I didn't pay much attention to them."

When he got older, Mel's feelings changed. Working in forestry management, he spent virtually every day in the woods, where he heard and saw things he couldn't explain. In 1995, he had his first Bigfoot encounter. Six years later, he had another. Then another, this one a sighting in clear day. He had no doubts. Bigfoot was suddenly far more real than he'd imagined. Before long, Mel became an investigator for the BFRO, leading expeditions to the Pacific Northwest.

But in 2020, another change overcame him. "I'd been told for years by my elders that I wasn't supposed to be chasing Bigfoots," he said. "They told me, 'You hunt these beings, and you shouldn't be. Just leave them alone.' I was trying to prove Bigfoot existed. But my elders were saying, 'They don't want to be known.'" On his desk, Mel kept a clump of hair he'd found that he suspected belonged to a Bigfoot. A medicine man said to him, "You took something that doesn't belong to you and [Bigfoot] wants it back. And if you continue to [chase Bigfoots], he'll attach himself to your family members, your children, your grandchildren, until he gets back what he wants." After returning the hairs to the hillside where he'd found them, and hopefully repairing his relationship with Bigfoot, Mel gave up the chase.

"I've corrected myself," he said, adding that he was still a one hundred percent believer in Bigfoot. "I no longer research. I no longer collect anything. I just go out into the woods to share my time with them."

Reflecting on his stint in the BFRO, Mel, now fifty-five, lamented that today's Bigfooters went about things in the wrong way, as he once did. "I tell them, you're me fifteen, twenty years ago. At one point, you'll come to terms with opening yourself up more fully to what's going on." Bigfooters' unending search for "proof," their sensationalistic TV shows, their paid expeditions, all of it, he felt, was uncomfortably akin to a marketing blitz. It preempted a respectful, organic approach to Bigfoot. "It reminds me of the Ian Malcolm line from *Jurassic Park*," Mel said, "when he goes, 'Ah, now eventually you do plan to have dinosaurs on your tour, right?' Bigfooters are doing the same thing. They've gotta have Bigfoot on their Bigfoot outings, right?"

Joe Bruchac told me something similar. His son, Jim, a professional animal tracker in Maine, had been asked several times over the years to participate in TV shows about Bigfoot, but he always turned them down. He thought it was disrespectful to pursue forest walkers. That, Bruchac implied, was the white man's game.

———

Before hiking the AT, I'd called an experienced outdoorsman I knew named Philip Werner. Philip had hiked the Hundred-Miles twice, northbound and southbound, and lived to tell the tale. He didn't think it was anything a semi-able-bodied man with maps and rain gear couldn't handle. Its challenges, he said, were largely self-made: "People can no longer comprehend what it's like to live in a world without GPS systems telling them when to turn left or right. We've lost our ability to navigate and our faith in our ability to work through it when we get lost. We've been coddled to death by civilization." His parting words: "Bring a compass and know how to use it."

One undertakes such journeys for selfish reasons. "All travel is a lesson in self-preservation," wrote Paul Theroux (the other Thoreau). For some, this means wallowing in five-star decadence while basking in the salutary effects of jalapeño margaritas and broad-shouldered masseurs. We need to unplug now and again, trade in our overlit, under-ventilated cubicles for same day laundry service and the minibar. Others seek hardship, enlightenment, a cleansing of wounds, or perhaps a sweeping of mental cobwebs. Married and with two young kids, I'd attained a measure of domestic stability I'd never imagined possible. Even so, as the rule goes, I was curious about what I was missing. One day, my wife granted me leave. That was why I hiked the Hundred-Miles. It had less to do with a desire to claim kinship with Thoreau than it did with the idea of the place, a place one could only visit, soak in, and leave.

One hundred is a fashionable number for pilgrimages. Each summer, tens of thousands of Catholics travel one hundred miles to the Black Madonna shrine at Jasna Góra in Poland. The "marathon monks" of the Tendai Buddhist sect in Japan, wearing straw-and-linden sandals, run fifty-two miles a day for one hundred consecutive days, followed by eighteen miles a day for another one hundred straight days, hoping to achieve enlightenment in the process. Many pilgrims on the Camino de Santiago in Spain opt for the last one hundred of the journey's five hundred kilometers.

Mine too was a pilgrimage of sorts, if a far chiller one, and as such drew on blind faith; a pilgrimage both to a place and in service to an idea: that by escaping my homebound life, my sunup-to-sundown errand running, I could somehow, without espressos or antidepressants, wake up and feel more alive. "We must learn to reawaken and keep ourselves awake," Thoreau wrote, "not by mechanical aids, but by an infinite expectation of the dawn, which does not forsake us even in our soundest sleep."

I had little inkling of Bigfoot then, certainly not the cannibalistic vein, until Friar Tuck happened along. His vision of terror paled in comparison to Maine's Barren-Chairback Range. After jotting it down, I quickly forgot about it. Circling back to it all these years later, I'm still trying to wrap my mind around its meaning.

———

On this more recent Bigfoot-related visit, I went to see Michelle Souliere, author of *Bigfoot in Maine*. Michelle owns the Green Hand Bookshop on Congress Street in downtown Portland, and I met her there. She had sharp blue eyes, chin-length dark curls, and a forearm tattoo of a mouse hoisting a pumpkin on a stick. She wore plaid gray shorts, sneakers with ankle socks, and a black T-shirt of the film *Tucker & Dale vs. Evil.* I hadn't browsed in a bookstore since pre-pandemic times, and as we spoke, my eyes drifted greedily to the shelves. Thomas Hardy, bell hooks, James Baldwin, Harry Crews, Roberto Bolaño, Julia Child!

Bigfoot in Maine is a combination of oral history, reportage, and folklore that moves easily between the past and present in an effort to say something meaningful about our debt to wild places. Most impressively, Michelle had coaxed eyewitness testimonies from famously reticent Mainers.

"It's something that's barely talked about here," she said. "Mainers aren't going to share this kind of stuff, generally. *Finding Bigfoot* made it more socially acceptable to talk about, but there's still a lot of stigma attached to it. People think you're either crazy or a fool. And not just your neighbors but your coworkers, relatives, and friends. Some of [my subjects] put up with decades of ridicule. A lot of them were retirement age and only talked to me because they didn't have a workplace to worry about anymore. Or they'd gotten to the point where they didn't care any longer what people thought of them."

She hadn't had such luck with Maine's Native Americans. No one from the Wabanaki Confederacy would speak to her. She'd said as much in the book, appending a disclaimer about her reluctance to add to the pile of white interpreters usurping and miscasting Indigenous stories. This is mine: It took me a year to find Joe Bruchac and Mel Skahan. Gathered here are selections from our conversations. Nobody else at the Wabanaki, Potawatomi, and Mashpee Wampanoag tribes wanted anything to do with me or my questions. Understandably so. Not that long ago, the U.S. government's official policy toward

Native Americans was to erase their way of life. Sacred and ancestral lands were plowed under. Children were enslaved and leased out to white families as indentured servants. Among the things officially forbidden to Native people were the healing stories and myths that formed their understanding of the world. White campaigns of eradication meant that much of Indigenous folklore was lost. Whites now offering themselves up as experts on that folklore—an expertise they didn't, in fact, possess—strikes many Native people as a bit rich.

"I didn't want to be another white person yammering on about something they've only read about," Michelle said. "It's a really complex and intriguing history that's not mine to talk about. There are traditions the tribes don't want out in the world at large and that shouldn't be commodified because they're extremely sacred."

Bigfooters, who had an understandable weakness for those traditions, rarely got a chance to discuss them with Indigenous people. Whichever stories they glommed onto tended to be ones that substantiated their beliefs. Hundreds more—about thunderbirds and river serpents, murderous dwarves and flying disembodied heads, mermen and underwater panthers—were superfluous. Seatco, Omah, Skookum; those fit the mold and got passed around the way so many stories do these days: online, where they could crossbreed haphazardly with others and where questions of appropriation could be comfortably dodged. As Joe Bruchac told me, "You can't trust the internet."

"[Non-Native] people are curious about those stories, and they should be," Michelle said. "But are they ours to 'ooh and aah' at for a few minutes while not really comprehending what they're about?"

In my last days on the trail, I ate almost nothing. Unable to stomach the trail bars I'd brought, I deposited them in a corner of a lean-to, thinking another hiker might be brave enough to choke them down. Oatmeal, prunes, I Frisbeed those into the trees, saving only coffee, beef jerky, and Caramellos. Weaving southward, I trod well-worn paths dramatically overhung with hemlock and birch. There was mountain juniper, wild lady slipper orchids, blueberries, huckleber-ries, and in a section called the Great Bog, sherbet-orange pitcher plants. Elsewhere I saw blackburnian warblers with flaming orange crests, white-throated sparrows, blackpolls, cedar waxwings, and a shirtless, long-haired man wearing noise-canceling headphones while meditating on a rock.

As a Michigan Cub Scout, I'd scrambled through woods a lot like these. I recall an afternoon with my father and a Webelos Handbook, fashioning a birdhouse from Popsicle sticks while contracting poison ivy and whining like the child I still am. Even if I'd never been to Maine, I knew these woods intimately. Northern deciduous forest is my foundational forest. The nodal points are the same—the swaying, soaring trees and crisscrossing paths, the feeling of being enclosed in a vaguely threatening realm.

But then the land rose again, un-Michiganly, in a series of sharp hills, the trail narrowing as I climbed. At one point, it disappeared altogether and I had to double back to scan for white blazes. I climbed. I backtracked. I sweated through my underpants. The higher I went, the better the visibility. At the top, the air was stunningly crisp. As I walked, dark forest gave way to a brightly lit canopy. Baneberry, white trillium, and a few violets collected in tangles of exposed roots. The views, it must be admitted, were spectacular. From barren and windswept outcrops, I encountered Lester Kenway's bounty: a storyboard sprawl of young pineland and crenellated rock faces, lakes glinting and wobbling under the shadows of passing clouds. It was only slightly marred by squared and burnt treeless patches, scenes of "sustainable woodland management," which made the hills resemble a tartan jacket. In two or three patches, harvested timber lay stacked and ready to haul out.

To the west, I could see Moosehead Lake, where Thoreau launched two canoe expeditions, in 1853 and 1857. He'd also glimpsed the lake from a hilltop, though one closer by, calling it "a suitably wild-looking sheet of water, sprinkled with small, low islands, which were covered with shaggy spruce and other wild wood." Per his Penobscot guide, Joe Polis, he reported the tribe's name for the lake was Sebamook, which is surely wrong. He also said the lake was ten miles wide by forty miles long. Close enough. Many years later, in the same month the Statue of Liberty was dedicated in New York City, Moosehead Lake featured in a prominent Bigfoot story, one that Friar Tuck had hinted at and Michelle mentions in her book. I'll elaborate on it a tad.

One evening, "an affrighted Frenchman from over the line" arrived at a small hamlet outside Waterville, weaving a frightening tale of woe. He'd been hunting and trapping with friends near Moosehead Lake, 115 miles to the north, when he returned to camp to discover the dead body of one of his companions. The dismembered corpse was propped up against a tree, its eyes and tongue gouged out. In the Frenchman's telling, "which is implicitly believed," says a 135-year-old newspaper article about the incident, the killer was a "terrible wild man" with seven-foot-long arms and brown hair growing over his face and body. Such stories were familiar to Mainers. Sightings of apelike beasts went back decades and included lumbermen's tales of

"Indian devils" and other bipedal figures of Indigenous legend. The Frenchman took no time forming a posse of a dozen men, which marched to Moosehead Lake, where it managed to locate the creature. "The party fired several shots at him and finally succeeded in reaching a fatal spot, laying the monster low." The story was picked up by New England papers, none revealing what happened to the creature's body. One Vermont editorial eerily cautioned its readers: "The wild man is coming to the front this fall."

———

Bruchac had mentioned the windigo, which appears in myths and legends of most Algonquian-speaking people. Like the Kiwakw and Chenoo, it's a human being who was transformed into a cannibal, either by a malevolent spirit or because of its own bloodlust. For the Anishinaabe, who live in the Great Lakes region of the United States and Canada, a windigo is typically ten feet tall with massive arms and frost-white hair. Its bite is infectious, its heart a block of ice. According to Ojibwe scholar Basil Johnston, the windigo "looked like a gaunt skeleton recently disinterred from the grave. What lips it had were tattered and bloody from its constant chewing with jagged teeth. Unclean and suffering from suppurations of the flesh, [it] gave off a strange and eerie odor of decay and decomposition, of death and corruption." With its ravenous, zomboid hunger, the windigo embodies greed, self-indulgence, the breaking of social norms. Johnson thinks the root of windigo may come from *weenin n'd'igooh*, meaning "fat" or "excess," or *ween dagoh*, "solely for self." In *Braiding Sweetgrass: Indigenous Wisdom, Scientific Knowledge, and the Teachings of Plants*, Robin Wall Kimmerer, a member of the Citizen Potawatomi Nation, says windigo is "the name for that within us which cares more for its own survival than for anything else."

Such boogeymen tales, Kimmerer notes, arose in a society where starvation was an ever-present threat and sharing was crucial to survival. Like European wild man tales, they're widely understood as symbolic and meant to frighten children into toeing the line while reinforcing taboos against cannibalism. They also help build "resistance against the insidious germ of taking too much," Kimmerer wrote.[1]

Once confined to the north woods, the windigo, Kimmerer says, has recently expanded its range. We're now living in an age of "windigo economics," a global system of unsustainable overconsumption in which every one of us is complicit. "The footprints are all around us, once you know what to look for," she wrote. "They stomp in the industrial sludge of Onondaga Lake. And over a savagely clear-cut slope in the Oregon Coast Range where the earth is slumping into the river. You can see them where coal mines rip off mountaintops in West Virginia and in oil-slick footprints on the beaches of the Gulf of Mexico. A square mile of industrial soybeans. A diamond mine in Rwanda. A closet stuffed with clothes. Windigo footprints all, they are the tracks of insatiable consumption. So many have been bitten."

At this point, we should emphasize a chronic divergence between white and Indigenous Bigfoots. According to Richard Erdoes, who wrote extensively about Native American life, particularly among the Rosebud Lakota, Native legends are where "history enters the mythic world obliquely." That is to say, they're paradoxically "believed" as actual "emblems of a living religion" while being intuited as symbolic

---

1 There's a two-millennia tie-in here to the miserly, gold-hoarding dragons of Beowulf, Norse legends, and beyond. Tolkien, in *The Hobbit*, refers to greed as the "dragon sickness."

and cultural lodestars—"magic lenses," Erdoes calls them, through which one's identity and social milieu can be perceived—rather than as literal representation of the world as it is. History and myth, in Native storytelling, become woven together, with reality slipping into the domain of folklore. Similarly, in his book about Bigfoot legends of British Columbia's central coast, *In the Valleys of the Noble Beyond: In Search of the Sasquatch*, Canadian journalist John Zada describes a nuanced intertwining of Indigenous belief, with the endemic "wild man"—"Bigfoot," we'll recall, is a nonnative term—defined more often than not as a hybrid of the real and allegorical. Zada also mentions how contemporary pop-cultural Sasquatch narratives have reshaped Indigenous views, muddying the traditional folkloric waters. The Algonquin people's ravenous and polymorphous windigo, for instance, has been soft-boiled into an Equestria villain on *My Little Pony*. Some readers, maybe even some Bigfooters, will find these distinctions compelling, others less so or not at all, given what Mel and Bruchac have said. What matters is to note the discrete versions of "Bigfoot" in Indigenous legends that aren't always synonymous with white beliefs and practices.

———

On my last afternoon, I heard what I took to be a moose, but on second thought, I wasn't so sure. The woods are like that. You hear things.

I'd reached the top of a ridge dotted with three-story white pines and was catching my breath on a landing perched over a granite staircase that descended to the valley floor. At such moments, I often paused for a rest, slinging off my pack and collapsing on top of it, wondering what horrors the next mile would bring. Here I decided to push on, as the sky was promising rain. I could see ahead of me a series of gently rising hills, gentler, anyway, than the scene of glacial upheaval through which I'd just ascended. Over the prow of the most distant hill, I guessed, was that night's camp. I was midway down the staircase when something at the edge of my vision raised a mean hackle, stopping me cold.

The mind longs for simple answers. In my youth, I was plagued by dogs. Dead-eyed, uncollared beasts burst from yards and fields as I pedaled past. Our own potbellied mutt, Brutus, fell into this category. Twice I was caught and bitten, once viciously, by outlaw dogs. This thing, whatever it was, sneezed houndlike, as if its head was filled with slobber and no brains. It gave off an almost chemical smell, like spent matches. Moose was the next obvious answer. Rarely do you see them, even in Maine, and I'd already filled my quota. Black bear, rarer still. One nonetheless took shape in my imagination—the sloping haunches and palsied, frothy lips—charged, and chewed my face off.

The forest floor was overgrown with brambles and grassy thickets, the trees becoming denser and darker farther down the staircase—a hillside extravagance no doubt courtesy of Lester Kenway—which skirted the bottom slope of Chairback Mountain. Without warning, a figure stepped out of the shadows below and began carefully picking its way toward me. I could hear its heavy breathing, branches swooshing against its body. It was a weighty moment. Then I heard what I thought was metal plinking granite: trekking poles. A woman with an ultralight pack, her dark hair pulled back and tied loosely at the nape, buttoned flannel soaked to the waist, approached with her head down. She didn't look up and passed without a word. I turned back to the woods. After what seemed like ages, the animal, whatever it was, found a path roughly parallel to the staircase and, snorting as it descended, veered off to the east. I never saw what it was. It seems reasonable to think it was nothing more than a raccoon.

———

When I returned from my hike, I sensed I wasn't finished with Thoreau and drove out to Walden Pond. In summer, we swim and fish there, staking out a crescent of beach in an underused cove near Thoreau's cabin site—now a pile of rocks, the original structure having been torn down ages ago. Usually we can hear traffic on U.S. 2—the Concord Turnpike—and trains whistling by on the Fitchburg line farther west. Near the main entrance sits a replica of Thoreau's cabin. Next to it is a bronze statue of the man himself, midstride and stoically regarding his sinewy left hand, as if puzzled to find it there. This presents an irresistible photo op: with a cell phone balanced in the empty palm, you have the bard of living deliberately scrolling his Twitter feed.

Tributes that urge us to remember the past today carry unintended baggage about the personal or cultural legacy of what we're honoring. Thoreau, a conductor on the Underground Railroad who helped ferry fugitive slaves to Canada, is worth memorializing. But it's odd that there's no statue to the Wabanaki, no mention at all of other Merrimack Valley Indians whose home this was for thousands of years before Thoreau.

That afternoon, a March day of smudged skies and late-winter trees casting deep shadows, the parking lot was surprisingly busy. I always forget that lunatics swim in this weather. Though I seemed to be the only walker, the beaches swelled with people in dark wetsuits carrying pilon-orange buoys. Somewhere a car alarm shrieked. A jet grumbled distantly.

I'd never caught the *Walden* bug myself. Like so many, I took a stab at it in college and understood nothing. Reading the book now, you see what a mess we've made of it. Even in Thoreau's time, Walden was far from pristine. Commuter trains passed twenty times a day, depositing bathers and anglers. Irish immigrants, railroad men, and freed slaves like Zilpah White, whose home at the edge of Thoreau's bean field the fine citizens of Concord saw fit to burn down in 1813, filled out the neighborhood. Emerson, it seems, was always dropping by unannounced. When he didn't, Thoreau dutifully reported to his parents' house for supper. *Walden Light*, he might've titled it. I'm not sweating the dude. He merely wanted to chill. It took guts, his guerilla counteroffensive in our multifront war against silence and solitude. We'll never forgive him for it. "No other male American writer," his biographer Laura Dassow Walls wrote, "has been so discredited for enjoying a meal with loved ones or for not doing his own laundry."

Walking, I was reminded of Thoreau's essay "Walking," in which he wrote, "I believe that there is a subtle magnetism in Nature, which, if we unconsciously yield to it, will direct us aright. It is not indifferent to us which way we walk. There is a right way; but we are very liable from heedlessness and stupidity to take the wrong one." The fact that this is so patently false—nature has no opinion about which way we walk; there are no right or wrong directions, only the ones we choose—doesn't detract from its power. Faith in a natural order of things, that the directions we take have larger meaning, seem part of consciousness itself.

Much of this Thoreau cadged from Emerson: the transcendentalist idea of nature as threshold to an upper spiritual realm, an inbuilt hyperbaric chamber of individual expression uncorrupted by the mania of city living. I'm summarizing, obviously, but to Thoreau, who was recapitulating sentiments that go back to Ovid's pastorals, civilization ran an interference of sorts on our consciousness, cock-blocking us from communion with the natural world and, by extension, from reaching a truer understanding of ourselves. It's a notion that today's proto-hippy ATers have thoroughly imbibed, boiling Thoreau's complex ideas into prepubescent, Hallmark schmaltz: "Live the life you've always imagined." But there's a curious twist to Thoreau, who thought of nature as a sidebar to the main narrative of becoming yourself. To "reawaken" didn't mean caving to bottomless adulation of the ego or taking vigilant note of every chipmunk and pin oak, as the philosopher John Kaag has said (and of which I'm as guilty as anyone). It simply meant waiting and watching, looking at the world and the other people in it, remaining alert to its strange and vivid uncertainties.

Bigfooting, in that respect, is more properly Thoreauvian than solo hiking the Hundred-Mile Wilderness. "Nature is a natural draw for us," Cliff Barackman once told me. "It's an inclination we [Bigfooters] all have. On a spiritual level, it's good for the soul to see ourselves in a wilder state. But we lose something profound if we look at wild places and don't imagine a hidden creature there. It's how we connect to the mystery." It was no accident, Cliff said, that Bigfooting drew the faithful into some of our most iconic and rugged landscapes, places where "you can't just hop in your car and drive very far into. You have to get out and walk." Wilderness, as you might expect, was the field's default setting. Part of its role was to remind us how much more fun and exciting the world could be.

I'd heard variations on this from others, some of whom stressed the solitary aspect of Bigfooting. "I don't think anybody ever finds Bigfoot in a big group of people," Bob Pyle had told me. "When I'm out there with others, even if they have the same objectives as I do, they talk. I can't even hear the birds." It's nice being with friends and all, but solitude and silence, Pyle said, were two key ingredients to successful Bigfooting. "Experiencing the solitude of it," he'd advised, "with as little extraneous noise as possible, that's half of the reason for doing it."

7

THE CENTER
OF THE WORLD

"There is science, logic, reason; there is thought
verified by experience. And then there is California."

—EDWARD ABBEY

C an you see this motherfucking sky? I mean, have you
fucking been to California?" Dave Eggers memorably
wrote. I could see it, I could! And no, I hadn't been. Not
really. I mean, never north of Smiley's in Bolinas or west of Chando's
in Sacramento, both during the Napster decade. Correction: I'd been
to Santa Rosa, specifically the IHOP on Fulton Street, which, as far
as IHOPs go, was lovely. That pretty much exhausts my experience
of California. Only Smiley's, where the oversalted margaritas were on
the house, do I still regret.

Northern California? Some kinetic force had kept me away.
Until now, at the tail end of my Bigfoot year. It was fall when I
arrived. A pulse of warm pavement underfoot. Sun blasting over the
horizon. Coming down I-5, the landscape wasn't immediately iden-
tifiable as California. More like Sergio Leone's vision of the American
West, which was actually Spain. Cresting a ridge, I gazed down a
long gorge of pinyon-dotted hills, any one of which could've served

as backdrop for the cemetery shootout at the end of *The Good, the Bad and the Ugly*. But overhead, that Eggerdian sky. It was as if Leone had enhanced even further his palette of highly concentrated beige and added the sweep of heavenly blue from Corbucci's *Compañeros*. California, per William Carlos Williams, is where "the whole weight of the wild continent" hauls up and dumps into the sea.

The land began teetering, the trees growing taller. Across upper-west California and southwestern Oregon, covering eleven million acres, runs the Klamath-Siskiyou wilderness. It contains some of our last truly ancient forests, making it a top contender for Squatchiest locale in the country. Turning off the highway, I was bluntly decanted into a maze of logging roads lightly dusted with pine needles. When I rolled down a window, the aroma of sweet pine, which I mainly associated with the health food aisle, swept in. The path snaked westerly along a slim, corkscrewed ridge, past heaps of rockfall and errant, center-lane boulders, to an altitude of about four thousand feet. No guardrails or anything. Just a drop into nothingness. Then, out of the blue, snow. Three to four inches laid out brightly before my windshield. The effect was like looking through the 3D viewfinder I had as a kid, where in a few clicks I traveled from the Swiss Jungfrau to the Wisconsin Dells and back again. Mile after mile of indescribably beautiful, infernally disorienting terrain.

Roughly a million acres of the Klamaths once belonged to the Karuk Tribe. In the early nineteenth century, when white miners and settlers swarmed in, the Karuk lost sovereignty over all but a sliver of it. Most of their ancestral home eventually fell under Forest Service control, where it remains. In 1918, District Ranger F. W. Harley, bemoaning a straggling Indian presence here, referred to Karuks as a "pure cussedness class" and, writing to a subordinate, suggested a policy of extermination: "Every time you catch one [an Indian] sneaking around in the brush, like a coyote, take a shot at him."

When Ivan Sanderson visited forty years later, the region was in the throes of another calamity:

> All along this mountainous trail there are the stumps of vast trees cut and hauled out, and great slides of friable shales, gray, brown, blue, or even green that have been sliced out of the sheer valley side. The great dozers and crawlers clank and roar in the hot summer sunlight as they gnaw their relentless way into this timeless land. The great trees seem to recoil at little from their mechanical jangling and screeching, but day by day these bright yellow and red monsters munch away ever deeper into one of the last of America's real wildernesses.[1]

You still see signs of it everywhere. On and on it goes. The syphilitic machinery of timber interests poking and prodding the last of the old growth, haranguing the Forest Service and the Bureau of Land Management to cull every last inch. It's never enough. The Karuk Tribe and conservation groups like the Klamath Forest Alliance fight for what remains. What remains is spectacular. But there's a question of how long it will last.

My target was Bluff Creek, a tributary of the Klamath River, in the Six Rivers National Forest. Fifty-four years ago, practically to the day, filmmakers Roger Patterson and Bob Gimlin—if "filmmakers" is the noun we're after; they'd rented a Cine-Kodak K-100

---

1 Dude could write.

from a Yakima camera shop—recorded a Bigfoot walking through a clearing on the creek's sprawling sandbar. You've seen the footage: a wobbly, sepia-toned fifty-nine seconds of a bearishly stout Bigfoot, darkly furred like an otter, throwing a sidelong glance over its shoulder and holding the camera's gaze before striding purposefully away. Whatever it is, you can't quite take your eyes off it. A prelapsarian Adam, or Eve, as it turned out (a close viewing reveals prominent breasts). The film is the single most infamous and contested piece of Bigfoot evidence in existence, with an audience divided between those who've dismissed it as a hoax and those who believe it has never been convincingly debunked. Patterson and Gimlin always stuck by it. (Patterson passed away in 1972 at age forty-six. Gimlin is in his nineties.) Their brilliance was in selling us the idea of Bigfoot convincingly enough to last for half a century.

If not for the Patterson-Gimlin film, chances are Bigfoot would've faded into history's back pages, a dustbin relic no better known than the Vegetable Lamb of Tartary.[2] From the Pattersonian stage, however, it trod audaciously into the American vernacular, embodying, in its homespun gigantism and subversive charm, the myth of America itself. Such is the talismanic regard for the film among Bigfooters that Bluff Creek has become something of a pilgrimage site, but only recently. The actual location was lost decades ago, misplaced at the foot of a troglodytic gulch. In 2011, a group of researchers calling themselves the Bluff Creek Project (BCP), referencing old sketches and photographs, located the unrecognizably overgrown site.

_____

2 Also known as the "barometz"—from the Tartar word for lamb—it was dreamed up by the fourteenth-century voyager Sir John Mandeville, who you may recall from chapter 3. Mandeville, in his fantastical *Travels*, claimed that lambs, unfamiliar to most medieval Europeans, grew on trees. That's not a typo. This was accepted fact in enlightened Europe for three hundred years. When evidence is lacking, legend fills the vacuum.

In the intervening years, the BCP has reshot the film several times to try to determine its veracity. Hamstrung by the fact that the celluloid "Patty," as she's known, is only about two millimeters tall and by the film's poor quality, they'll be the first to tell you they haven't succeeded. After the promise of rediscovery, Bluff Creek relinquished a few clues. The film, however, remained dauntingly unknowable, its 954 frames occluded by a pestering question: Could Patty possibly be real? There's more than the usual tension around the truth. Bigfooting's guiding credo, it could be said, hangs in the balance. BCPer Robert Leiterman has this to say about Patterson and Gimlin's legacy: "Either one of the most intriguing wildlife films of all time or the greatest hoax of a complicated century."

All the same, the BCP illuminated an important pop-cultural moment at risk of falling into obsolescence. Wanting to see their work, I reached out. They kindly agreed to let me tag along on a shoot. From member Rowdy Kelley, I'd received a GPS pin to their Bluff Creek camp. But the little blue arrow had crashed through some alders and Thelma and Louise'd over a cliff a few miles back. The sun was setting, the snow piling up, the road forking this way and that.

"Whoever takes to the woods and water recreation should learn how to shift himself for an emergency," wrote Horace Kephart in his 1906 classic, *The Book of Camping and Woodcraft: A Guidebook for Those Who Travel in the Wilderness*. While the wealthy "may employ guides and a cook," for the rest of us, "the day of disaster may come, the outfit may be destroyed, or the city man may find himself some day alone, lost in the forest, and compelled to meet the forces of Nature in a struggle for his life."

My central malfunction was that I'd bargained on the wrong vehicle at Avis: a sagging, dusky red hydrofoil on wheels, far cheaper than the SUV I needed, but with Formula 1 clearance. The chassis was practically tilling the earth, causing the whole car—I'm blanking on make and model; "Compact: Nissan Versa or Similar" is all that remains—to tremor like a subway. I slalomed along in a northerly direction, skidding on snowpack, thinking I'd probably shed the muffler.

At last I came upon another vehicle, a sand-colored Dodge Ram, idling in a turnout. Inside, James "Bobo" Fay from *Finding Bigfoot* and Rowdy Kelley were chewing burritos with hot air blasting. They'd been waiting for me.

"Glad you made it," Rowdy shouted from the passenger seat. "Any trouble?"

"Eh."

We spiraled down a rutted lane to a berm roosted high above Bluff Creek. A few trucks were wedged around a four-corner farmer's market tent. I've sold cheese under this identical type of tent. I know intimately its assemblage quirks, also the musical finesse required in disassembling it and the thin veil separating success from desolation. We warmed ourselves at a propane heater underneath. On cue, it began to rain. Rowdy, fifty-four, a film producer and location scout with a grizzled face like the actor Timothy Olyphant, sparked a camp stove for a round of hot chocolates. Daniel Perez, fifty-eight, an electrician who publishes a monthly newsletter, *Bigfoot Times*, and Robert Leiterman, sixty, a retired park ranger, introduced themselves. Daniel wore a gray hoodie, jeans, and a camo ball cap over shoulder-length black hair. Robert, in wire-rim glasses and fleece vest, leafed through a galley copy of his new book, *The Bluff Creek Project: The Patterson-Gimlin Bigfoot Film Site, A Journey of Rediscovery*. All were from California and had been involved with the BCP in one way or another for years.[3]

Bobo, though not officially of the group, had been to Bluff Creek a bunch and was instrumental in the film site's rediscovery. He was much thinner and more rangy looking than on TV. His dark hair was cut short. His deep-set eyes glittered with intelligence and shyness, as if he understood something I did not and never would. He was sixty-one years old and well over six feet tall. Aside from Barackman, his *Finding Bigfoot* costar, perhaps no living Bigfooter has a reputation to compare with Bobo's. Before it ended in 2018, the show ran for nine seasons and one hundred episodes, snaring 1.3 million weekly viewers and spawning two spin-offs (*Finding Bigfoot: Further Evidence* and *Finding Bigfoot: Rejected Evidence*), despite failing to make good on the promise of its title. It remains one of Animal Planet's most-watched shows.

The fame it bestowed irked Bobo to no end. "Being recognizable sucks," he said as we passed around a bag of beef jerky. "I can't even go to [Bigfoot] conferences and hang out with my friends." He'd get mobbed. People wanted something from him. They thought he'd struck it rich when he'd just made a living. They didn't realize the guy on the show wasn't even him. "It's embarrassing. [Animal Planet] wanted me to be what they wanted me to be. It was formula television." You've no doubt heard it before, celebrity proving more toxic than tonic. Erica Jong: "Fame means millions of people have the wrong idea of who you are." Reality TV lines up poorly with reality. So widespread is its reductive pabulum that we fail to notice the transfiguration of a bright, articulate guy into a subliterate stoner.

---

3 The Bluff Creek Project also includes Steven Streufert, Ian Carton, and Jamie Schutmaat.

Bobo couldn't stay. He had somewhere to be. Before leaving, he loaned me a winter sleeping bag. I'd brought only my summer bag ("It's California. How cold could it be?"). Unlike mine, Bobo's was a downy, puffed-up miracle, good to below thirty degrees and, by the looks of it, brand spanking new. Without it, I would've frozen.

———

In the morning, Robert, Daniel, Rowdy, and his dogs, Chloe, a fox-rat terrier, and Daisy, a Westie, tramped down to the film site. We passed under rare Port Orford cedars and three-hundred-year-old Douglas firs. I lagged behind with Robert, who paused to point out flora with a trekking pole. Under his gaze, the muddle of greenery burst to life.

"That's Pacific dogwood. That's red alder. That's big-leaf maple. That's vine maple. That's ocean spray, also called ironwood."

I had on nearly every item of clothing I'd brought. Long underwear: check. Second pair of long underwear: check. Robert, meanwhile, was scantily clad in papery athletic shorts, Baja hoodie, and hiking sandals over white socks. When we reached a feeder stream to Bluff Creek, he splashed in unhesitatingly, impervious to the cold, while I practically had to be airlifted over. Daniel, inchworming his way over the same treacherous snarl of felled trees, improved only slighting on my crossing.

The film site was in a densely timbered wood of alder and maple. It bore little resemblance to the sun-washed glade in the original film. When Patterson and Gimlin visited in 1967, the place had been scoured by a flood. The BCP had cleared brush and saplings to return the site to a semblance of its former self, but it remained marked by time's current. Obscurities lingered. Using measurements made in 1971 by Bigfooter René Dahinden, they set themselves the task of reconceptualizing the film site, laying out a surveying grid, remeasuring, and formulating ideas about what had happened here. "Trying to locate the landmarks through a fur coat in a lousy film is a losing proposition," a skeptical David Daegling has written. But Daegling had never been to Bluff Creek and had not seen the landmarks for himself. In fact, the BCP had located landmarks, or "artifacts," as they called them—tree stumps, fallen logs, a big Douglas fir over Patty's shoulder in frame 352, taking bore samples to assess their age—and confirmed some of Dahinden's data, such as Patty's approximate pathway and the distance, roughly, between her and Patterson (one hundred feet). In 2011, Gimlin came down to eyeball where he'd seen Patty slouching toward infamy all those years ago. It was about twenty feet off the BCP's estimation.

This afternoon, they were tinkering with camera lenses. Dahinden, who died in 2001, thought Patterson's camera had a 25-mm lens. It's a signal detail, Rowdy said. If you know the lens size plus focal length, aperture, and distance between the camera and subject, you can guesstimate the latter's height with something called a field of view formula. Patty's height has been reckoned at between six feet and seven feet three inches, but no one really knows. "If she's six feet, it could very well be a man in a monkey suit," Daniel explained. "But if she's seven three, then the probability of a monkey suit radically diminishes because how many seven foot three people do you know?" Patty's height, then, was indicative of the film's plausibility. "Skeptics want Patty to be shorter so they can throw the whole film out," said Daniel. The hope was, by reshooting with 15-, 20-, and 25-mm lenses, the BCP could, once and for all, settle the question of Patty's height. You can't remake the past, but you can try to make it make sense.

I'll be perfectly frank. To get a grip on whether this is actually possible would be to truly understand things I don't care to understand. Daegling, who specializes in primate physiology, told me that to calibrate Patty's size, you'd need a scalar—an object of known dimension occupying a good chunk of the film frame[4]—and to know precisely (not roughly) how far apart Patty and Roger Patterson were. (Canadian Bigfooter John Green visited the site soon after the film was made and couldn't establish the distance with any certainty.) Even then, Daegling doubted whether determining Patty's size after so many years was possible. "The bottom line," he wrote, "is that the thing in the Patterson film might be eight feet tall, it might be five feet tall, but nobody is ever going to figure that out. There is a minimum of information that must be known outside of the film to estimate anything within the film, and it is intellectually dishonest to pretend that we have it."

It was decided that I'd play Patty. The guys insisted on this. I flipped my raincoat inside out so the white lining reflected the light. Rowdy, the director, manned a vintage Kodak movie camera with a pistol grip similar to Patterson's that Daniel had found on eBay. He was perched precariously atop a stepladder, which was perched precariously atop a crudely laid platform of alder branches, which was perched precariously over the eroded riverbank at the point where Patterson had maybe/maybe not stood. Robert was spotting Rowdy in case it all came crashing down. It was impossible to see how, if Rowdy's position indeed foundered, Robert could do anything except scream while being crushed.

---

4 For the BCP, the big Douglas fir fit the bill. For Daegling, not by a long shot.

Daniel coached me on how to walk like Patty, how to turn my head just right for the "money shot" of frame 352, the one that gave us our iconic profile of Bigfoot and which the BCP was today trying to duplicate. When Rowdy hollered "Action!" I did my method best, clomping apishly across Bluff Creek while swinging my uncannily apish arms. "Let's try again!" We reshot half a dozen times. Changed lenses. Shot again. By the end, I was frozen stiff. But it was a thrilling departure from sitting around in the dark listening to acorns drop. And it came with the welcome knowledge that, by nightfall, I'd be snug in my tent.

———

By most accounts, Roger Patterson was a con artist who struck on a Bigfoot "documentary" as a money-making scheme and roped in his pal Bob Gimlin to assist (they were scouting for tracks along Bluff Creek when they happened upon Patty, so the story goes). These are suppositions, but to skeptics, Patterson's case doesn't look great. The fallout commenced immediately. In 1968, Bigfooter Bernard Heuvelmans, a friend of Sanderson's, was among the first to declare the film a patent fraud, noting an odd likeness between it and an illustration for an old Sanderson article in *True* (the illustrated Bigfoot also had breasts and threw an over-the-shoulder glance). British primatologist John R. Napier, otherwise sympathetic to Bigfooters, thought the biomechanics of Patty's gait pointed to a hoax—"The creature shown in the film does not stand up well to functional analysis. There are too many inconsistencies." Although he did admit he "could not see the zipper." Daegling, after analyzing the film frame by frame with an expert in hominid locomotion, came to an analogous conclusion: "It is

a testament to human ingenuity and mischief rather than to the presence of an undiscovered species." It didn't help matters when, in 2004,
a costume maker named Philip Morris told writer Greg Long he'd sold
a gorilla suit to Patterson for $435 shortly before the film came out.
Or when Rick Baker, a special effects and makeup artist who created
Harry in *Harry and the Hendersons*, said the Patterson-Gimlin Bigfoot
looked like it was made with "cheap, fake fur." Or when a Pepsi bottler
from Yakima, Bob Heironimus, claimed he'd been the one wearing
the suit. Or when Bigfooters Cliff Crook and Chris Murphy, using
computer enhancements, enlarged the film to reveal what appeared to
be metal fasteners on Patty's back. Even Robert Leiterman, in his Bluff
Creek homage, concedes, "I'd rather it were otherwise, but the case for
Bigfoot just isn't looking strong to me these days."

Admittedly, it's hard to watch the film and not see a singing tele-
gram. But enthusiasm for it has in no way dimmed. Meldrum, in
Sasquatch: Legend Meets Science, mounts a vociferous refutation of the
above. Not only do the gait biomechanics, musculature, and physical
dimensions hold up to scientific scrutiny, he wrote, but the costume
technology available to Patterson in 1967 couldn't have fabricated a
creature as sophisticated as Patty. Nor could it today, he claims. "Isn't
it curious that such a hypothetically skilled costume designer had
never been employed in the Hollywood film history then or since?"
For some Bigfooters, Meldrum's word is enough.

The Bluff Creek Project tended to be more laid-back about the
whole thing. They neither wanted to debunk the Patterson-Gimlin
film nor make excuses for it but simply to account for how it'd been
made. "I just focus on what I know," Rowdy told me, "which is film."
It required a stubborn attentiveness to detail bordering on obsession,
a near-Calvinist work ethic, and a stomach for truly shitty weather.

The guys had more to do. I puttered around, taking photos of the creek and film site. Chloe licked my boots with a tongue that unspooled all the way to the ground. There was, happily, no news of the coronavirus. Bluff Creek was all but cut off from the outside world. Cell reception: zilch. Given time, it would return to its old stolidity, to its manifold uselessness. For now, it lay somewhere between pristine and cultivated, wild and tame, permitting a fleeting respite from our internet brains.

I crouched on the streambank and watched for animals. A kingfisher popped into view, sketching an elliptical arc at eye level. Through the bearded limbs of a young hemlock, its trunk displaying a calligraphic scribble from bear claws, a raft of cirrus clouds slid by. Ambient air shook the leaves and pearled the water's surface. Although I never found any of them, I knew the BCP had trail cameras scattered around. In 2014, one of them captured footage of a Humboldt marten, a cat-size cousin of the weasel, then thought to be extinct. More images turned up. They helped establish that the Klamath region held a viable population of about two hundred martens, enough to get them included on state and federal endangered species lists. "One has only to climb above four thousand feet in the Klamaths to see how profoundly the world can change," wrote David Rains Wallace, "and to be glad that the evergreen forest's venerable tangle has persisted in its accommodating primitiveness."

You can trace the etymology of "Bigfoot" to this tangle. Just upstream from us, on August 27, 1958, a cat skinner named Jerry Crew found sixteen-inch footprints in the dirt near his bulldozer on Bluff Creek Road, then being cleared for logging access. Other men at the worksite had seen similar tracks. After the *Humboldt Times* reported the story, the Associated Press picked it up: "Who is making the huge 16-inch tracks in the vicinity of Bluff Creek? Are the tracks a human hoax? Or, are they actual marks of a huge but harmless wild-man, traveling through the wilderness?"[5] Crew referred to the print's owner as "Big Foot." They gradually petered out, along with the news coverage, but the name stuck.

A decade later, Patterson's film fused Bigfoot into our perceptual milieu. The film's success lies as much in its medium as in its timing. When it landed in theaters in 1968, packaged as a feature-length documentary, *Bigfoot: America's Abominable Snowman*, moviegoing was experiencing a seismic shift away from small, urban movie houses to suburban multiplexes and rural drive-ins. That's inadequate to describe a decade of white flight, exclusionary zoning laws, and quasi-legal segregation that left African American neighborhoods like Chicago's South Shore in havoc. But suffice it to say that seven-hundred-seat suburban/rural theaters meant the Patterson-Gimlin film could be seen by millions of Americans.

In its wake came a flotsam of Bigfoot movies, both fictional and non, playing to predominantly white audiences. All but one were flesh-obsessed, bottom-feeder schlock of chartless, tsunamic stupidity, including *Schlock!* (1973), about a Bigfootesque serial killer who terrorizes a California suburb while falling for a witless blind girl with a heart of gold. Directed by *Animal House*'s John Landis, it starred Landis in a Rick Baker-tailored gorilla suit, their first collaboration. (Baker later won an Oscar for his work on Landis's *An American Werewolf in London*.) There was *Bigfoot* (1970), *Shriek of*

---

5   It was long rumored that Ray Wallace, a local construction worker, had faked the Bluff Creek tracks as well as several other Bigfoot prints in California and Washington. After his death in 2002, Wallace's family acknowledged it was true, revealing to members of the press the carved wooden feet Wallace had used to fake Bigfoot tracks over the years, including those found at Bluff Creek in 1958.

the Mutilated (1974), *The Beast and the Vixens* (1974), *Sasquatch: The Legend of Bigfoot* (1976), *Creature from Black Lake* (1976), *Yeti: Giant of the 20th Century* (1977), *Snowbeast* (1977), *Curse of Bigfoot* (1978), *The Capture of Bigfoot* (1979), *Screams of a Winter Night* (1979), and *Night of the Demon* (1980), to name a few. The single watchable release of this gaggle, and the Patterson-Gimlin film's closest aesthetic heir, was Charles Pierce's *The Legend of Boggy Creek*. The illustrator of *Boggy Creek*'s poster art, Ralph McQuarrie, later had a hand in designing Chewbacca for George Lucas.[6]

By the late '60s and early '70s, Bigfoot took on an increasingly starring role outside the multiplex too. No doubt emboldened by Patterson's film, eyewitnesses, seeking validation and perhaps more, sprang forth from Florida glades, the Jersey Pine Barrens, delta bottomland, the Colorado Plateau, Kentucky hollows, and Texan hill country, bearing both cogent and overcooked accounts. John Green, in his migratory treasury of sightings, *Sasquatch: The Apes Among Us*, claimed to have dug up fifteen hundred "confirmed" Bigfoot encounters in the United States prior to 1978, including a swollen nine-year sweep from '68 to '77. "Bigfoot was entering its halcyon days, the 1970s," wrote Joshua Blu Buhs, "when it was an entertainment icon, object of ardent devotion, and subject of scientific inquiry."

Something that's all but unavoidable yet bafflingly absent from the Bigfoot literature, save a solitary, fugitive reference, is that Patty slunk across Patterson's viewfinder barely six months before Martin Luther King Jr. was slain in Memphis. Todd Gitlin has called 1968 a fulcrum point in American history. On one side sat the old, moneyed,

---

6 Bigfoot also made cameos in three episodes of *The Six Million Dollar Man* in 1976 and 1977, played by Andre the Giant in one and by Ted Cassidy (Lurch on *The Addams Family*) in another as a robotic Sasquatch from outer space.

racist white order; on the other a heretical new wave "pushing the young forward, declaring change was here." Curiously, just as that change was coalescing behind the civil rights movement, Black Power, antiwar, feminist, gay, Chicano, Native American, and environmental activistism, Bigfoot started popping up all over rural and suburban America. The late '60s and early '70s were also a time of dwindling social and economic fortunes for Bigfoot's fan base. "The working-class white man feels trapped and, even worse, in a society that purports to be democratic, ignored," wrote Pete Hamill in 1969. "The tax burden is crushing him, and the quality of his life does not seem to justify his exertions." Hamill presciently warned that the white working class "is beginning to look for someone to blame. That someone is almost certainly going to be the black man," and "if the stereotyped black man is becoming the working-class white man's enemy, the eventual enemy might be the democratic process itself."

What's hard to fathom even now is the tension and terror of that age. In one eighteen-month period during 1971 and 1972, some twenty-five hundred bombs were set off by revolutionary groups in the United States, almost five a day. American public life, Gitlin wrote, devolved into "scene after scene of revolt, horror and cruelty, of fervor aroused and things falling apart, and overall, the sense of a gathering storm of apocalypse, even revolution." To everyone, it must have felt cataclysmic.

The late anthropologist Bronislaw Malinowski theorized that religious faith and cultic attachments can rise during "crises of human existence," such as periods of convulsive social change. Hence the uptick of messianic figures in the '60s and of UFO sightings in the decade after 9/11. The people seeing Bigfoot then, as now, were almost exclusively white, rural, and working class, a demographic deeply embittered by the hydra of progress and fearful of their own cultural extinction. Nixonian re-entrenchment in white supremacy (or what conservatives dubbed "law and order") may have convinced some of them they could forestall the worst. But the futility of their position would soon become apparent.

By the late '70s, white working-class fortunes began a precipitous decline, falling year after year in a wave of misery and misfortune unparalleled in modern U.S. history. In *Deaths of Despair and the Future of Capitalism*, Princeton economists Anne Case and Nobel Prize-winner Angus Deaton describe in depressing detail the "other pandemic," the one before COVID-19, that by the 1990s was killing alarming numbers of Americans, most of them white men and women without a college degree. By 2018, suicide, drug overdose, and alcoholic liver disease among this demographic was claiming 158,000 lives annually, the equivalent of "three fully loaded Boeing 737 MAX jets falling out of the sky every day for a year." At the same time, mortality rates among college-educated Americans, including African Americans and white working-class people in other countries, sharply declined.[7]

The culprit? According to Case and Deaton, America's winner-take-tall, casino-style capitalism, which, they write, is "toxic" for everyone except the rich and "more like a racket for redistributing upward than an engine of general prosperity." Adjusted for inflation, the wages of American men have hardly budged for half a century. And for white men with only high school diplomas, median earnings lost 13 percent of their purchasing power between 1979 and 2017, even as overall income per household head rose by 85 percent

---

7 The authors note that similar hardships previously befell African Americans.

during the same period. These numbers line up with research by the Economic Policy Institute's Valerie Wilson, who found that the real median hourly wage for white men without a college degree *declined* from $19.76 in 1979 to $17.50 in 2014. No wonder people long for a vanished past, one better by far than the present.

"Jobs are not just the source of money," Case and Deaton note. "They are the basis for the rituals, customs, and routines of working-class life. Destroy work and, in the end, working-class life cannot survive." Wage deflation, out-of-control health care costs, an absent safety net, rapid technological change and globalization have become an effective killing machine of the white working class. The people pulling the levers, Case and Deaton argue, are the predatory bankers, real estate swindlers, and lobbyists who were allowed to rewrite bankruptcy and tax laws in their own interests, the pharmaceutical cartels that profited enormously by getting vulnerable people addicted to drugs (90 percent of overdose deaths since Purdue Pharma introduced and aggressively marketed OxyContin in 1996 are among those without college degrees), and the politicians on both sides of the aisle doing their bidding. "Working-class whites do not believe that democracy can help them," wrote Case and Deaton. "In 2016, more than two-thirds of white working-class Americans believed that elections are controlled by the rich and by big corporations, so that it does not matter if they vote." When they did vote, they cast their lot overwhelmingly with Donald Trump, a nostalgia merchant who promised (and failed) to restore their status and stability.

Bigfoot, in this context, materialized out of California timberland as a great white hope, expressing and repressing titanic disquiet at the unwinding of the white working-class world and fulfilling a desire for magical reassurance that the old regime, despite appearances, would endure. Malinowski: "Both magic and religion open up escapes from such situations and such impasses as offer no empirical way out except by ritual and belief into the domain of the supernatural."

———

Before we left Bluff Creek, Robert shoveled clumps of dirt into sandwich bags for souvenirs, taking care to refill each divot he made. "You wouldn't want a Bigfoot to twist its ankle," he joked. We huffed back to camp, Rowdy and I carting a wheelbarrow of filmmaking tackle up and over the Sisyphean ground, every bend revealing a calamitous rock scree or miasmic worm ball of roots and mud. Chloe and Daisy darted ahead, darted back, darted up ahead again, back and forth, clearly showing off. Due to erosion and tectonic recession, the Klamaths are shrinking by as much as an inch a year, I'd read, their features slowly wearing away. So even though we were technically headed up, we also were, in a sense, headed down.

At my car, I produced a six of Coors, ice-cold and glistening magnificently. I handed one to Rowdy. We toasted the day's labor. "Very cool" was his verdict. I couldn't have agreed more. With Bobo's sleeping bag rolled out in my tent, the aches of the day subsiding, the roar of wind quieted by the trees, I didn't want it to end. Even in my frozen-catatonic state, it was electrifying. In my notebook, I scribbled: "I could stay out here a hundred nights!"

Wolfing my beer, I cracked another. Rowdy was hitting the road and stopped after one. Neither Daniel nor Robert drank. Perhaps not unrelated to that math, I woke in the night having desperately to pee. Unzipping my sleeping bag, which I'd stuffed inside Bobo's for double the warmth, I fumbled for my headlamp, finding instead an empty water bottle. Half-asleep and chilled by alpine air, a decision was made. Sure, things could've gone better. But you learn by doing. In the dark, my aim was off. The initial salvo clanged off the rim, sprinklering Bobo's wonderful bag. Cursing, I found my target but lipped out and swamped my undies. Unable to recenter, I resorted to a desperation lob, which again veered astray, the return volley, in a final muddling of sports metaphors, catching me square on the chin.

Bizarrely, there was no trace of it the next day. No agglutinative dregs or barroom stench. I recalled the famous conclusion of *Alice's Adventures in Wonderland*: maybe it had all been a dream? Just in case, I laid Bobo's bag in the leaves, scrubbed it hood to foot box with disinfectant wipes, and left it to dry over a camp chair. Bobo, if you're reading this, sorry man.

———

I had wanted to visit the Redwoods Monastery in Whitethorn, two hours away, because Thomas Merton once stayed there. I'd also wanted to see the coastal redwoods, Russian Peak, the Marble Mountains, and fourteen-thousand-foot Mount Shasta, the state's tallest volcano, which was formed, along with the rest of the Cascadia range, during the last ice age and was reportedly home to *matah kagmi,* a Modoc Indian term for a Bigfootish ogre. Shasta is a nexus of far odder occult beliefs, namely the lost continent of Lemuria and a race of reptilian humanoids called, appropriately, "lizard people," said to reside within its core. Lenticular clouds that irregularly gathered over its summit were thought to be either UFOs or cloaking devices to disguise their coming and going. But I ran out of time. Mostly I regretted not seeing the Redwoods Monastery. Merton, an American monk and writer, last visited in 1968, shortly before his death. He'd planned to move there permanently, chucking the chaos of the maddening world for a life of Byronic solitude—"the natural life" of "true inwardness," in Marcus Aurelius's words—the Redwoods Monastery being the most solitary place he could find that had a working toilet. He died before he could make it happen, in Thailand, accidentally electrocuted after stepping from a shower onto a terrazzo floor and grabbing hold of a badly wired fan. He was fifty-three.

Merton's jones for solitude isn't unrelated to the subject of this book, solitude being what drives so many Bigfooters into the wild, as Cliff and Bob Pyle had told me: uncubicled immersion in nature, a refuge from the iPhone noodling din. It's what drives me. For Merton, solitude was no weekend lark. Hard to picture him in sniper camo and night vision goggles. He regarded his California move as nothing short of an ontological vision quest, a challenge to his spiritual condition that might as well have come directly from God. "More than anything I want to find a really quiet, isolated place—where no one knows I am (I want to disappear)," he journaled, "where I can get down to the thing I really want and need to do." That thing is tough to parse. It had something to do with love, with heady contemplation of the human condition, with the paradoxical Zen logic that knowledge of self can be achieved only through negation of the self. Not solitude for solitude's sake, then, but withdrawal from the legible world and its problems in order to address them in the silence of his calling. "The best thing I can give to others is to liberate myself from the common delusions and be, for myself and for them, free. Then grace can work in and through me for everyone." Merton wasn't playing a metaphysical dress-up game. He truly believed solitude begat a Stargate wormhole to universal compassion. If only we could all stake a claim to it, he said, we'd see ourselves as we really are, and "there would be no more war, no more hatred, no more cruelty, no more greed."

Merton's journals are some of my favorite reading. The guy was nothing if not conflicted. At one point, he even hedges over California, wondering if Alaska or New Mexico were better repositories for his earthbound angst. Scratch that, make it Bhutan! Or perhaps "a wandering life with no fixed abode" was the thing? Either way, he'd go it alone, somewhere he could obliterate his ego and pick up the pieces at his leisure. He couldn't wait to get started. He loved flying. The anonymity. The time to sit and read. Everyone smoked backed then. Smoke in the cabin. In your hair and clothes afterward. Somehow it didn't bother him. As long as he stuck to his rules for airline survival: "1. Get the last window seat in the back, next to the kitchen. 2. Get Bloody Mary when the girls start off with their wagon… 5. Get second Bloody Mary when girls come back down the aisle." His restlessness feels comically innocent today, when even in the face of imminent climate apocalypse, we can't sit still. We gotta be out there, spanning the globe, posting selfies.

But it's painful to read of Merton's desire to become master of his own life within the institutional coil of faith. As Mark Shaw tells us in *Beneath the Mask of Holiness*, Merton was an "imposter of sorts," tormented by the monastic life he'd entered twenty-seven years earlier at Gethsemani, a Trappist order in Kentucky, quarrelling with church censors as much as with himself, mapping out competing territories of selfhood and devotion, desire and compliance. The journals are themselves a literary sham, a "private" confession Merton always intended to publish. By '68, he'd had enough. In the back of

his mind, California beckoned: "I dream every night of the West." A
man with a plan. And such expansive hopes. Above all: transforma-
tion. Whatever that means. To Merton, it meant everything. If only
he could locate it, in California or Thailand or wherever, the rest was
gravy. Then, he said, it wouldn't matter "one way or the other if I
never come back."

Like a vacation but not really. No boardshorts and sombrero for
Merton. No stumbling through a colada fog, having somehow misplaced his hotel room. More of a Steve McQueen moment: his get-
away. "I really enjoyed being in the wild, silent spot where no one
as yet goes," Merton wrote of his western sojourn, when he passed
several weeks of near-perfect solitude. I'm glad he had this moment
and was able to savor it, because there wasn't much time left. In three
months, he'd be dead. Merton was often urging us, and himself, to
think of solitude not as a passive act or as some kind of New Age
swan dive into self-conceit, but as a way of seeing more clearly. "In
solitude," he wrote, "I become fully able to realize what I cannot
know." If he were alive today, he'd no doubt be shocked and a little
dismayed by Bigfooters' claims. But I like to think he'd also sympa-
thize. What Merton sought in solitude, after all, is basically the same
thing that Bigfooters seek: a deeper understanding of reality itself.

———

"I have always had a great need for solitude. I require huge swaths
of loneliness, and when I do not have it, which has been the case
for the last five years, my frustration can sometimes become almost
panicked, or aggressive," Karl Ove Knausgaard grumbles at the start
of *My Struggle*, his six-volume love letter to himself. He's mostly

referring to childcare, to the drudgery of diapers and double strollers and three a.m. wakeups and grocery-aisle meltdowns, of always "living on the brink of chaos." It so overwhelmed him, so completely detonated his solitude (a different species of solitude than Merton's, perhaps, but the same genus) and rendered null and void the necessary time to write that it nearly broke him. It got so bad, Knausgaard wrote, that "everyday life, with its duties and routines, was something I endured, not a thing I enjoyed, nor something that was meaningful or that made me happy… I always longed to be away from it." Yet it was these duties and routines that sparked a renewed commitment to writing and eventually brought *My Struggle* into focus. In spite of parenthood's totalitarian contours—it often feels like serfdom, like punishment for an unnamed crime, a sentence of hard labor in an emotional gulag indentured to your kids' megalomaniacal whims—it was also the regime under which Knausgaard produced his greatest work. As if to fill the joyless, time-sucking void of childcare, his mind spurred him to capture the passage of time more intensely, more permanently, through narrative.

To extend the metaphor a bit further, being with my children for a fair stretch rarely fails to put me in mind of the scene in *Back to the Future* when Doc Brown dangles precariously from a clock tower as he and Marty await a lightning strike they know is coming. I don't mean that a DeLorean time machine would tempt me to alter the past and therefore the present, where I'd no doubt encounter a version of myself still living in New York City, minus wife and kids, strapped to a wheel in a Midtown corporate dungeon, finding perverse sustenance in a shell of bitterness, like Mickey in *Sabbath's Theater*: "How could he leave? How could he go? Everything he hated was here." Nor do I mean I'd be tempted to alter the future and therefore the even more distant future, which is the premise of *Back to the Future II*, when Marty zaps forward to 2015, a halcyon age not of binge-watching and social media trolls but of hoverboards and self-tying shoelaces. What I mean is, with children, life becomes a string of lightning strike moments, erratic upheavals of terror and triumph on an otherwise plodding continuum. Even when I know what's coming, what blow may fall next, how long approximately the pauses between blows will last and what I might've done to prevent them, time ceases to pass as it once did. Because it's no longer mine to do with as I please—time becomes aggregate: my wife's, my children's, my own, to be used collectively, as a unit—the velocity at which it's consumed changes utterly. Time's passage, in the Einsteinian sense, grinds to a halt while simultaneously hurtling you toward your death. Or in philosopher Jim Holt's words, "As the past slips out of existence behind us, the future, once unknown and mysterious, assumes its banal reality before us as it yields to the ever-hurrying *now*." Parenthood, by backing you into opposing corners that force you to view your children both as the tiny miracles they're portrayed to be in the wider culture and as ongoing personal disasters, accelerates this feeling.

I've spoken to other stay-at-home dads about this (we are legion) and am always shocked to hear them complain not about the loss of privacy but its opposite: the pain of social isolation. Even pre-pandemic, they said things like "I miss going to bars" and "I just want to hang with my peeps." Which is INSANE. One of the only perks of parenthood (and of a global pandemic) is the built-in excuse to excuse yourself from virtually every social obligation imaginable. "Sorry I missed your wedding. The kids were sick." How many times have I used some version of that? Suddenly, thanks to the lockdown, there was no need. I was momentarily liberated from being invited to things I never intended on going to in the first place and therefore from having to bow out of them at the last second. My solitude was, in a way, more secure than ever. In another, it was a perfect shambles, as my family and I lived out our domestic Thunderdome, baking sourdough loaves while clawing each other's eyes out.

My wife hates this kind of talk. The very name "Knausgaard" triggers a Pavlovian eye roll and finger gag, *My Struggle* being, in her mind, a case study of the precious male ego and "solitude" synonymous with white boy privilege. Touché. Were she inclined, she could extrapolate this to encompass certain niches of magazine writing, from "outdoor adventure" publications like *Outside*, *Men's Journal*, *Backpacker* (field guides, you might call them, to peckerwood fantasies of seclusion and self-reliance and pretending you know what a piton is for), to glossy "travel" rags for the aspirational rich, like *Travel + Leisure* and *AFAR* (whiter than fox hunting, whiter than Duke basketball). Call it what you will. Self-enrichment. Experiential catharsis. A purifying theme park of the soul. In a certain light, solitude exists only for those who can afford it, in service to the hard-dying idea that the nonwhite world is ours for the taking.

Let me back up a bit. Catholics, it's worth remembering, have a long history of social isolation. The first "desert father" was Saint Paul, who hermitted himself away in a cave in the Theban desert around AD 250, seeking peace and a little quiet from his in-laws. He stayed for one hundred years, give or take, living off fruit from trees and bread brought to him by a kindly raven. A few centuries later, Saint Cuthbert chose to social distance at Inner Farne Island, a slightly more upscale retreat than Saint Paul's, off the English coast, where he built himself a crypt out of stones and turf and had much cuter puffins for company. Like Merton, Cuthbert seesawed between monkish austerity and entanglement in worldly affairs, at times practically commuting between his hermitage and a bishopric at Lindisfarne, before dying at age fifty-three, the same as Merton. I seem to recall the latter making a point somewhere that the desert fathers (and by extension himself) weren't world-loathing frontiers-men lost to a decadent solipsism. Unlike me, their thirst for solitude wasn't about opening the ego's floodgates to drown out society in idle distraction. Fleeing a godless, corrupt state to meet head-on the problems of the day was the task at hand. Through solitary prayer—plus charity, poverty, daily labor, etc.—they sought to harness divine power for the common good, believing the ego turned outward, toward others, could hasten a more just and equitable world. Or as another good Catholic boy, W. H. Auden, put it, "To pray is to pay attention to something or someone other than oneself. Whenever a man so concentrates his attention—on a landscape, a poem, a geometrical problem, an idol, or the True God—that he completely forgets his own ego and desires, he is praying." The desert fathers also sought to shed a life of mutual dependence and indulge "the urge to an ardent interiority, the necessary ache and drive to comprehend their own confusion," as William Giraldi wrote in another context. "This commitment to the nobility of human privacy, to the dignity of silence, is a manner of enacting [a] commitment to the soul." He could've been writing about Bigfooters.

Whatever deep reserves of joy it taps into, solitude must be the best feeling in the world, evoking something akin to Camus's "unconquerable summer," a private truth, not unlike Merton's idea of grace, that he carried within him, in the wilderness of the self, even in the depths of winter. The pandemic gave us all a hard lesson in solitude. But we're so poorly schooled in it, we resented it rather than considering it holy.[8]

We should recall that for much of human history, happiness and solitude were mutually exclusive. Nebuchadnezzar II, the sixth-century BC Babylonian king who was driven into the desert for the sins of idolatry and pride, turned beastly almost overnight: "He ate grass like an ox…his hair grew like feathers of eagles, and his nails likes birds' claws" (Daniel 4:30).

To American pioneers, who were well acquainted with the terrors posed by wilderness, solitude wasn't a passing fancy but a way of life. On the frontier, away from it all, a Manichean battle was daily being waged between civilization and "a waste and howling wilderness / Where none inhabited / But hellish fiends, and brutish men / That Devils worshiped," as Puritan minister Michael Wigglesworth put it. "There can be no doubt," wrote the Michigan politician Lewis Cass more than a hundred years later, "that the Creator intended the earth should be reclaimed from a state of nature and cultivated." Subtract the God stuff and this puts me in mind of an overquoted Werner Herzog line from *Burden of Dreams*: "Nature here is vile and base… I see fornication and asphyxiation and choking and fighting for survival and growing and just rotting away…the trees here are in misery and the birds are in misery. I don't think they sing; they just screech in pain." When Alexis de Tocqueville, visiting Michigan Territory in 1831, told his hosts he wished to see untamed, primitive forest, they thought him mad. "In Europe people talk a great deal of the wilds of America, but the Americans themselves never think about them," de Tocqueville wrote in *Democracy in America*. "They are insensible

---

8 To be fair, for many of us, solitude was a synonym for financial and psychological penury.

to the wonders of inanimate nature and they may be said not to perceive the mighty forests that surround them till they fall beneath the hatchet. Their eyes are fixed upon another sight…draining swamps, turning the course of rivers, peopling solitudes, and subduing nature." Unbridled immersion in nature might sound nice to a prissy city boy like de Tocqueville. But if a man truly wanted happiness, the French American writer J. Hector St. John de Crèvecoeur said in 1782, "he cannot live in solitude, he must belong to some community bound by some ties." Our foundational grudge against wilderness betrays a key feature of our national character: violence. The American, D. H. Lawrence observed, "has got to destroy. It is his destiny," the carnage wrought by our white forebears comprising an "Orestes-like frenzy of restlessness in the Yankee soul, an inner malaise that amounts almost to madness."

For Merton, real solitude, even Californian solitude, was never going to stick. As he wrote in his autobiography, *The Seven Storey Mountain*, "There was this shadow, this double, this writer, who had followed me into the cloister." That doubleness, a tension between recluse and writer, between a "solitude that was an impregnable fortress" and the desire to live beyond its walls, became a central drama of Merton's life. In 1966, while recovering from back surgery, he fell in love with a nursing student named Margie Smith. Merton was twice her age and, more to the point, had been celibate for twenty-five years. It was the kind of instantaneous, atom-splitting love, he wrote, "that can virtually tear you apart." He nearly left the order to be with her. In the end, he stayed. Smith moved on, becoming a wife and mother of three. There's lots of handwringing over her in his journals. Merton was honest enough with himself to know he wasn't cut out for domesticity, that like Philip Larkin, he was "too selfish, withdrawn and easily bored to love." But doubt pursued him: "The drab, futile silences of this artificial life, with all its tensions and its pretenses: but I know it would be worse somewhere else. And marriage, for me, would be terrible! Anyway, that's all over... Yet this afternoon I wondered if I'd really missed the point of life after all. A dreadful thought!"

We're not alike, Merton and me. For starters, having never attended a church service in my life, I cannot, in Paul Muldoon's words, "tell Gethsemane from the Garden of Eden." Part of what I love about Merton is that he was no Bible salesman. He was devoted to his order, sure, and to remaining a good monk. But he grew weary of hectoring from Rome. Lamenting his guilt by association with the church's meddling in the New World, indistinguishable at times from slave trading and scalp hunting, yet undertaken in the name of a just God, Merton dismissed the "official machinery of Catholicism. Dreadfully dead, putrid." He went from writing and thinking mostly about spiritual matters to writing and thinking about anything else. Eventually, he became drawn to Eastern methods of contemplation, especially to Buddhism. It was why he had Asia on the brain. Sufism, karmic cycles, bodhicitta, *The Ramayana*. His journals are full of this stuff. He even hung out with the Dalai Lama in Thailand. If we're being honest, I couldn't care less. What interests me is how Merton, after a quarter century, rather than deserting his faith, formulated an entirely new credo. Like Darwin, who late in life discovered his mind, so steeped in scientific rigor, had grown immune to art (Milton, Shelley, and Shakespeare had sustained him aboard the *Beagle*), Merton felt his bonds shifting. Pounded nearly to death by the hammer of belief, his thinking gave way to other modes or to ways of placating one version of himself to clear a path to another: "I am going home, to the home where I have never been in this body," he wrote on the flight to Bangkok. "May I not come back without having settled the great affair. And found the great compassion, *mahakaruna*." It was also a return journey, unmoored from the church, to the world he'd cast aside decades before.

While Merton's California trip was a passage between two lives, mine, whatever this is, isn't that. Watching Rowdy's truck putter away, I remembered that while in Thailand, Merton eventually grew homesick for Gethsemani, giving vent to Thomas Bernhard's axiom, "I always want to be somewhere else, in the *place* I have *just fled from*." I too wanted to return. To leave this high ground and hurry to the airport, have a fountain Coke and chimichanga before boarding a flight back to boring old Cambridge, to familiar mornings of overpriced coffee and maple-ginger scones and blood vendettas sworn over parking spots, to my germ pod.

———

Extricating myself took time. On the Hoopa Valley Reservation, I found the tribal museum closed. I'd been hoping to speak with its curator, Silis-chi-tawn S. Jackson, about Omah, the fearsome "Boss of the Woods" referenced in Kathy Strain's book. We'd traded emails, but Jackson brushed me off: "We have no 'Bigfoot' stories, myths, or legends that are traditional stories from our ancestors," he wrote. "That is why I personally do not believe in Bigfoot. There are some Bigfoot stories from tribal members, but they are all contemporary from the last few decades, which corresponds with white peoples telling of Bigfoot." Fair enough. It might've been a bum steer. If so, I didn't blame him. The history of white settlement, needless to say, isn't one that kindles trust between strangers.

Also closed was the Karuk Tribe Headquarters, seventy miles north, in Happy Camp. The phone rang and rang. From 1850 to 1852, mobs of white miners burned Karuk villages on the Salmon River, slaughtered inhabitants, and sold the survivors into slavery. Such first impressions being impossible to live down, I didn't expect to get far. Still, I was curious to know what role, if any, Indigenous California legends played in our popular conceptions of Bigfoot. Kathy Strain has documented "Hairy Man" stories of the Tule River Indians in the San Joaquin Valley. Described as a bipedal, shaggy humanoid with extra-large feet, Hairy Man (*Mayak datat*) is both a physical and spiritual being, a protector of the living and caretaker of the dead. Seeing one is considered a blessing. The Wintu of the northwest Sacramento Valley have a similar giant man (*Supchet*); the Shasta of Siskyou County, a cannibal monster (*Itssuruqai*) and owl-woman monster (*Tah tah kle'ah*); and the central Californian Me-wuk, numerous rock giants (*Che-ha-lum'che, La'-lum-me, Oo'-le*) and a cliff-dwelling ogre (*Sachacha*). But what of the Karuk?

In A. L. Kroeber and E. W. Gifford's collection of tribal folklore, *Karok Myths*, I'd read about dozens of magical beings, many with a strong anthropomorphic bent. There's Loon Woman. Ipashnavan the cat owl and his hunting dogs. Water Person. A man in the form of a huge black ant. A bird that carries off people in her talons. Excrement Child (the Karuk, you soon discover, take special joy in scatological humor). And poor, bumbling Coyote, trapped in a deer's rectum (trust me, he has a perfectly good explanation).

Many Karuk myths involve fire. To the tribe, I'd read, "Fire is life." For thousands of years, before their land was stolen, the Karuk practiced what today we'd call prescribed burns, targeting sections of forest with fire during low-risk seasons to burn off deadfall and restore vegetation. It's partly why the Klamaths are so ecologically rich. Fire is also central to the Karuk creation story:

> Coyote wanted to steal fire, which had been lost in a bet. He collected various animals, and placed them at intervals from the river to the mountains. Frog was in the first place— closest to the river. There was forest fire in the mountains, and he stole it by diverting the children who were in charge of it, and then pretending to fall asleep by the fire, having placed oak bark between his toes. At the right moment, he ran away with a piece of burning charcoal. The ember got passed from one animal to the next as each got tired. Turtle was able to escape by rolling down from a mountaintop towards the river, and then gave it to Frog. Frog hid the fire in his mouth, dived into the river and swam to the other side, and spat the fire out under a Willow. Dogs howled as the fire rose up, and mankind came into existence.

Of the hundreds of Karuk myths, there's a single, vaguely Bigfootish fellow named Madukarahat, a cannibal who dwelled on the upper Salmon River. One day, Madukarahat grew so irritated by an incessantly bawling girl that he scooped out her brains and replaced them with frogs. Hijinks ensued. None the worse for wear, the frog-brained girl torched Madukarahat's house with him inside. The end. Little else in *Karok Myths* strikes a Bigfoot chord.

The nearby town of Willow Creek, on the other hand, traffics heavily in Bigfoot lore. There's a Bigfoot Motel, Bigfoot Books, an annual Bigfoot Daze festival, and running through the Klamaths east of town, a four-hundred-mile-long Bigfoot Trail. I gassed up and drove down to the Salmon River, where I sat drinking undrink-able Nescafé while watching a bald eagle bank and wheel over stands of lodgepole pine. The sun shone like an acetylene torch, the light driving shadows from the water. Birds the color of sweet vermouth, others a Waffle House yellow, dipped past. Magpies and crows, those were easy. So many crows, cawing and flapping, in groups and singly, some standing apart, looking this way and that.

Not far away, near the village of Somes Bar, where the Salmon and Klamath Rivers collide, is a place the Karuk called Katimin, or "the center of the world," their axis mundi. The Hopi have an equiv-alent belief, expressed in the word *tuwanasaapi*, meaning the center of the universe, or the place where you belong. More than anywhere else, the Karuk felt the sadistic clamp of white justice most acutely at Katimin. In a purported effort to broker "friendship and peace" with the Karuk, the U.S. Senate authorized an 1851 treaty that essen-tially forfeited tribal access to Katimin, a place of incalculable spiri-tual significance. It was one of eighteen such treaties with California tribes at the time. "One cannot imagine a more poorly conceived, more inaccurate, less informed, and less democratic process than the making of the 18 treaties in 1851–52 with the California Indians," the anthropologist Robert F. Heizer wrote. When settlers took their land, the Karuk lost stewardship of it. The woods around Katimin, and elsewhere in the Klamaths, were clear-cut, creating fuel-heavy, highly flammable forest that burns longer and hotter today than anyone cares to remember.

"A journey is a bad death if you ingeniously grasp or remove all that you had before you started, so that in the end you do not change in the least. The stimulation enables you to grasp more raffishly at the same, familiar distorted illusions. You come home only confirmed in greater greed—with new skills (real or imaginary) for satisfying it." Classic Merton, in that the meaning is elusive. Perhaps he means how we're unable or unwilling to reshape our narratives about the world, even when the evidence suggests those narratives are little more than figments. Mired in nostalgia for the past, we lose sight of the present. So that even in this most remarkable landscape, awesome beyond belief, a scrim falls over our eyes, preventing us from seeing it as we might, if only we were more clear-sighted. Perhaps he means how we inhabit a kind of prison, a prison of the self, separated from others and from nature by our fears and convictions, each of us condemned through time to repeat and suffer the same mistakes.

Merton was a Trappist monk. Like Buddhists, Trappists talk of taking leave of the self, relinquishing attachments not only to physical objects but to the past, to our very identity, in order to bridge the gap between perception and reality. For Merton, this search for clarity, in a world darkened by unreason, was the central struggle of life. Viewed from one vantage point, it's the subject of this book, or a sizeable fraction of it. At the Salmon River, warming myself in the sun, I could only hope that I too, despite lingering doubts, had opened my mind to new possibilities and to the sense of wonder that Bigfoot invokes. One can see a connection to the way in which Lisa Feldman Barrett says we might sharpen our picture of the world: by remaining vigilant against the myths of memory. If we fail at that, we might as well have stayed home.

8

CONSOLATIONS
OF SQUATCHOLOGY

"We played with exaggeration as a means
of keeping reality at bay."

—JOHN BANVILLE

Mike Smith is a slim, red-bearded man in his early fifties, a retired Army Ranger from San Angelo, Texas, and a Bigfooter of uncommon intensity. After seeing combat during the U.S. invasion of Panama from 1989 to 1990 and again during the Gulf War, he developed PTSD, for which he was in treatment. It was serious enough that he couldn't work. Sudden movement, crowded rooms, parking lots, situations where there were "too many bodies and I can't get a head count and lose my concentration," agitated him. He was also manic depressive. We'd been speaking for a few minutes when he revealed this to me, adding that he often carried a sidearm because he didn't feel comfortable without one, but tonight he'd left it at home. He talked about what a typical day looked like. "If I go to the grocery store with my wife and there's too many cars, I'll say, 'Let's come back later.'" He wore a Realtree camo T-shirt, cowboy boots, and faded jeans with a Conch Republic key chain clipped to a belt loop. His eyes, pensive and watchful, put me in mind of the Theodore Roethke poem: "I have myself an inner weight of woe / That God himself can scarcely bear."

We were at the Twentieth Texas Bigfoot Conference in the small town of Jefferson, 167 miles east of Dallas. On that first night, a few hundred of us mingled in the visitor's center, eating middle-school tacos on paper plates and drinking pop and iced tea. Centerpieces of plastic Christmas ornaments with Bigfoot cut-outs inside occupied each table, although it was only October. People had on overalls, cowboy boots, Stetsons, Longhorns jerseys, stonewash jeans with prominent belt buckles, baggy cargo shorts, and NRA caps. I sat with Smith; a middle-aged couple from Sherman, Texas; and Ruth Young Thigpen from Tyler, an actor in her late sixties who had a bit part in the TV series *Yellowstone*, she said. All around us was the cicada-like hum of conversation, broken at intervals by chirping cell phones. When I asked Smith how he felt being in this room, with so many folks coming and going, his voice changed. "I'm comfortable around Bigfoot people. I don't know why, but I feel safe here." He thought about it for a second. "Tomorrow I'll probably wear my gun."

Guns seemed to be on people's minds. A woman standing next to our table wore a shirt with the words "When Negotiations Fail" printed above an AK-47 that had smoke curling from its barrel. A man and his son wore matching T-shirts with the Second Amendment on the back: "A well regulated Militia…" The boy was fourteen or fifteen. His ball cap, illustrated with two M-16s, read, "Come and Take It." I overheard a man behind me say, "I've got a gun and I'm not afraid to use it." Everyone was white.

At our table, the unhappy subject of NFL football came up. Smith loved the game but could no longer watch it on account of the kneeling, which he thought disrespectful. There was a general murmur of assent. Then a guy who said his name was Steven sat down with a plate of tacos and started in on ghosts. Jefferson, in addition to being "the official Bigfoot Capital of Texas," by decree of the city's mayor, billed itself as "the most haunted town in Texas." There were twice-weekly ghost tours to a dozen or so haunted places, such as the Jefferson Hotel and Schluter House. Steven told me that at his downtown hotel, you could rent a "spirit box" at the front desk, similar to a Mel meter, to detect the presence of ghosts in your room. To all of us, he announced, "I heard that earlier this year a couple staying in Room 17 checked out in the middle of the night because of something they saw. It spooked them pretty bad. So far, I'm getting only static."

Talk shifted to space travel. Two days earlier, Jeff Bezos, at the time the world's second richest person (net worth: $197 billion), had launched his dick rocket *New Shepard* into orbit with a crew that included William Shatner, the ninety-year-old *Star Trek* actor. Smith, a Trekkie, thought that was friggin' awesome. He owned two Captain James T. Kirk costumes, one with a gold long-sleeve shirt from the TV series and one for special occasions with a burgundy jacket that Shatner wore in *Star Trek II: The Wrath of Khan.* The couple from Sherman, who I guessed were in their late forties, leaned into each other sweetly as they recounted seeing Shatner at a Comic-Con.

Back in July, Bezos himself had entered space, spending $5.5 billion, or about $550 million per minute, for a four-minute trip. I'd read that a single flight of a Falcon 9 rocket ship, one of many owned by Elon Musk, then the world's richest person (net worth: $317 billion), cost $67 million. Meanwhile, in Texas, Americans have been ravaged by the opioid epidemic; wildfires have burned tens of thousands of rangeland acres; oil refineries spew cancer-causing benzene;

environmental laws are so brazenly violated by oil and chemical companies that residents joke the toxic air "smells like money"; unsur-
prisingly, life expectancy plummeted during COVID-19, which had
so far killed 88,311 Texans; even so, in 2021, the state legislature
rejected federal Medicaid expansion for its uninsured citizens, of
which there were more than five million, twice the national average.

After dinner, Jeff Meldrum gave a slideshow presentation called
"Bears and Bigfoot" that drew on his book, *Sasquatch: Legend Meets
Science*. Meldrum is large and lanky, with a deep, authoritative voice.
He wore brown slacks and a button-down shirt. His super-white
beard stood out in the darkened auditorium. He spoke of how closely
bears resemble Bigfoots, especially when standing upright, which
could account for misidentifications, he said. Their behavior, distribution, habitat, diet, vocalizations, and scat also mirrored Bigfoot's,
as did, most notoriously, their footprints and trackways. He mentioned something called a "midtarsal break," a foot characteristic
associated with nonhuman primates like gorillas and chimpanzees
that allowed for "grasping" flexibility. Some Bigfoot prints exhibited
midtarsal hallmarks that, Meldrum implied, would be impossible for
hoaxers to duplicate.[1] He gave pointers on distinguishing between
Bigfoot and bear tracks ("You too can become an expert on bear-foot
morphology!"), and extrapolated from the state's black bear numbers
(roughly five thousand) a Texan Bigfoot population of about sixty.

---

1   "This whole midtarsal break business is bogus," David Daegling told me. "Meldrum is simply recy-
    cling [late Bigfooter] Grover Krantz's arguments of fifty-plus years ago: 'I'm an anatomist and no one
    can fool me.' It's total baloney. You can create these 'breaks' by walking around on the beach or with
    phony, clumsily crafted Bigfoot feet attached to your shoes." Such fake footprints, Daegling suggests
    in his book, are rampant among a Bigfoot subset—"the hoaxers, the con artists, and the liars"—and
    play a crucial role in keeping the legend alive. Bigfoot, he wrote, "is explicable entirely in terms of
    human agency"—hoaxing, misidentification, hallucinations—with no scientific proof supporting
    the creature's existence. The myth's durability, he concludes, is owed almost entirely to the internet.

He then proceeded to a discussion about an orangutan's "chewing cycle," "gut passage," and "hindgut fermentation," the point being, I gathered, that history is littered with unlikely hominids eating and shitting in the woods ("We're drawing inferences"). Elizabeth Loftus's research on memory came up, with Meldrum conceding certain points while inferring a degradation of scientific standards in her work ("Bad science that gets elevated because it fits the skeptics' narrative.")

It surprised me that Meldrum didn't mention one of the more intriguing hypotheses in his book: that North American Bigfoots could be a surviving population of *Gigantopithecus blacki*, an extinct ape that lived in southern China until about one hundred thousand years ago. Standing ten feet and weighing upward of eleven hundred pounds, *Gigantopithecus* was the largest primate that ever lived. After roaming around for a million years, it went extinct, probably because of dwindling habitat and food resources. Unless, Meldrum proposed, it migrated across the Bering Land Bridge, as bison, mammoths, and humans once did, taking up residence in Alaska, Canada, and the Pacific Northwest, where they survived furtively. "This can only be suggested in a qualified manner, based upon the incomplete evidence at hand," he concedes, since nothing in the fossil record supports it. "Nevertheless, the *possibility* is certainly sound, and the *plausibility* is quite reasoned and tenable." Those are debatable terms, but even skeptics like Daegling concede there's no biological or evolutionary reason why Bigfoot couldn't exist, given that, with *Gigantopithecus*, it already has.

Meldrum then addressed the biggest bugbear of all: the puzzling absence of a Bigfoot body or bones despite decades of searching. There was, Meldrum explained, a logically good reason for this:

the remains of large mammals such as bear and moose decompose quickly in the wild, he said, with tissue and bones being consumed by insects and other scavengers inside a week of an animal's death. If those remains happened to be in remote areas, as Bigfoot's would presumably be, the chances of finding them before they vanished were slim. Judging from the response, Meldrum may have been beating a dead horse (or bear) here. I'd heard this narrative—a rhetorical sleight of hand that, even if true, elides other extremely compelling evidence we have that bear and moose do, in fact, exist—quite a bit. Nearly every Bigfooter I knew was familiar with it.

Nevertheless, Meldrum received a raucous ovation. There was a long pause as he strode to his table. He smiled wanly, stopping to shake hands with a middle-aged woman, his otherwise worried brow straining carefully upward. Fifteen years ago, Bigfoot nearly cost Meldrum his tenure at Idaho State, where faculty petitioned the university to conduct a review of his work, calling it "embarrassing" and "pseudo-academic." They accused him of preaching, not teaching. A lecturer in the physics department asked whether Meldrum planned to research Santa Claus next. Why, I wondered, would a tenure-track academic scientist, having labored through the scholarly equivalent of George Romero's *Dawn of the Dead*, choose such a lonely professional path? Surely not to be celebrated here, among rank-and-file Bigfooters? Their interest in him made sense. By lending an air of scientific gravity to the proceedings, Meldrum's mantras on things like bear bones and foot morphology spoke directly to the dignity of his audience, shrinking the chasm between their beliefs and mainstream respectability. He was, in a sense, the ideological shape and soul of the movement, embodying an eminent rejoinder to lamestream skeptics and tweedy know-it-alls. Which was why his name was on the lips of virtually every Bigfooter. Meldrum's investment was murkier. It required either extraordinary courage and disregard for professional repute, I thought, or a Herculean pandering to belief, energized by the room, by the people nodding along, confirmed in all the things they'd heard and witnessed. Or perhaps the answer lies someplace in between, where the truth usually resides.

I spotted Charlie and Lyndsey Raymond and went over to say hello. They were setting up a vending table for the following day. Charlie smiled and said, "Are you finished writing your book? You know, if they turn it into a movie, you've got your leading lady right here."

He squeezed Lyndsey's shoulders. Lyndsey said something like, "Shut it, Charlie."

Copies of Charlie's book were stacked next to some KBRO stickers. I grabbed a few stickers and held out five dollars to Lyndsey. She waved it away. "For your daughter," she said. We chatted about the Kentucky expedition. Charlie had been impressed by the level of activity and was already planning a return trip in the spring. He'd documented fifty credible sightings within a few miles from where we'd camped, he said. Lyndsey felt like they were closing in on a major discovery.

"We're gonna get one soon," she said. "I think it's gonna happen. We would've gotten one already but the government's holding something back. They know something they don't want *us* to know."

———

If you're interested in what Bigfoot signifies, you have to go to Texas. This is mostly self-evident. Texas is where our clichés of American enormity and self-reliance find their most vivid expression. It's a land, Larry McMurtry wrote, "rich in unredeemed dreams," and as such could be said to radiate America's vital signs. Texas is vast. Texas is voluble. Texas is, more than any other state, entirely its own. Texas, most decidedly, doesn't give a damn what you think.

Believing in Bigfoot is practically a civic duty here. Texans have written songs about Bigfoot. Outside San Antonio, they named a town after it. The state has the seventh-most BFRO-documented sightings in the nation, with 252 since 1995. It is home to the Sasquatch Genome Project, which claims to have sequenced Bigfoot's DNA. It is where, in 1836, Davy Crockett, while exploring Nacogdoches, met "a large ape man…covered in wild hair, with small and needling eyes, large broken rows of teeth, and the height of three foundlings [about eight feet]," and whose flatulence, evidently, could clear a trailhead: "The Creature spread upon the wind like the morning steam swirls off a frog pond." Even more remarkably, it spoke: "It told me to return from Texas, to flee this Fort and abandon this lost cause."

Texas is where, for two months in 1969, the Fort Worth Police Department was flooded with calls about a humanoid-goat thingy creeping around Lake Worth. It became known as the "Lake Worth Monster" and the "Goatman of Greer Island." It's also where, in 2009, Peter Matthiessen was persuaded to give a talk at the Texas Bigfoot Conference, then held in the city of Tyler. Still considering whether to continue with his Bigfoot novel, which had ground to a halt, he'd told a reporter from the *Texas Observer*, "People have a need for story and myth. Most scientists are very skeptical. And they should be. But they shouldn't have a completely closed mind about it. Remember the coelacanth, a so-called fossil fish? It was believed to be 200,000 years extinct and then turned up 20 years ago off the

Madagascar coast. I saw some myself in a tank while visiting the Comoros Islands. So, you know, stranger things have happened than Bigfoot."

For me, Texas was all but unavoidable. What fixed the idea in my mind, I confess, were the tacos. Not middle-school tacos, necessarily, though I enjoyed those. I mean tacos like the ones that appeared out of the mist off I-20 in Canton and later at Taco Reyes in Marshall. In the enviable position of having once been Mexico, Texas is bubbling over with tacos. McMurtry might have referred to it as a land "rich in taco dreams." If you happen to be fond both of Bigfoot *and* tacos yet inhabit the Bigfoot/taco desert of Boston, Texas presents a double bonus.

On Saturday, I walked the short distance from my hotel to the visitor's center, passing a startling number of antique shops. The air was dry, pleasantly hot. Despite the busy streets, there was plenty of parking. It was still summer in Texas. People wore short-sleeved shirts and sundresses. In October! On a wall outside Oils & More aromatherapy was a poster for an upcoming "History Haunts and Legends" conference, featuring the paranormal investigators "Wraith Chasers" and "After Party Paranormal." Behind the Marion County Sheriff's Office, on West Dallas Street, guys in white and orange prison jumpsuits sat on a curb, smoking cigarettes. On South Vale, beside the Jefferson Hotel, stood an actual GTE telephone booth. When I picked up the receiver, it had a dial tone. In a park across the street from the visitor's center was a walnut-colored Bigfoot statue of the type you find in whacky garden centers, except this one was about five feet tall with eyes painted a brilliant red. Nearby was an official-looking sign: "Warning. Bigfoot Area. Stay on Marked Trails."

The visitor's center was a shapeless, single-story building at the edge of town. Lots of folks were standing around the entrance talking on cell phones. On a bench in the lobby was a sealed package of cloth surgical masks and three unopened, 33.8-ounce bottles of hand sanitizer. Of the roughly three hundred people inside, I counted two besides myself wearing masks. Eventually I removed mine.

I hung around all day, striking up conversations with whoever would talk to me. Most of the people I met were believers of one stripe or another. Almost everybody had an amazing story to tell. I spoke with Tex Wesson, fifty-five, a maintenance worker from outside Fort Worth; Margaret Bradberry, seventy-three, a retiree living in the Mid-Cities; and her friend Deborah Aumiller, sixty-two, also retired and a resident of North Richland Hills. Here's some of what they said.

Tex Wesson:

I had an encounter when I was sixteen, but it wasn't no Bigfoot. It was what everybody calls a Dogman. Back then— this was 1982—that term hadn't been coined yet. So I didn't know what to call it except a werewolf. I grew up out in the country, west of Fort Worth. I was coming home from hunting when I saw it. The brush was so thick you had to travel by game trails, and the thing ran across the trail in front of me in broad daylight and jumped over a fence on our property that I was fixing to jump over. It was twenty-five to thirty feet away. The nearest thing I can think of to compare it to is the thing from *An American Werewolf in London*. He was shaggy and lean like a wolf, with black fur that had silver streaks in it, and a short black snout and brown eyes. His ears were pinned back, like how a dog or horse will pin their ears back when they're mad. What really stuck out was when he turned and growled at me. I could see he had a black, mottled mouth and tongue. I thought, "What in the world is that?" I'd been hunting and fishing and trapping in those woods since I was twelve and thought I knew every animal in them. When I got home, I went into the kitchen. My mom was washing dishes. One of her rules was, "No guns in the kitchen." But I was basically in shock. I wasn't in the right frame of mind, and I laid my gun on the table and collapsed in a kitchen chair. She turned around and was about to say something when she saw me. She goes, "Oh my God! What's wrong?" She couldn't get me to talk. She called my sister. It took them about 45 minutes to calm me down. When I told them what had happened, they tried to convince me it was something else, like a coyote, or that it was just my imagination. But over the years, I stuck to my guns. I said, "I know what I saw. He was up on *two* legs." A lot of people get traumatized by a sighting. My sister lived about fifty yards away, and whenever I'd go to her house, it was at a dead run. It took me about six months before I would go hunting again. And the reason I finally did is, I can't stand bullies. Just can't stomach them. And that's what I felt like, like I was being bullied. I got mad. I said, "I can't let this dictate where I can and can't go." Flash forward to 2017. I hadn't hardly told anybody about any of this. But I found people on YouTube who were encountering the same animal. I contacted some of them, just to talk, because I knew they wouldn't tell me I was crazy. One guy says, "Why don't you come up here to Brown Springs, Oklahoma, and go Bigfooting?" And I did. The first time we went out, I had a sighting. I was standing beside the truck, getting the lay of the land, because I'd never been there, and I was looking through a thin tree line when a Bigfoot jumped up out of a wheat field. This was in an area where three Bigfoots had been sighted before. My exact words were, "I'll be damned. There goes one right there." He was jet black, with slick hair and a round, not conical, head. Then he bolted. I saw him head to toe for a few steps. The wheat was about three and a half to four feet tall, and I could see him from the hips up, so he had to be seven and a half or eight feet tall. I thought, "Gosh, he's fast. Smooth and graceful like a dancer." That's what it reminded me of. We followed him into the river bottoms. We could hear footsteps up on a ridge above us. About every 150 yards, we heard wood knocks. We theorized it was a family group with a male leader pushing the rest before him. That was my first Bigfoot sighting, and I was hooked. I've been going after them ever since.

Margaret Bradberry:

I was eight years old. My mother and brother and myself were going over to Hicks Apple Orchard in Granville, New York, near Whitehall. We lived in Hudson Falls then. It was about ten o'clock in the morning. As we were going over Swamp Road, this thing—we didn't know what it was—ran out in front of us. My mom slammed on the brakes and my brother and I started screaming, "Turn around, Mom! Turn around!" Because it was coming right for us. It scared the living daylights out of us. I'm shaking just thinking about it. My mother wasn't an experienced driver, so it took her a while to get us turned around. My brother and I got a real good look at the thing. It was huge. Absolutely huge. You know how they say Bigfoots have the peak on top of their head? Well, it had that peak. And it was a brownish, sort of reddish color. We kept yelling, "Go, Mom! Go!" She got us turned around and we finally started moving. After my dad got home from work, he went down to Swamp Road and found footprints. We didn't tell anybody else about it. Back then, it didn't occur to us to do anything with the tracks. I eventually found out that whole area, from Whitehall over into Rutland and up through the Adirondacks, is known for Bigfoot sightings. But we didn't know that then. I don't know if Dad told anyone. I wish I had talked to him more about it, but I didn't. We just kind of left it alone. But I'll tell you this, from that summer on, I never went outside again without my dad. It just scared me to death. Much later, whenever I'd go visit him—he lived out in the country near where this happened—I wouldn't go to sleep without pushing the bed against the inside wall and I wouldn't sleep near the windows. Nobody could convince me it was anything but a Bigfoot.

Deborah Aumiller:

This was just yesterday. Margaret and I drove out to Caddo Lake for a swamp tour. We had lunch at the restaurant there before getting on the boat. It was sunny, bright skies, not quite hot but it sure was warm. We were sitting inside talking. I was looking out the window to my left, admiring the cypress trees, taking in the swamp. It's pretty thickly wooded, and if you're there when the trees start blooming, it's really wonderful. The restaurant is right at the edge of the water. On the other side of the water, 130 feet or so away, is government property. Nobody's allowed to go over there. Period. Our tour guide told us later that government folks regularly run people off that land. There was some dry ground there, and on that ground was a particular tree that I was using as a landmark, because its bark was darker than the trees around it. I was just gazing at the swamp. The sun was rising and lit those trees up pretty good. Then all of a sudden, I realized that I couldn't see the dark tree anymore. And then I saw there was something in the way; something had stepped in front of it. I'd never seen a Bigfoot before. But the way this thing was standing—stock still—I could see it was pretty tall. It had to be six or seven feet, big enough for me to notice at that distance. I worked around a lot of men for thirty years who were between five, six, and seven feet, so I've got a good sense for height. It didn't appear to be huge in mass, but it had wide shoulders. I could see a tiny delineation between its body and arms, like when you have your arms hanging at your side, and a rising in the middle where the head would be. His left shoulder was covered by leaves and branches. I didn't see a face, but I could just make out two little slits where the eyes would be. He was all beige. With the sun shining, it may have appeared lighter colored than it was. But it wasn't a deep, dark brown. It never turned to look at me directly. I don't think he could've seen through the window, and the sun would've been in its eyes. It was watching everybody outside the restaurant, people eating on the patio and walking their little dogs. I watched it for a good fifteen minutes. I didn't say anything to Margaret. At some point, I went back to my food and iced tea. When I looked again, it was still there. I was considering whether it could've been a hoax. But the simple fact is, it was across a big expanse of water that was not shallow and was also on government property. I didn't see how likely it was that somebody would create a hoax like that. Well, when I looked again, it was gone. I sat there and thought about it a while. Margaret could tell something was up. She said, "What's going on?" And I said, "I think I just saw Bigfoot." I'd been convinced for a long time that it was an actual animal, and an intelligent animal. But this I had to process. It left me feeling a little weirded out.

Nothing in their accounts struck me as disingenuous or duplicitous. On the contrary, I believed they were telling me the truth.

Around 11:30 a.m., Charlie Raymond gave a funny, meandering talk in which he referred to Bigfoots as "the ninjas of the forest" and said they could easily hurt us if they wanted but, for reasons we didn't understand, chose not to. With a slide titled, "Where are the fossils or bones?" he recast some of Meldrum's decomposition narrative from the night before, claiming the bones of large mammals were rare finds in the wild.

In a utility closet-like space off the kitchen, I found a curtained-off area with a sign that said "Sasquatch Session in Progress." A woman at an adjacent table told me it was for people to anonymously record a story of a sighting.

"Would you like to try?" she asked.

"Oh, I don't think I'm ready," I said.

"Well, come back if you change your mind."

Later on, I ran into Mike Smith. This time, he was wearing a sidearm on his right hip, a Glock, by the looks of it. The gun somehow made him appear smaller and more frightened, I thought. I asked if he felt better having it.

"Yeah, I don't know." He shrugged with Bartleby-like resignation. "I guess so. What can you do?"

A young man of perhaps twenty talked loudly on his cell phone beside us. "You wouldn't believe it!" he shouted. "It was like he commanded the devil to stop!"

Smith took a deep breath. We said nothing more, but the moment somehow felt significant. He wrote his email and phone number in my notebook. When we shook hands, I imagined a sadness running through his arm into mine. Looking back, I wondered if the feeling was mutual.

———

I remember first wanting to die when I was thirteen. I'd been thinking about it for a while without quite realizing that was what I was thinking about. It can creep up on you in a way, entering the mind secretively and unbidden. At some point, it dawned on me that I didn't experience the most ordinary moments without a feeling of crisis. I hadn't understood how quickly life can go haywire. You forget how to live. I began to worry I was going insane, that I'd be taken from my parents and locked away in the Kalamazoo psychiatric hospital. My fear over this became so great, the discord of daily life so concentrated, that killing myself seemed a perfectly reasonable exit. I never said it aloud. But my parents, unable to help and sensing I needed it, sent me to a psychologist. They were convinced, I think, that I was acting out because of their divorce. That wasn't it. I couldn't say what it was. The psychologist was a bald, stocky man with a thin nose and caterpillar eyebrows. He was fiftyish and liked jazz. Because I too claimed to like jazz but in fact knew nothing about it, he tried to educate me, playing Bill Evans and Lonnie Johnson records while we discussed inkblots. Everyone tells you it'll be all right, and of course that's the cruelest joke there is. But this man, this kind and cheery man whose name I forget, didn't tell me that. He merely held out a promise of hope that I wasn't alone. The struggle to endure pain went on all around us, he said, at all times. It was in every mode of human expression: art, literature, religion and philosophy, in Bill Evans's Steinway and Lonnie Johnson's Gibson guitar. The point being that not only is pain transcended through art but that a sense of connectedness, of human solidarity, can provide comfort. And to some extent it did. There was consolation even in imagining death, in seeing how others imagined postponing it. Giacomo Leopardi, the nineteenth-century Italian poet who contemplated suicide on more than one occasion, referred to a "philosophy of despair"—not wallowing in mental illness but trying to understand it.

I hadn't thought of this for a long time when I started reading Michael Ignatieff's book *On Consolation: Finding Solace in Dark Times*. Written during the pandemic, amid a global search "to give meaning to our shared feelings of disorientation, fear, loneliness, and raw grief," the book explores notions of consolation in Hebrew, Christian, Stoic, Enlightenment, and Marxist thinkers and artists. Ignatieff is interested in "how ideas and meanings are forged in the crucible of experiences at once singular and universal in their significance." Probably it's safe to say he didn't have Bigfoot in mind when writing of a "fellowship of witness" and "chain of meaning" that lets people "grasp the commonality of their experience," tells them they're not alone and are part of a "genuine community of brothers and sisters." But a feeling of mutuality and belonging, of placing one's experiences on a continuum, was on plain display in Jefferson. It's consoling to know that others have shared your hardships, just as its consoling to know that others share your convictions. Their candor and friendship, their validation, can give you hope to carry on.

In an earlier book, *The Needs of Strangers*, Ignatieff wrote, "We are the only species with needs that exceed our grasp, the only species to ask questions about the purposes of our existence which our reason is unable to answer." Grief binds us together. It's the kind of trouble none of us can get out of. But we've got to try. Next to love, he suggests, "metaphysical consolation and explanation" is our strongest need, "one which is utterly unreconciled to the limitations of our ignorance." Ignatieff knows we're all seekers of one kind or another. Many have reported that Bigfoot released them from fear and depression, that other Bigfooters nurtured them and gave them purpose. We might, then, see Bigfoot as a metaphysical consolation, a form of therapy and sustenance. Bigfoot's tribe sure can use it these days.

For millennia, people sought consolation in God (or several gods), either alone or in houses of worship among like-minded adherents. Some of us still do. But in recent years, Americans have abandoned the church in droves, with more and more choosing to identify as atheist, agnostic, or "nothing in particular." A Gallup survey found that in 2020, only 47 percent of us belonged to a church, mosque, or synagogue, the first time such affiliations dropped below 50 percent since Gallup began polling Americans about religion in the 1930s, when church membership was 73 percent. Over the past two decades, according to Gallup, those who professed no religious preference at all grew from 8 percent to 21 percent. Even among Americans who *did* have a religious preference, church attendance declined 13 percent. The Pew Research Center has chronicled similar trends away from organized religion, a decline that began around the turn of the twenty-first century and accelerated, not coincidentally, after 9/11.

As formal religious faith has dried up, our belief in the unreal has nonetheless persisted. A quarter of us, according to a Pew and Princeton University survey, say we believe in astrology (that the position of the sun, stars, and planets affect our characters and lives), reincarnation (that the essence of a person continues after their death to be reborn over and over in this world), and that physical things like trees, mountains, and crystals contain spiritual energy. Nearly 16 percent of Americans believe in the "evil eye" or the ability of people to cast curses and spells, and about a third say they've communicated with the dead. Our overall fondness for New Age spirituality[2] has risen sharply, more than doubling since the "high strangeness" of the 60s. In fact, "religious and mystical experiences are more common today among those who are unaffiliated with any particular religion (30%) than they were in the 1960s among the public as a whole."

To turn a Norman Podhoretz quote on its head, nothing defines the spiritual character of American life more saliently than contradiction. Our newfangled spirituality, animated less by anti-religion than pro-everything else, is a Bizarro World muddying of alternative

---

2 Merriam-Webster's defines "New Age" as "an eclectic group of cultural attitudes…and beliefs (such as reincarnation, holism, pantheism, and occultism) outside the mainstream, and that advance alternative approaches to spirituality, right living, and health."

practices and nostrums with trace elements of Judeo-Christian superstitions and Oprah-style kitsch. It's about having options, specifically the guilt-free kind. Liberated from the righteous packaging of formal religion—the humbug of sin and redemption and eternal hellfire—we're now eager to entertain whatever we want. People "don't so much abandon religious fantasy in favor of reason as find *different* fantasies that better suit their particular excitement and credulity quotients," wrote Kurt Andersen, "constructing bespoke packages of spiritual and worldly make-believe." So we join Wiccan churches, consult fortune tellers and psychics, contemplate mandalas, attend immortality retreats, try our hand at forest bathing, ayahuasca, spell candles, salt therapy, shamanic sound healing, homeopathic medicine, purging, or sweat lodges, or chart a path of "spiritual freedom" in the Eckankar cult. We believe in soul travel, extrasensory perception, ancient aliens, the lost continent of Atlantis, the positive energy of crystals, Nostradamus's predictions, yoga not just as exercise but as spiritual practice, Mayan end-time, astral projection, haunted houses, that coffee enemas cure mental illness, what the Ouija board says, or, like Tucker Carlson, in testicle tanning to replenish testosterone.[3]

I noted earlier that much hinges on how you define belief, which isn't monolithic and unchanging, like the New York Knicks' perennial shittiness, but a shifting and porous matrix (see the Knicks' 2019 defense) of the physical and metaphysical, objective reality and

---

3 It's probably worth stating the obvious here: some of these practices are part of organized religions with tens of millions, if not billions, of followers—reincarnation, for instance, being a tenet of the Dharmic faiths (Hinduism, Buddhism, Sikhism, and Jainism)—who'd no doubt cringe at the term "New Age." I'm not claiming that such practices are spiritually adjacent to testicle tanning, only that they might as well be to New Agers, who by definition aren't genuine disciples of any one faith but spiritual rolling stones, cherry-picking and reframing and discarding beliefs at whim.

subjective fancy. It's also worth stating that surveys like Gallup's and the Pew Center's, with their reductive, binary answers to complex questions—"Yes or No"—often fail to capture the "yes but..." intricacy of an individual's actual beliefs, providing only surface impressions of one's thinking, not a CAT scan.

But we can agree from the ample data and complimentary research that a New Age great awakening is afoot. A vast majority of us, roughly three out of every four Americans (nearly 250,000,000 people), say we believe in at least one paranormal or supernatural phenomenon. Many of us hold to more than one, and some 16,000,000 believe in a half dozen plus. Women are more likely to gravitate toward crystals, men toward UFOlogy, while more than half of millennials think "reincarnation is a very real possibility." Conservative white men, according to survey after survey, are especially prone to conspiracist politics and occultism, constituting large majorities of devoted believers. We need look no further than Donald Trump to see that Americans are having a damnably hard time distinguishing the empirical from opinion, that our "striking addiction to irreality," as James Baldwin once called it, has come off the rails. In dark times, some people double down on God while others drift further into the margins of belief, or into the arms of a madman.

Which isn't to say we don't need certain kinds of fantasies. They're a way of telling stories about ourselves, of tidying up our messy lives into meaningful plotlines. Just as superstition allows us to feel in control of the uncontrollable, fantasy can help us deal with anger, grief, love, and failure (again I'm tempted to analogize the Knicks) and name desires that can't be reconciled with reality. And, of course, they provide an escape hatch from the otherwise inescapable, soul-destroying mundaneness of everyday life. My seven-year-old daughter

is heavy into fairies, so heavy that her thinking about fairies (in particular fairy couture) absorbs upward of 70 percent of her cerebral
load. A twenty-one-year-old student of mine is, he freely admits, a
much sought-after Dungeon Master, refereeing online games among
other twentysomethings that drag on for days or weeks. Sentimental
fantasies of swooning, eternal love suffuse the romantic novel, to say
nothing of Hollywood. And that's a good thing, because how could
any of us have carried on living if Bella Swan and Edward Cullen of
Twilight hadn't returned to Forks in time for junior prom?

Most of us, hopefully, grow up, shed our waking fantasies about
the world, see the Twilight Saga for what it truly is—a crime against
humanity—and maybe even get married, settling into a love that
isn't a transcendent repository of unbridled eros, but a cage match
of blood, sweat, tears, and professional counseling. We reconcile our
sentimental narratives with a rationalist, sober worldview. Or we
don't. And that's when things get scary. As our last two presidential
elections have shown, when fantasies become real, when the unbelievable is the only thing people believe, rationalism turns to dust.

Which brings us to Michael Barkun, a political scientist at
Syracuse University. In his 2003 book, *A Culture of Conspiracy:
Apocalyptic Visions in Contemporary America*, Barkun traces an inces-
tuous web between paranormal/supernatural beliefs ("occultism"),
pseudoscience, and right-wing conspiracy theories. Such "stigmatized
knowledge," as he calls it—"the heretical, the scandalous, the unfash-
ionable, and the dangerous"—once occupied ideological backwaters
of American life, far removed from mainstream thinking. Until the
internet came along, circulating previously marginalized fantasies
among a vast and diverse audience and binding them together in a
common thread of conspiracism, with the potential to turn violent.

"Crank science, conspiracist politics, and occultism are not isolated from one another" but intimately linked, Barkun wrote, via a
technology that promised to build consensus but has, in fact, only
made truth harder to discern. "Someone seeking information on
UFOs, for example, can quickly find material on antigravity, free
energy, Atlantis studies, alternative cancer cures, and conspiracy,"
lending the impression that these beliefs represent a "unified domain"
instead of a random allotment of unconnected ideas. Such intermin-
gling, Barkun warns, is potentially catastrophic to our broader social
order. "The implication[s]...are disquieting, for they involve the creation of a larger community of belief whose view of the world is at
variance with the prevailing norm. And the variance goes beyond
mere eccentricity, because it involves a deviant view of authority."
He wrote that twenty years ago, when magical thinking appeared far
more benign than it does today.[4]

Believers in the paranormal and supernatural, Barkun's research
reveals, share a baseline worldview with conspiracy theorists.
"Alternative facts," in Kellyanne Conway's immortal phrasing, carry
serious crossover appeal, whatever their claims or motivations. If
you're inclined to believe in, say, "ancient wisdom" or Dr. Oz's "alternative" medicine, you're more likely than others to find it plausible
that the Apollo moon landing was a hoax, or that, contrary to all
evidence, Princess Diana faked her own death, or that Joe Biden had
SEAL Team Six members murdered to cover up a botched assassina-
tion of Osama bin Laden (as Trump once tweeted), or that you and
your dachshund Trixie are nightly abducted and probed by aliens. A
2014 study by two University of Chicago political scientists called

---

4 Trump appears to have taken some of Barkun's book to heart: "The more a story is told, and the
  more often people hear it, the more likely they are to believe it," Barkun wrote.

"Conspiracy Theories and the Paranoid Style(s) of Mass Opinion," drawing on years of research, found that belief in things like ghosts and psychic healing "significantly predicted belief in five specific conspiracy theories." The probability of supporting such theories, the authors wrote, "derived from two innate psychological predispositions": first, an "unconscious cognitive bias to draw causal connections between seemingly related phenomena" (i.e., jumping to conclusions based on shoddy evidence), and second, a natural weakness for melodramatic narratives that "provide compelling explanations for otherwise confusing or ambiguous events" (i.e., looking for explanations that justify our fear and uncertainty). Not only does magical thinking tend to beget more magical thinking, then, but seemingly innocuous paranormal and supernatural beliefs can be gateway drugs to dangerous conspiracy theories. They're opposite sides of the same coin.

Andersen again: "It's an instance of complicated, consequential synergy—apparently harmless fictions blending and growing and spreading through the culture, combining with particular religious and political mindsets to become dangerous, with impacts on the real world. There is a line extending from flying-saucer obsessives to 9/11 truthers to Donald Trump." All are a part of a new American religion, a surreal alchemy of hokum that may very well usher in another two thousand years of zealotry and superstition.

————

If you've ever pondered how many antique shops one small town can hold, you'll find the answer in Jefferson. To be honest, I lost count. There were two or three around every corner, it seemed, all of them doubtlessly with LPs of *Whipped Cream & Other Delights* by Herb

Alpert & the Tijuana Brass and back issues of *Ladies' Home Journal.*
Haley's Antiques, Three Rivers Antiques, Old Mill Antiques, The
Old Vault, GG's Antiques and Collectibles, Texas Treasures, Gold
Leaf Antique Mall, Granny Had It, Mason Dixon Line. I managed
not to buy any taxidermy, as I had a flight home in the morning
and didn't wish to repeat experiences with carry-ons that raised TSA
eyebrows (a stuffed rattlesnake, an alligator head). A special quirk of
TSA folks, who you'd think would've seen it all, is they don't appreciate certain kinds of surprises.

Wandering Jefferson's sidewalks, I paused to admire its languid,
tumbledown charm, its massive Victorian homes and redbrick streets,
its complementary allegiance to the old and the modern. I ducked
into a wine shop, thinking I might buy a beer. It looked like the kind
of place you'd find in Edgartown, Martha's Vineyard. Clean white
walls. Light streaming through high windows. Overpriced bottles
of zinfandel and chardonnay sweating on a marble countertop bar
beside long-stemmed glasses. Flannelled hipsters in Red Wings and
tight chinos. The closest thing to beer they had was hard cider. I'm
puzzled by this cider craze. Back home, our local shop has surren-
dered an entire cooler to "artisanal" and "craft" ciders. Who's drinking this crap? In namby-pamby Massachusetts, fine. But God help
us, there can't be a market for it in *Texas*?! Then again, a year ago, I
might've said something similar about Bigfoot.

Gun boosterism notwithstanding, politics remained mostly offstage in Jefferson. Whatever folks might've been feeling about House
Dems' new gun control bill or Biden's climate change agenda, they
didn't need to say it out loud. No party of strangers, the gathering
was, as always, a blindingly white, predominantly male affair, with
the usual thicket of cops and military, for whom a deeply rooted

conservatism came as naturally as camo detailing on a johnboat. But the vibe was church picnic, not Trump rally, with an air of solemnity, almost of reverence, that became more evident as the day wore on and the faithful trickled in and out in a muted processional, renewing their prayers and convictions. Scrums of awkward high schoolers with moms standing at a respectful distance. Provocatively bearded lummoxes dressed as if they'd just stepped from a duck blind. Codgers holding fast to canes and trailed by small, doddering wives. If it's no longer God that people want, then perhaps it's simply reassurance they're not alone in their beliefs, even when—especially when—the meaning of those beliefs isn't always intelligible.

As beguiled as I am by this vision, as I was by Jefferson, there is, to be sure, some nontrivial convergence, well apart from the Gandalf beards and Buddha paunches, between Bigfooters and Trumpers: extreme reactionary views, a tendency toward the sensationalistic, a fetishization of traditional masculinity, a hard-bitten mistrust of urban elites generally and the federal government and its scientific minions specifically, coupled with an inverse, reflexive flag waving and suspicion of "protestors" and "kneelers," as well as a depth of commitment we used to reserve for the church. That's not consistent among all Bigfooters, obviously, any more than wokester inanities like defunding the police are among self-hating liberals. But there seemed to be a disproportionate number of Trumpers in Jefferson, amounting almost to a homogeneity (it was Texas, after all). A key characteristic of both is that they trust themselves and themselves alone to parse fact from fiction, while at the same time, the language they share often doesn't register a difference between the two.

As the conference wound down, I said goodbye to Charlie and Lyndsey. We'd agreed to meet up again, and I hoped we would.

Outside, the streets were returning the heat from the day. Crowds spilled onto sidewalks from bars and restaurants. I was glad to see the tourist trade alive and well in Jefferson. The smell of barbecue and charcoal, muffled sounds of geriatric honky-tonk, followed me to my hotel just north of town. I sat on my room's little porch overlooking a garden filled of old, gnarled trees, as pleasant a place as any to have a beer. The sky, vacuumed of Texan stars, was completely black. There's more mystery up there, I thought, than down here, so much that we can't comprehend and so little that clarifies what we don't know, which is pretty much everything—an abyss, the theoretical physicist Carlo Rovelli called our ignorance of the elementary nature of the universe. Yet what mystery remains in our own world still manages to confound and deceive the human heart.

———

After I returned home from Texas, I called Chris Servheen, a grizzly bear biologist in Missoula, Montana. Chris is seventy-one and, judging from online photos, wears a bushy, late-era Nietzsche moustache. Before retiring in 2016, he led the U.S. Fish and Wildlife Service's grizzly bear recovery efforts, coordinating all the research and management of grizzlies in the Lower 48 states while working with biologists in Alberta and British Columbia. He did this for thirty-five years. He also dabbled in bear conservation in China, Japan, Malaysia, Laos, Taiwan, Greece, Austria, Spain, and France and was cochair of the Bear Specialist Group for the International Union for Conservation of Nature. He's one of the world's leading experts on bears.

I asked him if it was conceivable that an animal of Bigfoot's girth could survive undetected in the American West.

"No," he said. "It's not possible for a large animal to exist in these landscapes and not be seen."

Could they just be really good at eluding surveillance?

"No. There are lots of people in these landscapes and lots of ways to see these animals—aircraft flights, automatic cameras. Even rare animals like grizzlies or wolverines, we see them. And even in places where they're really low density, they show up on cameras. So the fact that [Bigfoot] is never detected just doesn't make any sense. What it tells me is that they're not out there, that it's another fantasy."

What about the bones and decomposed remains of bears? Were they as rare as Meldrum and others contended?

"No, no. They're quite common. People find grizzly bears skulls and bones, black bear skulls and bones, all kinds of bones, all the time. We've had hunters come in with grizzly bear claws from an animal that died years ago that they found in a really remote area with really low densities of grizzly bear populations. So no. Animal remains are found all the time. They don't dissolve and disappear."

In Jefferson, stories made the rounds of wildlife biologists and park rangers who'd had Bigfoot encounters but were afraid to speak out for fear of losing their jobs. I asked Chris if he'd heard such rumors. He sighed volubly.

"No. I know quite a few such biologists, as you can imagine, and I've never heard any such thing."

I sensed I'd touched a nerve. Chris had just published an op-ed criticizing proposals by the governors of Montana, Idaho, and Wyoming to delist grizzlies and gray wolves from the Endangered Species Act, partly so they could be hunted. The Montana legislature was also considering bills to place bounties on wolves and allow ranchers to kill grizzlies they thought were threatening livestock, essentially amounting to an open season. A hunter himself, Chris thought these ideas were dangerously misinformed and pandered to a small minority of special interests. "This antipredator hysteria is fueled by misinformation and barroom biology," he told me. "There seems to be a perception among some people that facts and science don't really matter and that beliefs are more important."

When the Endangered Species Act came into being in 1973, grizzlies and gray wolves were nearly extinct in the United States. Thanks largely to Chris's work, about twenty-three hundred grizzlies reside in the West today, down from fifty thousand or so in the mid-1800s. Removing them from the ESA, he said, threatened to undo all the gains that have been made.

"Unfortunately, we live in a time in which truth is strangely unaccepted. Lots of people believe in things that are nonsensical, that just aren't real, because somebody told them or they read about it online. It's kind of like saying certain people won the election. Well, no, that's not real either. It's a pathology."

I then called Lee Kantar, a moose biologist for Maine's Department of Inland Fisheries and Wildlife. Lee, fifty-five, is Chris Servheen's ungulate doppelgänger, right down to the Nietzschean 'stache. He has led Maine's moose research and management program since 2011. Before that, he was the statewide expert on deer, and before that, he studied elk in the southern Rockies. His pioneering field work on moose mortality has been modeled in several other states and Canadian provinces. It's a good guess that Lee knows more about moose than anybody else alive. I asked him about Bigfoot's chances of survival in Maine.

"As a biologist, as an outdoorsman, I find it very difficult to believe that an animal exists out there and leaves no evidence behind.

All animals leave sign. There's no question. Every animal defecates in the woods, every animal dies in the woods, and every animal leaves other types of evidence that they were there. We run into the same phenomenon with mountain lions in Maine. It's suspect whether they ever existed here, but people will swear they saw the animal. We've never had a body. We've never had a firm, confident track. We've never found feces. In the western United States, especially if there's snow on the ground, you can go out and find mountain lion tracks. You can find caches where they buried an elk they killed. You can find mountain lion turds. Here? You don't have to be a rocket scientist to figure it out. But smart people, observant people, will swear they saw a *black* mountain lion. We know from the trapping and fur records that there's no such thing as a melanistic mountain lion. They don't exist. But you can never convince people."

Like wolves and grizzlies out West, moose were nearly exterminated in Maine. By the early 1900s, there were only about two thousand left in the state. They've rebounded to around sixty thousand today. But their numbers are shrinking due to the winter tick parasite, which kills about half of Maine's moose calves every year and which climate change is worsening. A big part of Lee's job involves performing field necropsies on moose. When we spoke, he was tinkering with the engine of a snowmobile he rides to wintertime carcasses in Maine's outback. I asked him how long it takes for a moose to decompose.

"Let's put it this way. Fact: we investigate moose mortalities. That involves going into the woods within twenty-four to forty-eight hours of a moose death. We take the animal apart, leave guts all over the place, bones scattered around. We speed up the decay process. As soon as we're done, the scavengers come in. When we go back to these sites a year later, where the moose is buried in the duff, there are still bones that remain, for sure. The rest of the moose might disappear, but the bones are going to stay for quite a while. They take a long, long time, based on snow, rain, wind, rodents gnawing on them, to decompose."

Did any biologists or park rangers he knew express job insecurity over Bigfoot sightings?

"No. No. No."

But then Lee surprised me.

"I think the whole Bigfoot thing is really cool. I saw the Patterson film as a kid and absolutely loved it. So I make no judgments. There's something really attractive about Bigfoot. It's a mystery. We all love to search for stuff, whether it's hunting or looking for rare birds. It gives us purpose and adventure. And the one that got away, the one you just haven't been able to see, that's even more thrilling. If it was easy, like, you know, seeing a crow, who cares? But if it's uncommon, like a fish crow? Then that's a pot of gold."

Lee had cut right to the Matthiessenian chase, if you'll pardon the pun. The ties that bound together flesh-and-blooders with the woo'ers and idly curious had everything to do with pursuit of the extraordinary and in turn with a desire to understand the world. A commonality, it seemed to me, that hitched them to the rest of us and to the great folkloric heroes and heroines of the past. And even, in a sense, to scientific tradition. Up to a point.

"I've spent a lot of time in the woods, and I'll see things where I'll go, 'What in the hell was that?'" Lee said. "Maybe I couldn't make it out because of the distance, or it was a fleeting glimpse. But if you'd ask me to tell you what it was, I'd say, 'I don't know. Something black ran by.' And as soon as I'm not looking at it anymore, my brain starts filling in all of the blank spots to create in my mind what the animal was. I was turkey hunting the other day and something was making a vocalization that I'd never heard before. I'm going, 'Is that a bird or is it something on the ground?' I couldn't figure it out. I went to investigate. I kept looking and moving toward it and, long story short, it was two porcupines in a tree. They were mewling incredibly loud. I mean, you wouldn't believe how loud it was. Again, like with visuals, you hear something like that and you don't know what it is, your brain fills in the details. So I can understand why people mistake things. You see things in the gray light of morning or as it gets dark that you can't explain. And you make tree stumps out to be something else. It's human error. It happens all the time. But when you take the next step of saying, 'There's something that exists out there, a Bigfoot or an alien,' well, to me, that's the power of science. It's what I love about it. You can never prove anything. You can only disprove it."

Science, Lee went on, helps us explore what we don't understand, reconceptualizes our view of things in the hopes of acquiring the most reliable knowledge, free of "feeling" and ideological blinders and the pressure to ascribe to ascendant beliefs. "It's not a perfect system for discerning the truth," he said, "but it's as close as we can get."

———

At about the same time, I heard from Rowdy Kelley. He'd finished analyzing the film from our Bluff Creek shoot and had decided which lens Roger Patterson had likely used to capture Patty in 1967. "Looks like the 20-mm is the best fit," Rowdy said, adding that the

25-mm lens was a close second but would require moving the film-ing position farther back, nearer the creek, to make it work. With the 20-mm, things more or less measured up with what you see in frame 352 of the Patterson-Gimlin film, when Patty, scanning over her right shoulder, casts that brief, long-distance glare, which I'd tried awkwardly to duplicate at Bluff Creek. The old snag and tree stump "artifacts" the BCP had identified fit neatly within the frame's edges, while Patty's left-to-right bearing, with the slightly waggish stance, corresponded to the position of those artifacts. Although by no means conclusive—"We're going on old info for where Patty was during [frame 352] so we may not get an exact result," Rowdy clari-fied—it seemed to align. Daniel too called to say that, based on their experiment that day, the 20-mm lens correlated closely with the old film. Unless I was reading too much into it, Daniel seemed jazzed by the persuasiveness and beauty of what they'd done. "You don't have to be a scientist to do scientifically valuable work," he said.

There was one problem. If the BCP's verdict was correct and Patterson had indeed used a 20-mm lens, then Patty couldn't be seven feet tall, as many Bigfooters have long hoped. Instead, accord-ing to the field of view formula—which reckons with lens size, aper-ture, focal length, and more to estimate a subject's height—she was a far more plausible six feet tall. And if that were the case, Patty, as Daniel had put it to me at Bluff Creek, "could very well be a man in a monkey suit." I would've expected some hand-wringing over this, as it embodied a major kink in a timeworn Bigfoot narrative. But no. The Bluff Creek Project, Rowdy and Daniel agreed, would continue with their work, tinkering and reshooting the Patterson-Gimlin film to try and figure out what it meant. In a recent issue of his newsletter, *Bigfoot Times*, Daniel had written, "The result is only preliminary and nothing is set in stone… More experimentation is in order."

Rowdy had also sent along a still frame from our shoot. It was of Daniel, Robert, and me standing under a canopy of Bluff Creek alders, soon after filming had wrapped. My coat is still inside out, its white lining catching what remains of the sun. Daniel and Robert are close beside me, their faces halved by shadows. We don't have our arms across each other's shoulders, even though that's how I remembered it, as a scene of shared giddiness and pride of accomplishment. The photo itself is drained of color, with a bubble of late-autumn light at its edges, as if we're in a glass terrarium. Part of what I like about it is that it puts me in mind of Patterson's film—the huge trees with gold-tinted leaves, the scattered deadfall in the creek bed, the partial glimpse of something slowly filling the screen, then Patty bounding out of the frame mere yards from where we stood. It's a great story. I was glad to have participated in its ongoing moment. I didn't believe in Patty, not really, but I liked entertaining the possibility, the slightest possibility, that she'd once been real.

EPILOGUE

"But it is the shadow that is exciting, the
light that cannot be defined."

—JOHN CHEEVER

I first encountered my subject in New Mexico, where this story began.
One morning, I walked into the Chama River Canyon
Wilderness, through dawn shadows, past knots of cholla cactus with
hard yellow flowers clenched tight as fists. The trail rose over a shim-
mering plain, casting a view of the Jemez Mountains and the famous
Pedernal, a headless prominence that Georgia O'Keeffe painted eighty
years ago from her parcel at Ghost Ranch. At the top, the sun was
molten. The area beyond the trail was loose, sandy soil full of cactus
and brittle juniper shrubs. I discovered I had excellent cell reception.
Four bars! I called my wife. The day was March 3, 2020, soon after the
first coronavirus-related death in the United States was announced.
We discussed imminent school closings and details of a summer vacation that wasn't to be. It's difficult now to square my memory of the
place with what followed, with the waiting deaths, the encroaching
fear, with the bigger story that, unlike this one, has no beginning and
no end. My daughter, who was in a knock-knock phase, told a joke:

"Why do bees have sticky hair?" "Why?" "Because they use a honey-comb." After we said goodbye, feeling worked up, I burst into tears.

On the way down, I startled a flock of bluebirds. Hundreds of them. Rising and lowering my binoculars, I watched the wildest baby blue dart among stunted pinyons and careen skyward, cerulean boomerangs in an off-white galaxy. Below me I could see the trail punching through the rocks, curling in and out of view, abutting a canyon that straggled toward the Chama River many miles away. Somewhere down there was the trailhead. Wondering how far from it I'd wandered, about how much of what I thought I knew I really knew at all, I caught sight of my rental car, its windshield warping the sunlight so the whole vehicle seemed spectrally lit, a distant caramel orb plopped down in an immense redness. With a running jump, I could've almost parachuted to it.

I sensed movement, a man or an animal standing at some distance from the car. I could make out a brownish blur and at least two reedy legs poking through long desert grass. An elk? I'd seen a whole bunch the day before—a "herd," I suppose it's called—crossing a road not far from here. I considered if I should try shooing it away. Then I thought I saw, in slanting sunlight, more movement, a deliberate striding, grass rippling beside it. Tweakers? I was three hours from Albuquerque, home of *Breaking Bad*. I stowed my binoculars and hurried on. By the time I reached the bottom, the sun had mellowed. I had no cell coverage. The air was still. It was then that I began to wonder. I stood, I recall, beside the car, fixing my eyes on the ground behind it, on the yam-red clay dappled with strange, oblong, foot-like patterns, thinking of what it might've been.

Never mind tweakers. Change the setting, I thought, add explosions and M. Emmet Walsh, and this could be a movie.

ACKNOWLEDGMENTS

I would like to thank Farooq Ahmed, Isaac Campos, and Amanda Petrusich for reading drafts and offering suggestions. Thanks also to Deborah Aumiller, Kimberly Baker of the Klamath Forest Alliance, Cliff Barackman, John Baranchok, Lisa Feldman Barrett, Paul Bartholomew, Jimmy Behel, David Boehmker, Margaret Bradberry, Joseph Bruchac, Peter Byrne, Richard Crossett of the U.S. Fish and Wildlife Service, David J. Daegling, Marc DeWerth, David Ellis of the Olympic Project, Tim Gallagher, Mike Gamble, Marge Gates, Miriam Goderich, Jason Grainger, Victoria Haydon, Lee Kantar, Leila Karge, Michael Kauffmann of the Bigfoot Trail Alliance, Rowdy Kelley, Robert Leiterman, the Brothers Lubavs, David Luneau, Lynne McNeill, Jeff Meldrum, John Mionczynski, Matt Moneymaker, Barbara Mueller, Daniel Perez, Lyndsey and Charlie Raymond, Lance Richardson, Lori Russell, Chris Servheen, Dustin Severs, David Allen Sibley, Mel Skahan, Mike Smith, Michelle Souliere, Richard Stenger, Kathy Moskowitz Strain, Steven Streufert, Nancy and Bobby Thompson, Dacus Thompson, Tex Wesson, Jeff Wheelwright, Jonathan Wilk of Team Squatchachusetts, and especially the Balanced Rock Crew.

I am indebted to Robert Michael Pyle for his hospitality and encouragement, to James "Bobo" Fay for a sleeping bag, to my parents for their love and generosity, to my agent, Jane Dystel, for believing in this book, and to Jenna Jankowski, my editor at Sourcebooks, for helping to make it better.

And most of all to my wife, Cassie Frank, without whom none of this would have been possible.

READING GROUP GUIDE

1. A large, ape-like figure can be found walking through plenty of historical accounts. Compare the indigenous stories with those of the early settlers. How, in each, is this figure characterized?

2. Trace O'Connor's journey across the country in search of answers. Which trip would you have liked to tag along on?

3. Discuss the various places Bigfoot appears: on t-shirts and magnets, movies and books. Where did *you* last see him?

4. O'Connor comes across plenty of believers, of all different demographics and backgrounds. Besides the obvious—they all believe in Sasquatch—how are they similar? Describe their differences.

5. What do you make of the countless eyewitness testimonies of Bigfoot? Do you think they make the case for cryptids more or less convincing?

6. Whether it's our faith in a higher power, ghosts, or crystals, everyone believes in something. Is there anything you believe in that falls outside the realm of "reality"?

7. If the Patterson-Gimlin film turned out to be a hoax, would that have any bearing on your belief in Bigfoot? Do you think it would make any skeptics into believers?

8. Consider the different reasons people want to believe in a figure like Sasquatch. Which do you find most compelling?

9. After all of this: do you believe in Bigfoot?

BIBLIOGRAPHY

Andersen, Kurt. *Fantasyland: How America Went Haywire: A 500-Year History.* New York: Random House, 2017.

Barkun, Michael. *A Culture of Conspiracy: Apocalyptic Visions in Contemporary America.* Berkeley: University of California Press, 2003.

Barrett, Lisa Feldman. *How Emotions Are Made: The Secret Life of the Brain.* New York: Mariner Books, 2017.

———. *Seven and a Half Lessons About the Brain.* New York: Mariner Books, 2020.

Bartra, Roger. *The Artificial Savage: Modern Myths of the Wild Man.* Ann Arbor: University of Michigan Press, 1997.

Bartholomew, Robert, and Paul Bartholomew. *The Mysterious Northwoods: Strange Tales from the Adirondack and Green Mountains.* Privately printed, 2020.

Beck, Fred, and R. A. Beck. *I Fought the Apemen of Mt. St. Helens.* Privately printed, 1967.

Bindernagel, John A. *North America's Great Ape, the Sasquatch: A Wildlife Biologist Looks at the Continent's Most Misunderstood Large Mammal.* Courtenay, BC: Beachcomber Books, 1988.

Blackburn, Lyle. *The Beast of Boggy Creek: The True Story of the Fouke Monster.* Charlottesville , VA: Anomalist Books, 2012.

Bord, Colin, and Janet Bord. *The Bigfoot Casebook.* Mechanicsburg, PA: Stackpole Books, 1982.

Braudy, Leo. *Haunted: On Ghosts, Witches, Vampires, Zombies, and Other Monsters of the Natural and Supernatural Worlds.* New Haven, CT: Yale University Press, 2016.

Brooks, Max. *Devolution: A Firsthand Account of the Rainier Sasquatch Massacre.* New York: Del Rey Books, 2020.

Bruchac, Joseph. *The Wind Eagle and Other Abenaki Stories.* New York: Greenfield Review Press, 1985.

Bryson, Bill. *A Walk in the Woods: Rediscovering America on the Appalachian Trail.* New York: Broadway Books, 1998.

Buhs, Joshua Blu. *Bigfoot: The Life and Times of a Legend.* Chicago: University of Chicago Press, 2009.

Byrne, Peter. *The Hunt for Bigfoot.* Privately printed, 2015.

Calloway, Colin. *Dawnland Encounters: Indians and Europeans in Northern New England.* Hanover, NH: University Press of New England, 1991.

Carranco, Lynwood. *Genocide and Vendetta: The Round Valley Wars in Northern California.* Norman: University of Oklahoma Press, 1981.

Case, Anne, and Angus Deaton. *Deaths of Despair and the Future of Capitalism.* Princeton, NJ: Princeton University Press, 2020.

Coil Suchy, Linda. *Who's Watching You? An Exploration of the Bigfoot Phenomenon in the Pacific Northwest.* Surrey, BC: Hancock House, 2009.

Coleman, Jon T. *Nature Shock: Getting Lost in America.* New Haven, CT: Yale University Press, 2020.

Coleman, Loren. *Bigfoot: The True Story of Apes in America.* New York: Pocket Books, 2003.

Critchley, Simon. *Bald: 35 Philosophical Short Cuts.* New Haven, CT: Yale University Press, 2021.

Daegling, David J. *Bigfoot Exposed: An Anthropologist Examines America's Enduring Legend.* Walnut Creek, CA: Altamira Press, 2004.

Dudley, Edward, and Maximillian E. Novak. *The Wild Man Within: An Image in Western Thought from the Renaissance to Romanticism.* Pittsburgh: University of Pittsburgh Press, 1972.

Erdoes, Richard, and Alfonso Ortiz. *American Indian Myths and Legends.* New York: Pantheon Books, 1984.

Faragher, John Mack. *Daniel Boone: The Life and Legend of an American Pioneer.* New York: Henry Holt, 1992.

Fort, Charles. *The Complete Books of Charles Fort: The Book of the Damned/Lo!/Wild Talents/New Lands.* New York: Dover Books, 1974.

Gallagher, Tim. *The Grail Bird: The Rediscovery of the Ivory-billed Woodpecker.* New York: Houghton Mifflin, 2005.

Gray, John. *The Silence of Animals: On Progress and Other Modern Myths.* New York: Allen Lane, 2013.

Green, John. *Sasquatch: The Apes Among Us.* Seattle, WA: Hancock House, 1980.

Heinrich, Bernd. *One Man's Owl.* Princeton, NJ: Princeton University Press, 1987.

Hufford, David. *The Terror That Comes in the Night: An Experience-Centered Study of Supernatural Assault Traditions*. Philadelphia: University of Pennsylvania Press, 1982.

Husband, Timothy. *The Wild Man: Medieval Myth and Symbolism*. New York: Metropolitan Museum of Art, 1980.

Ignatieff, Michael. *The Needs of Strangers*, New York: Picador, 1984.

————. *On Consolation: Finding Solace in Dark Times*. New York: Metropolitan Books, 2021.

Johnston, Basil. *The Manitous: The Spiritual World of the Ojibway*. New York: Harper Collins, 1995.

Kephart, Horace. *The Book of Camping and Woodcraft: A Guidebook for Those Who Travel in the Wilderness*. London: Outing, 1906.

Kimmerer, Robin Wall. *Braiding Sweetgrass: Indigenous Wisdom, Scientific Knowledge, and the Teachings of Plants*. Minneapolis: Milkweed Editions, 2013.

Krantz, Grover S. *Bigfoot Sasquatch Evidence: The Anthropologist Speaks Out*. Surrey, BC: Hancock House, 1999.

Kroeber, A. L., and E. W. Gifford. *Karok Myths*. Berkeley: University of California Press, 1980.

Leiterman, Robert. *The Bluff Creek Project: The Patterson-Gimlin Bigfoot Film Site: A Journey of Rediscovery*. Privately printed, 2021.

Loftus, Elizabeth. *Memory: Surprising New Insights into How We Remember and Why We Forget*. Boston: Addison-Wesley, 1981.

Long, Greg. *The Making of Bigfoot: The Inside Story*, Amherst, NY: Prometheus Books, 2004.

Malinowski, Bronislaw. *Magic, Science and Religion*. New York: Doubleday Anchor, 1954.

Matthiessen, Peter. *In the Spirit of Crazy Horse: The Story of Leonard Peltier and the FBI's War on the American Indian Movement*. New York: Viking Press, 1983.

————. *Shadow Country: A New Rendering of the Watson Legend*. New York: Random House, 2008.

————. *The Snow Leopard*. New York: Penguin, 1978.

————. *Wildlife in America*. New York: Viking Press, 1959.

McLean, Jason. *Metroplex Monsters: Dallas Demons, Fort Worth Goatmen & Other Terrors of the Trinity River*. Charleston, SC: History Press, 2020.

Meldrum, Jeff. *Sasquatch: Legend Meets Science*. New York: Forge Books, 2006.

Merton, Thomas. *The Journals of Thomas Merton. Vol. 3, A Search for Solitude, 1952–1960*, edited by Lawrence S. Cunningham. New York: Harper Collins, 1996.

———. *The Journals of Thomas Merton.* Vol. 7, *The Other Side of the Mountain, 1967–1968,* edited by Patrick Hart. New York: Harper Collins, 1998.

———. *The Seven Storey Mountain.* New York: Houghton Mifflin, 1948.

Murphy, Christopher L. *The Bigfoot Film Controversy.* Surrey, BC: Hancock House, 2005.

Napier, John. *Bigfoot: Startling Evidence of Another Form of Life on Earth Now!* New York: E. P. Dutton, 1972.

Nash, Roderick Frazier. *Wilderness and the American Mind.* New Haven, CT: Yale University Press, 1967.

Olson, Steve. *Eruption: The Untold Story of Mount St. Helens.* New York: W. W. Norton, 2016.

Paulides, David. *The Hoopa Project: Bigfoot Encounters in California.* Surrey, BC: Hancock House, 2008.

Perez, Daniel. *Bigfoot at Bluff Creek.* Norwalk, CA: Center for Bigfoot Studies, 2003.

Pinker, Steven. *Rationality: What It Is, Why It Seems Scarce, Why It Matters.* New York: Viking, 2021.

Powell, Thom. *The Locals: A Contemporary Investigation of the Bigfoot/Sasquatch Phenomenon.* Surrey, BC: Hancock House, 2003.

Pyle, Robert Michael. *Chasing Monarchs: Migrating with the Butterflies of Passage.* New Haven, CT: Yale University Press, 2014.

———. *Where Bigfoot Walks: Crossing the Dark Divide.* New York: Houghton Mifflin, 1995.

Quammen, David. *Monster of God: The Man-Eating Predator in the Jungles of History and the Mind.* New York: W. W. Norton, 2003.

Raymond, Charlie. *Bluegrass Bigfoot: Encounters with the Kentucky Wildman. Vol. 1. Privately* printed, 2021.

Rovelli, Carlo. *Helgoland: Making Sense of the Quantum Revolution.* New York: Riverhead, 2021.

Sanderson, Ivan T. *Abominable Snowmen: Legend Come to Life.* Philadelphia: Chilton, 1961.

Shaw, Mark. *Beneath the Mask of Holiness: Thomas Merton and the Forbidden Love Affair That Set Him Free.* New York: Palgrave Macmillan, 2009.

Shipton, Eric. *Eric Shipton: The Six Mountain-Travel Books.* Seattle, WA: Mountaineers Books, 1997.

Sibley, David Allen. *The Sibley Guide to Birds.* New York: Knopf, 2020.

Souliere, Michelle Y. *Bigfoot in Maine.* Charleston, SC: History Press, 2020.

Strain, Kathy Moskowitz, *Giants, Cannibals and Monsters: Bigfoot in Native Culture*. Surrey, BC: Hancock House, 2008.

Tanner, James T. *The Ivory-Billed Woodpecker*. New York: Dover Books, 2003.

Thoreau, Henry David. *The Maine Woods*. New York: Houghton Mifflin, 1864.

Wallace, David Rains. *The Klamath Knot: Explorations of Myth and Evolution*. Berkeley: University of California Press, 2003.

Walls, Laura Dassow. *Henry David Thoreau: A Life*. Chicago: University of Chicago Press, 2017.

Wiseman, Frederick Matthew. *The Voice of the Dawn: An Autohistory of the Abenaki Nation*. Hanover, NH: University Press of New England, 2001.

Zada, John. *In the Valleys of the Noble Beyond: In Search of the Sasquatch*. New York: Atlantic Monthly, 2019.

INDEX

ABOUT THE AUTHOR

 John O'Connor is from Kalamazoo, Michigan. His writing has appeared in the *New York Times, Oxford American, The Believer, GQ,* the *Financial Times, Creative Nonfiction*'s True Story series, and elsewhere. He has an MFA in nonfiction writing from Columbia University and presently teaches journalism at Boston College. He lives in Cambridge, Massachusetts, with his wife and children. This is his first book.